D0881209

Causes Won, Lost, and Forgotten

ALSO BY GARY W. GALLAGHER

Lee and His Army in Confederate History (2001)

Lee and His Generals in War and Memory (1998)

The Confederate War (1997)

Fighting for the Confederacy:
    The Personal Recollections of General Edward Porter Alexander (1989)

Stephen Dodson Ramseur: Lee's Gallant General (1985)

Miami Dade College
Kendall Campus Library
11011 Southwest 104th Street
Miami, FL 33176

Causes Won, Lost, and Forgotten

HOW HOLLYWOOD & POPULAR ART
SHAPE WHAT WE KNOW ABOUT THE
CIVIL WAR   Gary W. Gallagher

THE UNIVERSITY OF NORTH CAROLINA PRESS
Chapel Hill

THE STEVEN AND JANICE BROSE LECTURES
IN THE CIVIL WAR ERA
William A. Blair, editor

This book was published with the assistance of the Blythe
Family Fund of the University of North Carolina Press.

© 2008 The University of North Carolina Press
All rights reserved
Set in Quadraat, Egiziano, and The Serif Black types
by Tseng Information Systems, Inc.
Manufactured in the United States of America
The paper in this book meets the guidelines for permanence
and durability of the Committee on Production Guidelines for
Book Longevity of the Council on Library Resources.

Library of Congress Cataloging-in-Publication Data
Gallagher, Gary W.
Causes won, lost, and forgotten : how Hollywood and popular
art shape what we know about the Civil War / Gary W. Gallagher.
     p. cm. — (The Steven and Janice Brose lectures in the
Civil War era)
Includes bibliographical references and index.
ISBN 978-0-8078-3206-6 (cloth : alk. paper)
1. United States—History—Civil War, 1861–1865—Motion
pictures and the war. 2. United States—History—Civil War,
1861–1865—Causes. 3. War films—United States—History and
criticism. 4. Historical film—United States—History and
criticism. 5. United States—History—Civil War, 1861–1865—
Historiography. I. Title.
E468.9.G35 2008
973.7—dc22   2007042145

A Caravan book. For more information,
visit www.caravanbooks.org.

12 11 10 09 08   5 4 3 2 1

$ 28. 00

For JW
sesp

Contents

Causes Won, Lost, and Forgotten

Introduction

On October 4, 1993, a full house at Washington's National Theatre watched the world premiere of *Gettysburg*, a Turner Pictures film based on Michael Shaara's Pulitzer Prize–winning novel *The Killer Angels*. Because the Association for the Preservation of Civil War Sites had been given a few choice seats, I found myself, as president of that organization, in the row occupied by Ted Turner and a number of his employees. Jeff Daniels, Sam Elliott, and other actors who appeared in the movie sat in the next row back. During the four-hour epic, I was intrigued by reactions among what was predominantly an insiders' crowd of Civil War enthusiasts and people associated with *Gettysburg*'s production. My favorite moment came during the sequence devoted to Pickett's Charge, near the climax of which Mr. Turner appeared briefly as Confederate colonel Waller Tazewell Patton. As Patton's infantrymen reached the Emmitsburg Road just below the main Union defensive line, the camera focused on Turner, who waved his saber and shouted, "Let's go boys!" Several individuals to my right sprang up and clapped loudly upon hearing their boss utter his line—then lapsed into awkward silence when Union minié balls cut Patton down two or three seconds later. Hearty applause swept the house at the end of the film, and during the postscreening "gala" I heard innumerable comments about how director Ron Maxwell brought the battle and its leading characters to life—how the movie conveyed an immediacy and sense of action impossible to capture in prose.

As one who had read and thought a good deal about Gettysburg, I found much to consider in both the film and the audience's response. Scenes such as the Confederate artillery bombardment preceding Pickett's Charge impressed me, as did Stephen Lang's performance as General George E. Pickett. Other elements of the film proved less satisfying. For example, many of the 5,000 reenactors, whose involvement helped make the production possible, brought too many years and too much excess flesh to the task of portraying Civil War soldiers (one of the first Confederates with a speaking part bears a remarkable resemblance to Santa Claus). Whatever quibbles I had with *Gettysburg*, remarks from members of the audience reminded me that films strongly influence perceptions of historical events, and I wondered what larger understanding of the war viewers might take away from the movie. A colorful brochure handed out at the premiere caught my eye in this regard. On its cover (fig. 1), Union and Confederate battle lines face one another against a dramatic, cloud-studded sky. Six words located just above the film's title suggest that the soldiers were all Americans with more to connect than to divide them, who nonetheless found themselves trapped in a tragic war: "SAME LAND. SAME GOD. DIFFERENT DREAMS."

That brochure went into a large file of material I had been collecting on representations of the Civil War in the visual arts. Long fascinated by how the conflict shows up in popular culture, I have been especially intrigued over the past twenty years by films and contemporary paintings and sculpture that feature Civil War themes.[1] This book explores how interpretive traditions created by participants in the conflict appear in recent cinema and works of art. Seeking to reach both a general audience interested in the war and historians of the mid-nineteenth-century United States, I focus on four major traditions. (1) The Lost Cause tradition offered a loose group of arguments that cast the South's experiment in nation-building as an admirable struggle against hopeless odds, played down the importance of slavery in bringing secession and war, and ascribed to Confederates constitutional high-mindedness and gallantry on the battlefield. (2) The Union Cause tradition framed the war as preeminently an effort to maintain a viable republic in the face of secessionist actions that threatened both the work of the Founders and, by extension, the future of democracy in a world that had yet to embrace self-rule by a free people. (3) The Emancipation Cause tradition interpreted the war as a struggle to liberate 4 million slaves and remove a cancerous influence on American society and politics. (4) Finally, the Reconciliation Cause tradition—reflected in the brochure's "SAME LAND. SAME GOD. DIFFERENT DREAMS" text—represented an attempt by white people North and South to extol the American virtues both sides manifested during the war, to exalt the restored nation that emerged from the conflict, and to mute the role of African Americans.

The Union, Emancipation, and Reconciliation traditions overlapped in some ways, as did the Lost Cause and Reconciliation traditions. Yet each of the four can be examined as a quite distinct attempt to explain and understand the war. For example, Union and Emancipation joined in expressing joy at the destruction of the Confederacy but often diverged in discussing the end of slavery. For the Union Cause, emancipation represented a tool to punish slaveholders, undermine the Confederacy, and remove a long-standing threat to the development of the republic; for the Emancipation Cause, it stood as

FIGURE 1. Cover of the brochure from the premiere of *Gettysburg*, with text emphasizing how much Americans North and South had in common. Author's collection.

the most important, and ennobling, goal of the northern war effort, a mighty blow for the advancement of millions of black Americans. Union and Reconciliation similarly lauded the fact that one nation emerged from the conflict, and anyone who cherished the Union had to welcome, on some level at least, the reintegration of former Rebels into the national citizenry. Yet unlike reconciliationists, who avoided discussion about which cause was more just, supporters of the Union tradition never wavered in their insistence that Confederates had been in the wrong. Adherents of the Lost Cause and Reconciliation could agree to play down emancipation and the slavery-related politics of secession, but many former Confederates, whatever their public rhetoric about loyalty to the reunited nation, persisted in celebrating a struggle for southern independence that had nearly undone the Founders' handiwork.

I concentrate on the last two decades because they have seen a significant expansion of interest in the Civil War after a relatively dormant period between 1965 and the mid-1980s. The dormant stage followed a flurry of publications and public events tied to the war's Centennial in 1961–65. The glut of books during the Centennial, many hurried into print to reap a quick profit, convinced much of the publishing world that the Civil War was at least temporarily exhausted as a marketable subject. That perception—along with a national revulsion with the war in Vietnam, which fastened an added stigma to military studies of all kinds—severely curtailed the number of new books on the Civil War.[2] The University of North Carolina Press offers an excellent example of these trends. It had built a strong list of Civil War era titles between its founding in 1922 and the Centennial, including fifteen issued between 1960 and 1966. During the period 1967–84, however, North Carolina published just two new Civil War titles. Major attention to the field resumed at Chapel Hill in the mid-1980s and has carried forward to the present. Matthew Hodgson, director of the press from 1970 until 1992 and an ardent student of the Civil War, attributed Chapel Hill's renewed engagement with the field to "a resurgence of public interest."[3]

That resurgent interest, apparent to anyone who paid the slightest attention, stemmed from many factors. Increasing distance from Vietnam almost certainly played a role—though the precise effect would be impossible to quantify. The years of Ronald Reagan's presidency also had an influence, again hard to pin down, in changing public attitudes toward the use of military strength as a tool of national policy.[4] Three other factors specifically related to the war came together in the second half of the 1980s. A series of increasingly well publicized 125th anniversary commemorations of Civil

War events began in 1986, reaching a high point at Gettysburg in 1988, when 12,000 reenactors performed for 140,000 spectators and a host of newspaper and television reporters and camera crews.[5] Enthusiasts' observing 125th anniversaries spoke to the Civil War's unique place in the national imagination. Almost any other group would have waited until the sesquicentennial or bicentennial to commence their celebration. Civil War preservation also burst into the national news in 1988 after a developer announced his intention to build on hundreds of acres adjacent to Manassas National Battlefield Park in northern Virginia. Confrontations over Civil War battlefield preservation, which often centered on land near major metropolitan areas, soon became a permanent fixture on the American scene.[6] Finally, James M. McPherson's *Battle Cry of Freedom: The Civil War Era* received a glowing endorsement in the *New York Times Book Review* on February 14, 1988, and became a bestseller en route to winning the Pulitzer Prize for history.

In September 1988, the editor of *Civil War Times Illustrated*, the most widely read magazine in the field, analyzed burgeoning attention to the topic. Alluding to national coverage in such publications as *Newsweek*, *U.S. News & World Report*, the *Washington Post*, and the *New York Times*, he called the summer of 1988 "an emotionally charged season for history buffs." The commemoration at Gettysburg, national debate about the development at Manassas, and expanding subscription lists for magazines devoted to the war, among other things, pointed to "a significant growth of interest in the Civil War." *Civil War Times Illustrated*'s increased readership reflected the general rise in attention to the conflict after a low point in the post-Centennial years. In 1969, when William C. Davis assumed its editorship, *Civil War Times Illustrated*'s circulation had dropped so far that "owners were talking about euthanizing the magazine" because they believed "its heyday had passed."[7]

Momentum from the late 1980s received an enormous boost in 1990 with the airing of Ken Burns's documentary *The Civil War*. The eleven-hour series garnered the largest audience of any program in the history of public television, with an estimated 40 million viewers tuning in for at least one episode. It subsequently became a staple of PBS fund-raising drives, received wide use in classrooms, and sold well in video and DVD formats. Easily the most important factor in fueling the Civil War boom of the 1990s, Burns's series inspired large numbers of Americans to purchase books, visit National Park Service Civil War sites, and otherwise try to deepen their understanding of the conflict. *The Civil War: An Illustrated History*, authored by Geoffrey C. Ward, Ken Burns, and Ric Burns and chosen as a Book-of-the-Month Club main selection, appeared as a lavish "companion volume" to the series. Sales for Shelby Foote's trilogy, *The Civil War: A Narrative*, suggest the impact of Burns's documentary. The most prominent talking head in the series (he occupied more than twice the air time of all the others combined), Foote had sold 15,000 sets of his magnum opus between 1974, when the third volume was published, and 1990; six months after PBS first ran the documentary, prospective readers had purchased another 100,000 sets.[8]

Numerous television documentaries trailed in the wake of Burns's success. The wide availability via cable of the Arts and Entertainment Network and later the History Channel afforded ample opportunity for viewers to find these programs, which typically dealt with military aspects of the conflict. Probably most widely seen was the fifty-two-episode *Civil War Journal*, created by Greystone Productions and first aired on A&E beginning in 1993 before moving to the History Channel. Craig Haffner, executive producer for Greystone, explained that "the growth of the cable television industry and the success the Public Broadcasting Service achieved by scheduling its eleven-hour Civil War special as a week-long event" made *Civil War Journal* possible. He might have added that the size of the potential audience of Civil War buffs by the early 1990s also played a major role. Like Burns with his documentary, Haffner added a printed dimension to Greystone's project in the form of three volumes put together from comments by historians featured in the series.[9]

As the number of Americans drawn to the Civil War increased after the late 1980s, other trends pertinent to an examination of films and artworks developed. Confederate symbols that had been part of the public landscape for many decades in the form of monuments and representations of the St. Andrew's Cross battle flag, often mistakenly called the Stars and Bars, became hotly contested. Many Americans considered the symbols to be obnoxious relics from a slaveholding, racist past; others, perhaps a majority of whom had Confederate ancestors, insisted they represented honor and courage in a cause that had little to do with slavery. Georgia's and Mississippi's state flags incorporated the Confederate battle flag in their design, and the banner flew over South Carolina's capitol building. In all of these states, proponents and opponents of the Confederate flag engaged in well-publicized fights. A picture of Robert E. Lee among a group of portraits on a flood wall along the James River in Richmond, Virginia, provoked similar controversy, as did efforts to place Confederate symbols on license plates in Maryland and elsewhere. At the same time, complaints arose in many places concerning monuments that had been erected on courthouse grounds, university campuses, and other public spaces by the Lost Cause generation.[10]

The national press took notice. The *Wall Street Journal*, *U.S. News & World Report*, and *Time* covered various stories relating to Confederate symbols. "Rebel-Flag Battle Opens Old Wounds, Builds New Alliances," proclaimed a front-page headline in the *Wall Street Journal* in 1995; the story below explored the complicated racial politics of the issue. Two years later, as South Carolinians continued to argue, *U.S. News & World Report* featured the religious dimension of the story in a piece titled "The Flag and the Fury." "In South Carolina's escalating holy war over the Confederate flag," stated the article, "both pro-flag and anti-flag forces claim he [God] is on their side." That same week, *Time*'s "Winners and Losers" section included this on the "winners" side of the ledger: "Diehard Maryland Rebels. A federal judge lifts the state's ban on license plates that fly the Confederate battle flag."[11] Despite the Maryland ruling and Mississippi's decision to keep its existing flag (following a statewide vote that split along racial lines), the Confederate battle standard steadily lost ground amid debates over its presence at governmental and other public sites.[12]

Attention to emancipation and black participation in the war increased as Lost Cause symbols retreated. Release of the film *Glory* in 1989 inspired greater interest in the service of the United States Colored Troops—a phenomenon that reached a high point with the dedication on September 12, 1996, of the African American Civil War Memorial in the historic Shaw neighborhood of Washington, D.C. The monument features a sculpture by Ed Hamilton titled *The Spirit of Freedom*, around which a series of stainless steel plaques list the names of 209,000 black soldiers and 7,000 white officers who served in USCT units. In January 1999, a facility that offered exhibits and research materials operated by the African American Civil War Memorial Freedom Foundation and Museum opened a short distance from the monument. Although it remains to be seen whether Hamilton's sculpture and the museum will attract substantial annual visitation, the contrasting public trajectories of the Lost Cause and the Emancipation Cause, as we will see, seemed to affect films and artworks in different ways.[13]

Growing interest in the Civil War and wrangling over Lost Cause symbols helped define the period I explore in this book, but I still had to decide which films and artworks to examine. I eventually settled on fourteen movies, some that are specifically dedicated to the war and others that deal with it more obliquely: *Glory* (directed by Edward Zwick, 1989), *Dances with Wolves* (Kevin Costner, 1990), *Gettysburg* (Ron Maxwell, 1993), *Sommersby* (Jon Amiel, 1993), *Little Women* (Gillian Armstrong, 1994), *Pharaoh's Army* (Robby Henson, 1995), *Andersonville* (John Frankenheimer, 1996), *Ride with the Devil* (Ang Lee, 1999), *The Gangs of New York* (Martin Scorsese, 2002), *Gods and Generals* (Ron Maxwell, 2003), *Cold Mountain* (Anthony Minghella, 2003), *The Last Samurai* (Edward Zwick, 2003), *C.S.A.: The Confederate States of America* (Kevin Willmott, 2004), and *Seraphim Falls* (David Von Ancken, 2006). All but *Pharaoh's Army*, *Andersonville*, *C.S.A.: The Confederate States of America*, and *Seraphim Falls* were major releases shaped by leading directors, heavily advertised, and designed to reach a wide audience in theaters. I included *Pharaoh's Army* because it is a splendid smaller work that deserves serious attention and *Andersonville*, a made-for-television film, because the much-honored filmmaker John Frankenheimer directed it. *C.S.A.: The Confederate States of America*, a mock-documentary seen by very few people, made the list because it directly confronts the Lost Cause tradition, and *Seraphim Falls*, a western set in 1868, because an incident involving United States soldiers and a Confederate colonel's family supplies the explanatory key to the plot.[14]

Some readers will question my decision to exclude—apart from *Andersonville*—productions made specifically for television. These programs include Burns's *The Civil War* (which has spawned a fairly large literature to which I have contributed), dozens of shorter documentaries that have been staples on the cable networks, made-for-television movies, and miniseries. I hasten to acknowledge the popularity of *North and South*, which translated John Jakes's novels *North and South* (1982) and *Love and War* (1984) to the small screen. Aired in two parts of more than nine hours each in 1985 and 1986, the miniseries possibly inspired a mild growth of interest in the Civil War. Most viewers, however, almost certainly tuned in for the steamy soap operatic dimension of the episodes, which offered uncomplicated heroes and villains in all the usual categories—attractive plantation owner, vicious slaveholder, wild-eyed abolitionist, lustful young woman, mixed-race heroine, and so on. A few minutes into the series, I concluded that the principal direction must have been something like, "A little more over the top, if you please"—advice clearly heeded by Patrick Swayze, Kirstie Alley, David Carradine, and, in an inspired bit of casting, Wayne Newton as a sadistic Confederate prison commandant. Television's relationship with the Civil War, from Centennial era series such as *The Gray Ghost* (1957–58) and *The Americans* (1961) through more recent documentaries and other programs, deserves book-length treatment.

Doing justice to the subject would require more space than I can allocate here, so others will have to take on the task.[15]

I make no claim to offer a history of the Civil War in American film, but some comparative context is necessary. To that end, each of my chapters on the cinema includes discussion of movies produced before the late 1980s. *The Birth of a Nation* and *Gone with the Wind* most obviously require attention because of their singular influence over the span of many decades (a continuing influence in the case of *Gone with the Wind*). Other leading examples of the Civil War genre also proved useful as background for my analysis of the current state of the four interpretive traditions, including John Huston's post–World War II version of *The Red Badge of Courage*. Productions during the eras of the Civil War Centennial and the civil rights movement—among them *The Horse Soldiers*, *Raintree County*, and *Shenandoah*—shed light on the degree to which films since *Glory* have reinforced or repudiated earlier cinematic conventions. I hope my approach, while emphasizing the past two decades, will provide a clear sense of the interpretive arc of Hollywood's engagement with the Civil War.[16]

As I sought evidence of the four traditions, I remained fully aware that Hollywood's overriding goal is to provide entertainment that will earn profits. Studios, producers, and directors seldom have a didactic purpose. They focus on plots and characters that create and sustain dramatic momentum, often purchasing the film rights to successful novels such as *Gone with the Wind*, *Andersonville*, *The Killer Angels*, and *Cold Mountain*. David O. Selznick almost certainly never issued these instructions to an underling: "Find me a good piece of material laying out the Lost Cause interpretation of the Confederate experience. The dramatic potential is important but will be secondary to our getting the interpretation right." Neither would anyone in Hollywood insist that a historical drama, above all, reflect the insights of the best recent scholarship—at least not anyone who hopes to attract and satisfy paying customers. The complexity of scholarly investigation translates poorly to cinematic treatments in which images and sound often take precedence over dialogue. Freddie Fields, who produced *Glory*, spoke directly to this point in 1989. Reacting to complaints that the film got some historical details wrong, he observed: "You can get bogged down when dealing in history. Our objective was to make a highly entertaining and exciting war movie filled with action and character."[17]

Yet films undeniably teach Americans about the past—to a lamentable degree in the minds of many academic historians. More people have formed perceptions about the Civil War from watching *Gone with the Wind* than from reading all the books written by historians since Selznick's blockbuster debuted in 1939.[18] Even moderately successful movies attract a far larger audience than the most widely read nonfiction books dealing with the conflict. Among titles published over the past twenty years, only McPherson's *Battle Cry of Freedom* has reached hundreds of thousands of readers[19] — a figure far exceeded by box office sales and subsequent videocassette and DVD rentals for a number of Civil War–related films. Whether intentionally or not, films convey elements of the four interpretive traditions, and how well each of the quartet has fared sheds light on their comparative vitality.

In contrast to my using a relatively small number of recent films, I pursue a more expansive strategy with artworks. I created my sample by canvassing advertisements in three magazines devoted to the Civil War. *Civil War Times Illustrated*, the oldest publication of this genre, was established in 1962 and headquartered in Pennsylvania until recently moving its editorial offices to Virginia. *Blue & Gray Magazine*, second oldest of the three, has been published in Ohio since 1983. *North & South*, the magazine of the Civil War Society, has been based in California since its inception in 1997. All three reach a national audience and from the outset have claimed freedom from sectional special pleading. "*Civil War Times Illustrated* will be non-partisan," wrote the editor in the first issue, promising that it would be "carefully balanced in editorial content." *Blue & Gray Magazine*'s editors announced in their inaugural column a "pro-Union" and "pro-Confederacy" stance that recognized "the strengths and weaknesses, and the blunders and accomplishments of both sides." *North & South*'s editor pledged to embrace "many perspectives." "A good deal of wartime propaganda, north and south, still lurks within the pages of our history books," he observed. "It will be one aim of *North & South* to expose this for what it is, and to get at the historical truth." In sum, these magazines would seem to be perfect venues in which to present whatever pieces, Union or Confederate, artists thought would sell best.[20]

I examined more than 2,750 advertisements that appeared between 1962 and 2006, the vast majority of them for prints of paintings or for sculptures. I use the first twenty-five years for comparative context about how topics have gone in and out of fashion. As with the films, my emphasis is on art produced in the last two decades. The growth in the market for this art since the mid-1980s has been stunning. During the 1960s, *Civil War Times Illustrated* ran just 18 ads for art. The 1970s saw the number increase more than five-fold, to 92 — still an average of fewer than 10 ads per year. The total jumped to 567 in the 1980s, with the largest gains in the latter part of the decade. During the 1990s, after Burns's documentary, the film *Gettysburg*, and other factors spurred general interest in the Civil War, the magazine ran 1,471 ads. Based on the assumption that artists place ads for pieces they believe will sell best, I make judgments about the relative strength of the four interpretive traditions within the world of those who purchase artworks. In the absence of information from specific purchasers, I rely on discussions with artists, magazine editors, and gallery owners to venture some generalizations about the market.

Compared to films, these magazines and their advertisements touch a small number of people. *Civil War Times Illustrated* prints approximately 85,000 copies per issue and *Blue & Gray Magazine* and *North & South* fewer than that number between them.[21] Most of their readers, a large proportion of whom probably watch Civil War movies, possess a good deal more knowledge about the conflict than typical filmgoers. The two audiences offer very different prisms through which to examine how the four interpretive traditions survive in current popular culture.

My exploration of cinema and advertisements yielded two key themes. First, films and artworks deal very differently with the Lost Cause. Hollywood increasingly shuns it. The Emancipation Cause has become the most influential of the four traditions in an industry where the Confederate narrative long held sway with *The Birth of a Nation*, *Gone with the Wind*, and many less important films. Since the release of *Glory* in 1989, only *Gods and Generals* takes a predominantly Lost Cause interpretive stance. Leading characters in several of the other films oppose slavery, embrace emancipation, and manifest quite modern opinions about race. This trend aligns with, and probably grows out of, the post–civil rights movement shift away from public displays of the battle flag and other Confederate symbols.

Yet that shift seems to have strengthened the Lost Cause in the world of those who purchase Civil War art. Confederate leaders and topics completely dominate the advertisements, with Robert E. Lee, Stonewall Jackson, and the Army of Northern Virginia's campaigns heading the roster of most-painted subjects. Several factors probably contribute to this phenomenon. The romanticism long associated with Lee and Jackson and respect for plucky Confederates battling more powerful Union foes certainly boost interest in Lost Cause themes. The art usually ends up in private homes rather than in public places, allowing buyers who wish to express admiration for the Confederacy and its leaders to do so without fear of stirring up controversy. Antagonism toward "big government" and its impact on Americans' everyday lives may be important for those who claim the Confederacy favored localism, state rights, and the individual over central power—an ironic stance considering that the Richmond government was by far the most intrusive in American history until deep into the twentieth century. Robert E. Lee makes an especially poor artistic representative of small national government. He wholeheartedly supported conscription and other expressions of strong central power, demanding that state and local needs give way to those of the national military effort. Some purchasers—perhaps especially those enamored of works featuring Nathan Bedford Forrest—may be influenced in their choice of artworks by unhappiness with a changing racial landscape in the United States.

A second and more surprising theme confirms the weak presence of the Union Cause in movies and art. The most important tradition to the North's wartime generation, it lags far behind Emancipation and, to a lesser degree, Reconciliation. No scene in any recent film captures the abiding devotion to Union that animated soldiers and civilians in the North. This is somewhat understandable. Long pieces of explanatory dialogue about Union as an emotional and political focus would bring narrative momentum to a halt. Yet a number of films demonstrate what a single scene could accomplish. In *Casablanca*, the singing of *La Marseillaise* in Rick's bar as the camera moves from one passionate face to the next communicates devotion to a French nation humbled by German military power. More to the point, *Gone with the Wind*'s fancy ball, staged with Confederate flags and a huge portrait of Jefferson Davis much in evidence, creates a strong sense of the kind of national purpose that would prompt women such as Melanie Wilkes to contribute their wedding rings to support southern armies. Union Cause advocates of the Civil War generation would be most alienated by Hollywood's negative depiction of northern soldiers. More often than not, they appear as cruel and destructive racists who abuse black people, Confederate civilians, and Native Americans.

The Union Cause fares only marginally better in advertisements for artworks, which relegate Ulysses S. Grant, William Tecumseh Sherman, Philip H. Sheridan, and other great national heroes of late-nineteenth-century paintings and sculpture to a decidedly secondary position. Apart from Gettysburg, which looms large for reasons unrelated to the Union Cause, famous northern military victories such as Shiloh, Vicksburg, Chattanooga, and Cedar Creek also receive scant attention from modern artists.

Why have the Union Cause and its military forces reached such a point?

Part of the answer lies in the nebulous nature of a fight to save "the Union." The other two northern traditions lend themselves to simple formulations: emancipation meant freeing the slaves, and reconciliation meant bringing Americans back together after a period of sectional alienation and slaughter. Both traditions focus on clear outcomes almost all modern Americans see as desirable. A tougher challenge awaits anyone who tries to explain why Union, a word and concept no longer part of our political vocabulary, mattered so much. In a nation that has stood first among world powers at least since World War II, most Americans take their form of government for granted and cannot imagine an internal threat of the kind that galvanized the northern people in 1861. Both students and adults often ask why hundreds of thousands of northern men, in the absence of a challenge to their immediate well-being (Confederate armies never threatened to conquer large chunks of United States territory), risked their lives to safeguard the work of the Founders and preserve America's democratic example to the world. Yet anyone who does not appreciate that untold citizens believed Confederate independence would scuttle the American experiment in democracy cannot grasp what was going on in the North.

Ambivalence about the kind of nation that developed after the war exacerbates the problem. For most Americans, the Union (i.e., the North), with its factories and large population and substantial urban development, looks very much like the current United States. Unhappiness with various dimensions of the modern state often translates into a harsh critique of the Union. For example, conservatives and libertarians wary of too much control from Washington sometimes accuse Lincoln and the Republicans of using the war to build a powerful and intrusive state—thereby robbing the Union Cause of any uplifting purpose.[22] Some Americans unhappy with the global projection of United States military and economic power in the years since the end of World War II credit Union victory with making possible an avaricious state that embarked on imperialistic ventures. This formulation has allowed Hollywood to treat United States armies, whether rampaging through the Confederate countryside or in Vietnam, as largely malevolent expressions of national policy.[23]

Disappearance of the Union Cause highlights the degree to which recent popular culture, at least as expressed in film, has lost sight of nationalism as a motivating force. Nation stood at the center of the mid-nineteenth-century American crisis—on the one hand a mighty effort to confirm and redefine the United States, and on the other an even more all-encompassing struggle to establish the Confederate slaveholding republic. Conceptions of Union, the place of emancipation, the patriotic obligations of citizens, and the meanings of liberty and freedom all came into play on the northern side. Confederates wrestled with equally weighty issues while coping with the need to make far greater sacrifices than their enemies. Despite the example of the ball from *Gone with the Wind*, Confederate national sentiment typically gives way in modern understanding to a combination of localism, state rights, personal valor, and loyalty to family and friends. Among recent films, only Ron Maxwell's *Gettysburg* and *Gods and Generals* engage nationalism in a serious way—and even someone who watched both of them would come away with only a vague idea about a central part of the war's fundamental meaning for many of its participants.[24]

I will offer four final comments before moving on to the substance of my arguments. First, I wrote the book while the United States has been fighting the war in Iraq. Because it is too soon to gauge the impact of more than four years' conflict in the Middle East on how Americans relate to the Civil War, I have not brought Iraq into my analysis. Second, I am trained as neither a film critic nor an art critic. The aesthetic merits of the movies and artworks I discuss are irrelevant to my purpose. Third, filmmakers and artists interest me for how they present the Civil War—how they define and explain it, and how, in turn, their definitions and explanations likely shape and reflect Americans' understanding of the war. I do have strong opinions about artistic merit and historical accuracy, some of which will be obvious. But they are tangential to my principal purpose and probably will be dismissed by at least some readers as idiosyncratic and highly subjective. Fourth, few projects in my career as a historian have been as much fun as this one. I took delight in revisiting films and images important in my youth. As a fourteen-year-old entranced by the Civil War, I was among the first customers to purchase a ticket when *Shenandoah* came to the Rialto Theater in Alamosa, Colorado, in 1965. I watched the film three times in a row (a friendly usher allowed me to remain seated while the rest of the patrons filed out after the first and second showings). The pure pleasure of that day remains a treasured memory.[25]

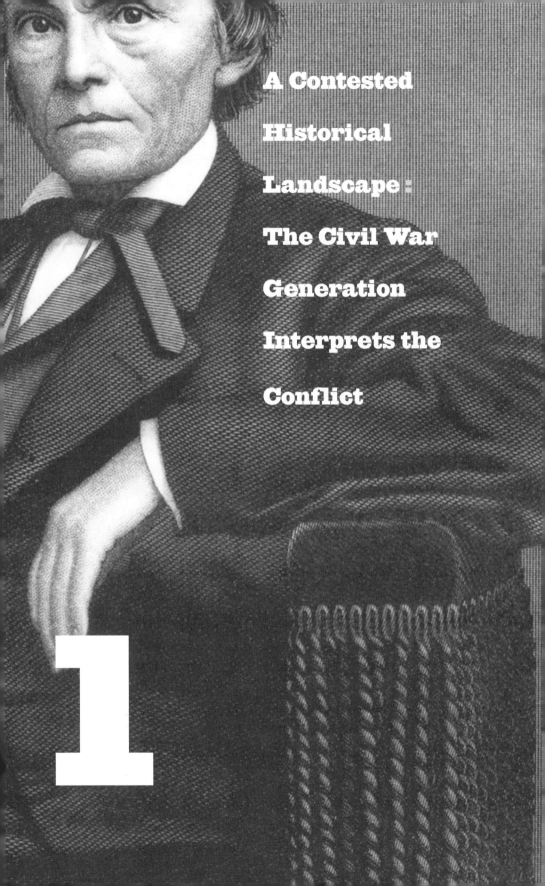

A Contested
Historical
Landscape :
The Civil War
Generation
Interprets the
Conflict

1

Americans began their struggle to define the historical meaning of the Civil War as soon as four years of slaughter ended in the spring of 1865. Their quest frequently took the form of heated debates that continue despite the passage of nearly 150 years. Many of the debates carried out by the Civil War generation focused on details relating to military operations. Some pitted former Confederates against former Federals, as when partisans of Generals Ulysses S. Grant and Robert E. Lee engaged in strident exchanges about manpower during the Virginia campaigns of 1864–65. Lee's defenders sought to magnify Union strength and minimize their own. They portrayed Lee as a noble chieftain who struggled against hopeless odds and Grant as a graceless butcher who triumphed only because he could draw on almost limitless men and matériel. Grant's partisans reacted predictably, also manipulating the numbers to insist that there had not been a huge difference in strength and claiming that Grant's superior generalship had been the key to Union victory. Other debates witnessed former soldiers from the same side assaulting each other in print. Most notable of these was the no-holds-barred controversy among ex-Confederates over culpability for the defeat at Gettysburg—a long-lived affair that came to center on the actions of General James Longstreet. For their part, Union veterans argued about leadership among their commanders at Second Bull Run, Gettysburg, and elsewhere. Most of these debates—which filled the pages of magazines, memoirs, and regimental histories for several decades after the war—revealed far more about the literary combatants in the postwar years than about the wartime events their prose dissected.[1]

Another set of debates shifted the spotlight to how the war's broader meaning would be interpreted by subsequent generations. Many people North and South cared passionately about how history would judge their actions in a struggle that had sent more than 3 million men into military service (out of a population of about 31.5 million) and claimed more than 600,000 lives. Here the stakes were much higher than in literary jousting over such relatively minor points as whether Longstreet dragged his feet on the second day at Gettysburg. These larger debates brought the poisonous issue of slavery into the picture, both as a precipitant of secession and war and, in the form of emancipation, as a factor that altered the character of the conflict and helped define its aftermath. They raised questions about comparative sectional virtue, moral right, and even divine approbation.[2]

Thumbnail treatments of four major interpretive traditions will provide background for the examination of films and artworks. One of the four formed almost immediately after the war in the South and two others in the North. Among them, the three offered starkly contrasting versions of the Civil War era, and all have modern counterparts that echo their arguments. The fourth tradition appeared somewhat later, won numerous adherents throughout the nation by the end of the nineteenth century, and remains widely evident today.

"A Record of Achievement, Endurance, and Self-Sacrificing Devotion"

What came to be called the Lost Cause school of interpretation arose in the South and contained several elements that have proved to be remarkably tenacious. Former Confederates confronted the postwar world as a people thoroughly beaten on the battlefield but defiantly unapologetic about their attempt to establish a slaveholding republic. The conflict had killed one in four military-age white southern men (American fatalities in World War II would have been approximately 6.5 million, rather than 400,000, if the ratio of dead to total population in the United States had matched that of the Confederacy), left much of the region's economy in ruin, wrought dramatic changes in the landscape, and, most important by far, destroyed the South's slave-based social system. Ex-Confederates sought to take something positive away from their catastrophic experiment in nation-building. They embraced a public memory of the Civil War era that celebrated their antebellum civilization with little reference to slavery, justified secession on constitutional grounds, highlighted their undeniable wartime sacrifice, and insisted that defeat in the face of impossible odds entailed no loss of honor. Refined and repeated endlessly during the post-Appomattox decades, Lost Cause arguments reached a wide audience through participants' memoirs, speeches at gatherings of veterans, and commemorative programs orchestrated by Ladies' Memorial Associations at the graves of Confederate soldiers. Various artworks, including prints published in the North, also celebrated the Confederate struggle, as did a large number of public monuments.[3]

Architects of the Lost Cause hoped to provide their children and future generations of white southerners with what they called a "correct" narrative of the war (women were especially diligent in monitoring school textbooks). Some Lost Cause writers specifically sought to create a published record that would influence later historians.[4] In terms of shaping how Americans have understood the Civil War, former Confederates succeeded to a remarkable degree. One need look no further than Robert E. Lee to find an obvious example of that success. Lee functioned as the preeminent Lost Cause hero. Ex-Confederates could focus on him and his famous victories without engaging the noxious issue of slavery or some of the messier political and social dimensions of the war. By the second or third decade of the twentieth century, Lee stood with Abraham Lincoln as one of the two most popular Civil War figures. In what must be reckoned a great irony of Civil War memory, Ulysses S. Grant, who did more to forge United States victory than anyone save Lincoln, came to inspire far less admiration across the United States than the principal Rebel chieftain.[5]

Although there was no official Lost Cause interpretation, several themes stand out as crucial for later explorations of films and artworks. Former Confederates faced the challenge of salvaging honor amid devastating defeat and horrendous human and material loss. Toward this end, they argued that northern numbers and material resources had been too great to overcome and stressed the enormous amount of physical destruction in the Confederacy. The United States had enjoyed an advantage in manpower of approximately two-and-one-half to one, but Lost Cause advocates typically lengthened even those odds. Confederate armies, they insisted, had waged a gallant but hopeless fight that bequeathed to subsequent generations of white southerners a noble legacy. In July 1876, the editor of the *Southern Historical Society Papers* called for increased attention to this subject. Pronouncing the "relative strength of the Federal and Confederate armies . . . a matter of great importance," he suggested that "even our own people are in profound ignorance of the great odds against which we fought, while Northern writers have persistently misrepresented the facts." Few Lost Cause warriors devoted more attention to northern numbers and industrial advantages than Jubal A. Early. A highly influential figure in debates about the memory of the conflict, he characterized the campaign Lee and Grant waged in 1864 as "a contest between mechanical power and physical strength, on the one hand, and the gradually diminishing nerve and sinew of Confederate soldiers, on the other, until the unlimited resources of our enemies must finally prevail over all the genius and chivalric daring, which had so long baffled their mighty efforts in the field." Early's juxtaposing outnumbered Confederates against limitless, mechanistic northern power resonated immediately among vanquished white southerners, and among later generations of Americans as well.[6]

The theme of admirable striving against irresistible United States power found expression in stone as well as in print. In 1903, for example, veterans dedicated an imposing monument on the capitol grounds in Austin, Texas, that underestimated Confederate strength by about 300,000 and overestimated that of United States forces by more than 650,000. The text read in part: "The South, Against Overwhelming Numbers and Resources, Fought Until Exhausted. . . . Number Of Men Enlisted: Confederate Armies, 600,000; Federal Armies, 2,859,132." Contending against odds of almost five to one, as the Texas memorial would have it (the seeming exactness of the Union figure lends verisimilitude to the invention), set a standard that could be used to instruct later generations. A monument erected in 1909 in Charlottesville, Virginia, offered such a lesson: "Warriors: Your Valour; Your Devotion to Duty; Your Fortitude Under Privations; Teach Us How to Suffer And Grow Strong."[7]

Lost Cause writers understood that slavery posed the greatest obstacle to their constructing a version of secession and war that would position them favorably before the bar of history. They knew their slaveholding society had been out of step with the tide of Western history, and they sought to remove that stigma from their record by presenting slavery as peripheral to the decision for secession and to the establishment of the Confederate nation. They said they had fought in defense of constitutional principles as the true inheritors of a revolutionary tradition that invested great power in the states and localities and viewed central governmental authority with alarm. Among the most prominent Lost Cause writers were Jefferson Davis and Alexander H. Stephens, who had served, respectively, as president and vice president of the Confederacy. Stephens evidently coined the term "War Between the States," which soon achieved wide currency among former Confederates. The two men had become implacable political enemies during the war (Stephens believed Davis exercised too much national power in the course of trying to mount a military effort capable of securing independence), but their postwar writings complemented one another.

Those writings underscore the ways in which Lost Cause figures attempted to rewrite history regarding the centrality of slavery. In the spring of 1861, as the Confederate government began its stormy life, both Stephens and Davis acknowledged slavery's importance to their experiment in nation-building. On March 21, in his famous "Cornerstone Speech," Stephens observed that the new Confederate constitution "put at rest *forever* all the agitating question relating to our peculiar institution—African slavery as it exists among us. . . . *This was the immediate cause of the late rupture and present revolution*," Stephens averred, adding without equivocation, "*Our new government is founded* upon . . . , its *foundations are laid, its cornerstone rests, upon the great truth that the negro is not equal to the white man; that slavery, subordination to the superior race, is his natural and moral condition. This, our new Government, is the first, in the history of the world, based upon this great physical, philosophical, and moral truth.*" Shortly thereafter, Davis justified secession on the grounds that Abraham Lincoln and the Republican Party planned to exclude slavery from the territories, in turn rendering "property in slaves so insecure as to be comparatively worthless, and thereby annihilating in effect property worth thousands of millions of dollars." Confronted with this threat to economic "interests of such overwhelming magnitude," added Davis, "the people of the Southern States were driven by the conduct of the North to the adoption of some course of action to avert the danger with which they were openly menaced."[8]

The two men's postwar memoirs told a different story. In *A Constitutional View of the Late War between the States*, a tedious two-volume work published in 1868 and 1870, Stephens did his best to push slavery into the background. He claimed that the "war had its origin in *opposing principles* . . . a strife between the principles of Federation, on the one side, and Centralism, or Consolidation, on the other. Slavery, so called, was but *the question* on which these antagonistic principles, which had been in conflict, from the beginning, on divers *other questions*, were finally brought into actual and active collision with each other on the field of battle." Davis took a similar tack in his two-volume memoir titled *The Rise and Fall of the Confederate Government*. He asserted that the South waged war solely for the inalienable right of a people to change their government—to leave a Union into which, as sovereign states, they had entered voluntarily. "The truth remains intact and incontrovertible," Davis stated, echoing Stephens, "that the existence of African servitude was in no wise the cause of the conflict, but only an incident."[9]

Where Lost Cause writers engaged slavery, they did so with an eye toward proving African Americans had demonstrated great loyalty to their masters amid the war's upheaval. Memoirs and histories of Confederate military units abound with examples of slaves assisting wounded masters, helping white women and their families on farms and plantations, and spurning Yankee invaders. The pages of *Confederate Veteran*, the official magazine of the largest Confederate veterans' organization, offers ample evidence of this dimension of the Lost Cause version of the war. One representative article in the *Veteran* discusses a proposed monument, to be erected in either Montgomery or Richmond, that would pay tribute "to the memory of the old-time Southern negro. The loyal devotion of the men and women who were slaves has had no

FIGURE 2. Portrait of Alexander H. Stephens that served as the
frontispiece for the second volume of *A Constitutional View of the
Late War between the States*. Author's collection.

equal in all history." Beyond individual examples of such "loyalty," Lost Cause advocates usually insisted that slavery as an institution had "Christianized" and otherwise benefited the African American. "In his native land he has never reached the dignity of a civilized being, and he has never been civilized until transplanted into slavery," wrote one former Confederate. "Whatever of eminence any individual of the race has attained, is due directly or indirectly to the civilizing influence of the institution of slavery. It was the master of slaves who accomplished the greatest missionary success and the progress of his ward since is due to the training and influence of the past."[10]

Robert E. Lee took the place of slavery at the center of much Lost Cause literature. This centrality continued a trend that by the war's midpoint had seen Lee assume the position of being by far the most important Confederate figure. During and after the war, white southerners often compared Lee to George Washington, and between 1863 and 1865 Lee and his Army of Northern Virginia had functioned as the Confederacy's most important national institution. Lee represented the best card the Lost Cause writers could play in seeking a sympathetic audience. Widely praised even in the North as a self-effacing Christian gentleman, Lee had won almost all of the Confederacy's great military victories. He sometimes contended against odds as great as two to one, which allowed Lost Cause warriors to cast him and his soldiers as stalwart heroes engaged in a valiant but hopeless struggle. Stonewall Jackson, a deeply religious and personally idiosyncratic subordinate of enormous talent, usually stood at Lee's right arm. The Lee-Jackson partnership, which lasted just eleven months, between June 1862 and May 1863, inspired Lost Cause authors and speakers to search for superlatives that conveyed the duo's greatness. The final act of their collaboration closed with Jackson's death in the wake of southern victory at Chancellorsville and became one of the iconic moments of Confederate remembrance.

Yet it was not enough to praise Lee and Jackson. Lost Cause adherents often deprecated Grant in the course of assigning military virtue to their heroes. In 1878, for example, a piece in the *Southern Historical Society Papers* mounted a shrill attack on Grant in response to the Union general-in-chief's observation that he "never ranked Lee as high as some others of the army." The Overland campaign of 1864 left Lee's utter supremacy beyond doubt, suggested the author of the piece indignantly: "Lee foiled Grant in every move he made, defeated him in every battle they fought, and so completely crushed him in that last trial of strength at Cold Harbor, that his men refused to attack again . . . and the government at Washington would have been ready to give up the struggle if its further prosecution had depended alone on 'the great butcher.'" Such assertions overlooked the fact that Confederate casualties during the six-week campaign had been proportionately heavier than Grant's and that by mid-June Lee faced the type of siege at Petersburg he most feared.[11]

The emphasis on Lee and his army gave precedence to military events in Virginia and the rest of the Eastern Theater. Gettysburg became a retrospective dividing point for many ex-Confederates, and the battle took on much greater importance in Lost Cause writings than it had enjoyed during the conflict. Former Confederate general John B. Gordon's widely read memoirs exemplify this point: "Whatever differences of opinion may now or hereafter exist as to the results which might have followed a defeat of the Union arms at Gettysburg, there is universal concurrence in the judgment that this battle was the turning-point in the South's fortunes." Seeking a scapegoat to absolve Lee of responsibility for the defeat at Gettysburg, Lost Cause writers in the mid-1870s began a long campaign to fix blame on James Longstreet (Second Corps commander Richard S. Ewell and cavalry chief Jeb Stuart also came in for criticism). In an argument at odds with the notion that the Confederacy never could have won because of northern numbers and industrial strength, former Confederates accused Longstreet of losing a battle at Gettysburg that would have propelled the Confederacy to ultimate victory. This gave an especially bittersweet tinge to Gettysburg and made the Pickett-Pettigrew assault of July 3 a transcendent Lost Cause example of southern courage — the hugely important "High Water Mark of the Confederacy."[12]

Beyond Gettysburg, the Lost Cause highlighted Lee's other famous campaigns of Fredericksburg, Antietam, Second Bull Run, and Chancellorsville. Jackson's fabled 1862 Shenandoah Valley campaign also received detailed attention. Overall, operations in 1862–63, when almost all of the Confederate victories took place, proved more attractive to the Lost Cause than the standoffs and defeats of the period beginning with Gettysburg and extending to Appomattox. The Western Theater, scene of an almost unbroken string of Confederate defeats that included the loss of Vicksburg and Atlanta, naturally offered less useful grist for the Lost Cause mill.[13]

Whatever the geographic region in which they fought, United States soldiers frequently served in Lost Cause writings as brutal foils to heroic southern opponents. Union generals Benjamin F. Butler, William Tecumseh Sherman, and Philip H. Sheridan provoked some of the harshest comments during and after the war, and many Confederate accounts described their troops, as well as other Federals, as "barbarians" or "vandals." In late July 1864, a woman in northern Virginia pronounced it "doubly hard to live as a Christian in times when all one's feelings of indignation, hatred and revenge are daily roused by tidings of some fresh atrocity perpetrated by the Yankees in the once happy homes of the South." She added that the "ruffians who have ravaged our land can only be punished fitly by those who could equal them in baseness." Such wartime opinions resurfaced in the work of Lost Cause writers such as Jubal Early, Sheridan's opponent in the 1864 Shenandoah Valley campaign. Early's 1866 memoir bristled with harsh language regarding Union destruction of civilian property and "wanton and barbarous" actions against various Confederates. North Carolinian Cornelia Phillips Spencer's reminiscence similarly cast the Federals as cruel invaders. "Not a farm-house in the country but was visited and wantonly robbed," she wrote of Sherman's operations near Goldsboro in the spring of 1865. "Many were burned, and very many, together with the out-houses, were pulled down and hauled into camps for use. Generally not a live animal, not a morsel of food of any description was left, and in many instances not a bed or sheet or change of clothing for man, woman, or child."[14]

Beyond the battlefield, the Lost Cause generally overlooked contentious debates on the home front to depict a united Confederate people determined to resist Yankee oppressors. Women often received extravagant praise as the staunchest Confederate partisans—an interpretive convention that contained a good deal of truth. George Cary Eggleston's widely cited *A Rebel's Recollections*, first published in 1875, offered this valentine: "The women of the South could hardly have been more desperately in earnest than their husbands and brothers and sons were, in the prosecution of the war, but with their woman-natures they gave themselves wholly to the cause. . . . To doubt its righteousness, or to falter in their loyalty to it while it lived, would have been treason and infidelity; to do the like now that it is dead would be to them little less than sacrilege." The introduction to a collection of Confederate women's narratives that touched every Lost Cause base, titled *Women of the South in War Times*, stated that "it may truly be said of the Southern women of 1861–1865 that the simple narrative of their life and work unfolds a record of achievement, endurance, and self-sacrificing devotion that should be revealed and recognized as a splendid inspiration to men and women everywhere." Patriotic women thus joined gallant soldiers and loyal slaves as allies in the Lost Cause's tripartite depiction of the Confederate population.[15]

"The Happy Re-establishment of the Union"

A second school of interpretation developed in the North and pre-sented a direct challenge to the former Confederates' portrait of secession and the war. This northern equivalent of the Lost Cause has never been given a convenient name (perhaps winners worry less about such things than losers),[16] but an accurate label would be the Union Cause. It argued that slave-holding secessionists sought to undo the work of the founding generation by dismantling a Union that afforded white citizens wide economic and political opportunities and stood as a democratic example to the world. For Ameri-cans infused with a sense of national exceptionalism, the stirring rhetoric of Daniel Webster had gotten to the heart of their sense of Union. "I speak to-day for the preservation of the Union," Webster famously had proclaimed on March 7, 1850, "Hear me for my cause." The Massachusetts senator went on to affirm, "We have a great, popular, constitutional government guarded by law and by judicature, and defended by the affections of the whole people. No monarchical throne presses these States together, no iron chain of military power encircles them; they live and stand under a government popular in its form, representative in its character, founded upon principles of equality, and so constructed, we hope, as to last forever." Twenty years earlier, countering what he claimed was South Carolina's support for nullification, Webster had thundered on the floor of the Senate, "Liberty and Union, now and forever, one and inseparable." The printed version of that speech sold nearly 150,000 copies and influenced generations of American schoolchildren.[17]

Republicans and Democrats across the North united in opposing seces-sion after Confederates fired on Fort Sumter in April 1861, and first to last most white northerners would have said the war was about restoring the Union. Republicans and many Democrats eventually accepted emancipation as a useful tool to help defeat the Rebels and punish the slaveholding class most northerners blamed for secession and the outbreak of war; however, except among abolitionists and some Radical Republicans, liberation of the slaves took a back seat to preservation of the Union. Abraham Lincoln spoke eloquently for all those who loved the Union. His first inaugural address, delivered on March 4, 1861, insisted the Union was perpetual; with seces-sion, which meant rejection of the principle of majority rule, "anarchy, or despotism in some form, is all that is left." Summoning images of a shared democratic destiny implicit in unionism, Lincoln closed on a lyrical note:

"The mystic chords of memory, stretching from every battle-field, and patriot grave, to every heart and hearthstone, all over this broad land, will yet swell the chorus of the Union, when again touched, as surely they will be, by the better angels of our nature." Four months later in a message to Congress, Lincoln staked out lofty ideological ground in arguing that secession "presents the whole family of man, the question, whether a constitutional republic, or a democracy—a government of the people, by the people—can, or cannot, maintain its territorial integrity, against its own domestic foes." Much deeper into the war, at Gettysburg in November 1863, Lincoln recalled the Founders and expressed his hope that the shining American democratic example of "government of the people, by the people, for the people" would endure in a restored Union.[18]

Countless United States soldiers during the war articulated themes related to the Union Cause that would be carried forward in the postwar era. Four of their voices, three from the Midwest and one from New England, capture the tenor of Union-centered sentiments that often linked the struggle of 1861–65 to that of 1776–83 and are worth attending to here. These four soldiers, like so many of their comrades, fit very comfortably in the tradition exemplified by Daniel Webster, and eloquently advanced by Lincoln, that accepted as an article of faith the importance of preserving the Union.

"Our Fathers made this country, we, their children are to save it," wrote an Ohio lieutenant. "Without Union & peace our freedom is worthless." Another Ohioan explained that to "admit the right of the seceding states to break up the Union at pleasure" likely would result in "military license, anarchy, and despotism." A month before he was killed at Gettysburg, a Minnesotan informed a friend that he was willing to risk his life "for the purpose of crushing this d——d rebellion and to support the best government on God's footstool." A Vermonter named Wilbur Fiske, writing letters for publication in a newspaper, spoke in early 1862 about the many "sober, thoughtful young men who have come here for the sole purpose of putting down the rebellion." More than three years later, Fiske cheered "the great and glorious victory of Gen. Grant with the army of the Potomac, which resulted in the complete overthrow of Gen. Lee and his rebel host. . . . We knew that the great serpent of secession whose poisonous fangs had been struck at the nation's life, was about to lose its power for evil forever."[19]

Retrospective accounts from the pens of soldiers and officers highlight the importance of Union to thousands of recruits and their commanders in 1861–62. William Tecumseh Sherman, who cared little about the fate of slaves and had been living comfortably in the South on the eve of the conflict, explained that President James Buchanan's irresolution in the face of the Lower South's dismantling of the Union had scared him. "I confess this staggered me," he wrote in his memoirs, "and I feared that the prophecies and assertions of . . . [various European] commentators on our form of government were right, and that our Constitution was a mere rope of sand, that would break with the first pressure." Chaplain Frederic Denison of the 1st Rhode Island Cavalry remembered that the "rebel shot that smote Fort Sumter . . . was answered by the clarion of liberty on all the hills of the Free States, summoning the loyal and brave to the support of the Union." A "great people" risked "their lives in defence of law and order," continued Denison in his history of the regiment. "It had not been believed that republicanism was capable of such spirit and voluntary self-defense."[20]

The historian of the Army of the Potomac's Irish Brigade echoed Lincoln in placing the importance of Union within an international context. "The Irish people in New York, and throughout the Northern States," observed David Power Conyngham in 1867, "were not slow in declaring for the Union and volunteering for its defence. . . . The Irish felt that not only was the safety of the great Republic, the home of their exiled race, at stake, but also, that the great principles of democracy were at issue with the aristocratic doctrines of monarchism." Conyngham remarked that Irish soldiers remained indifferent to the plight of slaves and had no desire to fight for emancipation. They fought because "the safety and welfare" of their "adopted country and its glorious Constitution were imperilled."

A private in the brigade chose words reminiscent of Daniel Webster's great speeches in seconding Conyngham's explanation of Irish motivation during the war. "I owed my life to my whole adopted country," wrote William McCarter of the 116th Pennsylvania Infantry in 1879, "not the North nor the South, nor the East nor the West, but the Union, one and inseparable, its form of government, its institutions, its Stars and Stripes. . . . My full determination was to assist in any way that I could to prevent the Union's dissolution by the traitors of the North, as well as those of the South." Sentiment for emancipation played no role for McCarter, who insisted that exposure to slavery during his time campaigning in Virginia and Maryland had persuaded him that the institution "was not the 'hideous monster' that I had previously heard it represented."[21]

Just as the Lost Cause celebrated Lee and his army, so also the Union Cause lauded United States military forces as a mighty agent that crushed the rebellion and ensured the republic's future. After the martyred Lincoln, Ulysses S. Grant stood as the preeminent Union idol. His victories at Forts Henry and Donelson, Shiloh, Vicksburg, and Chattanooga had broken Confederate power in the Western Theater, and his decisive confrontation with Robert E. Lee in Virginia had ended triumphantly at Appomattox. William Tecumseh Sherman, the victor at Atlanta in 1864, and Philip H. Sheridan, who that same year thrashed Confederates in the Shenandoah Valley, emerged from the conflict as Grant's premier lieutenants, filling the role opposite Grant in the Union Cause that Jackson occupied vis-à-vis Lee in Lost Cause memories of the conflict.[22]

A few witnesses will suffice to suggest how deeply northerners valued what their soldiers had accomplished in saving the Union. Herman Melville put the case very directly in the dedication for his collection of war poetry: "The Battle-Pieces In This Volume Are Dedicated To The Memory Of The THREE HUNDRED THOUSAND Who In The War For The Maintenance Of The Union Fell Devotedly Under The Flag Of Their Fathers." The wife of a Democratic judge in New York City composed an entry in her diary on April 10, 1865, that revealed joy and a belief that saving the Union opened magnificent possibilities for the soon-to-be reunited country. "Glory be to God on high; the rebellion is ended!" wrote Maria Lydig Daly upon hearing of Lee's surrender. "A Western man said," she continued, "speaking of the Union victories and our indifference hereafter to public opinion in Europe, 'The United States . . . will now be bounded by the Atlantic, the Pacific, and the Aurora Borealis.'" On June 18, 1865, Republican politician Roscoe Conkling spoke to members of the 117th New York Infantry, who had stopped in Utica on their way home from service in Virginia and North Carolina. He congratulated the "victorious soldiers of the Republic" for their role in defending "the life and glory of your country. . . . In all this career of glory, of duty, and of daring exploit, a common purpose has inspired you, a common hope has led you on. What was it? Peace. Peace with the Government and the constitution our fathers established, has been the object of the war, and the prayer of every patriot and every soldier." The regimental historian pronounced Conkling's remarks "appropriate and eloquent."[23]

William Swinton's popular history of the Army of the Potomac, published just a year after Lee's surrender at Appomattox, anticipated innumerable other accounts in focusing on restoration of the Union as the war's most notable outcome. "Thus the Army of the Potomac—that mighty creation of the patriotism of a free people, which for four years had waged a struggle unparalleled in its continuous intensity—ceased to be," wrote Swinton in a summary paragraph that made no mention of emancipation, "closing its career in the world and the world's wars by the happy re-establishment of the Union for which it had fought." In Swinton's Union Cause interpretation, soldiers in the Army of the Potomac, together with "their illustrious sister-army from the West," had matched their foes in courage and sacrifice but far exceeded them in results.[24]

Many monuments erected by participants in the war similarly celebrated the Union Cause. Two in New England, one in Kansas, and one in the far Southwest offer sentiments typical of many others. In Meredith, New Hampshire, a soldier at parade rest stands atop a granite base that honors "The Twelfth Regiment New Hampshire Volunteers Who Fought In The War Of 1861–1865 For The Preservation Of The Union." A cemetery in Freedom, Maine, boasts an imposing obelisk for "Those Who Died In The Service Of Their Country During The Late Rebellion, Sacrificing Their Lives for The Honor Of The Flag And The Integrity Of The Union." In September 1898, Junction City, Kansas, unveiled a memorial arch, atop which stands an infantryman flanked by a pair of mortars. It commemorates soldiers and sailors "Who Inspired By Patriotism Freely Offered Their Lives For The Maintenance Of An Undivided Country." More than thirty years before the dedication ceremony in Junction City, residents of Santa Fe had placed an obelisk in the city's plaza, erected by the "people of New Mexico through their legislatures of 1866–7–8," that carries the words "May the Union be Perpetual." A number of northern monuments draw on Lincoln's Gettysburg Address, as with the Grand Army of the Republic statue in Macomb, Illinois, that remembers the men of McDonough County who "Voluntarily and Freely Gave Their Lives That Government Of The People, By The People, And For The People Shall Not Perish From The Earth."[25]

"No Longer Cursed by the Hell-Black System of Human Bondage"

A third interpretive tradition, the Emancipation Cause, emerged shortly after the war from black and white abolitionists and Radical Republicans. Its adherents almost always paid homage to the Union, but they considered the emancipation of more than 4 million slaves to be the conflict's most important outcome. They joined Union Cause brethren in laying full blame for the outbreak of war on the seceding states and tied the rebellion directly to a "slave power conspiracy" that had wielded inordinate power in the antebellum decades. Many northerners monitored the growing Lost Cause literature in the 1870s and sensed that it was earning respect even above the Mason-Dixon Line. Those devoted to the Emancipation Cause deeply resented what they saw as a tendency among some northerners to forgive ex-Rebels too easily. They also worried that those who trumpeted reunion above all else failed to give due attention to the death of slavery as a pathbreaking accomplishment.[26]

Abraham Lincoln's second inaugural address foreshadowed two crucial parts of the Emancipation Cause. Delivered on March 4, 1865, it left no doubt about slaveholders' role in precipitating the war and held up emancipation as an outcome that, to a significant degree, preceded final restoration of the Union. "One eighth of the whole population were colored slaves, not distributed generally over the Union, but localized in the Southern part of it," Lincoln said in regard to the situation in 1860. "These slaves constituted a peculiar and powerful interest. All knew that this interest was, somehow, the cause of the war. To strengthen, perpetuate, and extend this interest was the object for which the insurgents would rend the Union, even by war; while the government claimed no right to do more than to restrict the territorial enlargement of it. Neither party . . . anticipated that the *cause* of the conflict might cease with, or even before, the conflict itself should cease." At Gettysburg fifteen months earlier, Lincoln also had acknowledged the centrality of emancipation, placing "a new birth of freedom" alongside restoration of the Union as a fundamental goal of the United States war effort.[27]

By the early 1870s, Frederick Douglass had embarked on a crusade against what he perceived as northern complicity in spreading, or at least tolerating, Lost Cause arguments. Douglass, who had been the most famous black abolitionist, knew that most former Confederates believed their failed cause had been just. He complained in 1871 that the "spirit of secession is stronger today than ever," characterizing it as "a deeply rooted, devoutly cherished sentiment, inseparably identified with the 'lost cause,' which the half measures of the Government towards the traitors has helped to cultivate and strengthen." In an address at Arlington Cemetery on Decoration Day in 1871, Douglass recognized the importance of Union, stating that loyal Americans should never forget that "victory to the rebellion" would have "meant death to the republic." But he added that "the unselfish devotion of the noble army who rest in these honored graves" had made possible a far better republic—"a united country, no longer cursed by the hell-black system of human bondage," that could look forward to "a long and glorious career of justice, liberty, and civilization." For Douglass, the admirable goal of restoring the Union had been ennobled by the achievement of emancipation.[28]

Douglass found particularly distasteful the manner in which some northerners responded to Robert E. Lee's death in the autumn of 1870. Indeed, many newspapers in the North were so admiring of various elements of Lee's life and career that J. William Jones, one of the general's indefatigable hagiographers, later quoted from them in his *Life and Letters of Robert Edward Lee: Soldier and Man*. For example, the *New York Sun* termed Lee "an able soldier, a sincere Christian, and an honest man," while the *New York Herald* breathlessly stated that Lee "came nearer the ideal of a soldier and Christian general than any man we can think of." The *New York Times* mentioned Lee's "unobtrusive modesty and purity of life" after the war, noting that he had "won the respect even of those who most bitterly deplore and reprobate his course in the rebellion." Douglass would have none of this. "Is it not about time that this bombastic laudation of the rebel chief should cease?" he asked. Offended by "nauseating flatteries of the late Robert E. Lee," Douglass sarcastically suggested that "the soldier who kills the most men in battle, even in a bad cause, is the greatest Christian, and entitled to the highest place in heaven."[29]

Although not as widely popular as the Union Cause, the Emancipation Cause was well represented in postwar writings. Henry Wilson's massive *History of the Rise and Fall of the Slave Power in America*, published in three hefty volumes between 1872 and 1877, laid out a direct challenge to the Lost Cause. A leading Republican during and after the war, Wilson attacked slaveholders who had "organized treasonable conspiracies, raised the standard of revolution, and plunged the nation into a bloody contest for the preservation of its threatened life." Like Douglass, Wilson considered emancipation rather than reunion to be the great triumph of the conflict—a triumph that "opened the continent to the forces of a fresher energy and a higher civilization." Seldom read or cited by historians, Wilson's trilogy is less well known than the standard Lost Cause texts.[30]

The regimental history of the 153rd Pennsylvania Infantry, a nine-month unit mustered into service in the summer of 1862, similarly found in emancipation the touchstone of the war. Noting that the "fixed policy of Lincoln primarily was the preservation of the Union, the dissolution of which was to him (and to every true American), the greatest calamity which could befall the nation," the book's author, a musician named W. R. Kiefer, went on to stress that the president's antislavery feelings most impressed the Pennsylvanians. "They had helped to elect him; they knew how he stood on the great moral question of human slavery; for largely the men were religious in practice or at least in proclivity," he explained. "Probably the majority had imbibed the anti-slavery sentiment which had become the burning sectional issue. Many of them sealed their convictions with their blood on the sacred soil of Gettysburg." The men carried out their duties in behalf of Lincoln's Emancipation Proclamation, stated Kiefer, "the most immortal moral edict known to any nation. . . . Lincoln caused the shackles to drop from the arms, intellects and souls of about four millions of American citizens."[31]

While writers such as Douglass, Wilson, and Kiefer helped keep alive Emancipation Cause sentiments, African American communities across the South established traditions that marked the achievement of freedom. Although often held on January 1 to honor Lincoln's Emancipation Proclamation, these commemorations did not follow a rigid pattern. In parts of Texas, for example, word of freedom arrived on June 19, 1865 — giving rise to "Juneteenth" celebrations. "African Americans' particular understanding of the war, borne out of their actions," notes one student of these events, "was also reflected in their later remembrances. Black southerners never did recall the 'War of Northern Aggression' or the 'War Between the States' or even the 'War for Union'; rather, the war, for them, was the 'Freedom War,' the 'Slavery War,' or the 'Holy War.'"[32] Seldom openly antagonistic toward those who praised the Union Cause but scarcely mentioned emancipation, they argued for the addition of emancipation to preservation of the Union as an imperishable outcome of the bloody labors carried out by United States soldiers and sailors.

Among those uniformed men had been more than 180,000 African Americans, who held a special position in the Emancipation Cause narrative. They had taken the most direct action possible in the struggle for freedom, imperiling their lives to stake a claim for political and legal equality in a restored Union. Joseph T. Wilson, a black veteran, gave voice to what innumerable African Americans undoubtedly felt. "What a picture for the historian's immortal pen to paint of the freemen of America," he wrote, "whose sufferings were long, whose struggle was gigantic, and whose achievement was a glorious personal and political freedom!" Luis Emilio, a white officer in the famous 54th Massachusetts Infantry, wrote movingly about the final scene in the regiment's Civil War service. Assembled on Boston Common, the soldiers heard their commander, Bvt. Brig. Gen. Edward N. Hallowell, express thanks for "the brave manner in which they had supported him in many trying times." The men of the 54th had returned home with their colors, tattered from long campaigning but intact "enough to show how bravely they had been defended." Hallowell assured the men that they "had proved good soldiers in the field; now he hoped they would become good citizens." "When they left Massachusetts," proclaimed Hallowell, "it was the only State which recognized them as citizens. Now the whole country acknowledged their soldierly qualities."[33]

"Enemies No Longer, Generous Friends Rather"

The achievements of black men in blue uniforms went largely unnoticed in the fourth interpretive tradition—a movement toward reconciliation that gained power in the late nineteenth century and remains widely evident today. The Reconciliation Cause included major military and political figures who advocated a memory of the conflict that muted the divisive issue of slavery, avoided value judgments about the righteousness of either cause, and celebrated the valor and pluck of white soldiers in both Union and Confederate armies. It was because of *American* traits showcased on Civil War battlefields, the reconciliationist interpretation maintained, that a United States economic colossus stood poised by 1900 to assume a central position on the world stage. Reconciliationists often pointed to Appomattox, where Grant and Lee behaved in a way that promoted peaceful reunion, as the beginning of a healing process that reminded all Americans of their shared history and traditions. Although sometimes combining with elements of the Union Cause and even the Emancipation Cause, the Reconciliation Cause most often was characterized by a measure of northern capitulation to the white South and the Lost Cause tradition.[34]

Although reconciliationists achieved considerable success, it is important to stress that many Americans, South and North, remained resolutely unreconciled into the twentieth century. They had been bitter at the end of the war and remained so long thereafter. A pair of examples will illustrate this phenomenon. Reconstruction, with its Fourteenth and Fifteenth Amendments conveying political and legal protections to freedpeople, deepened the white South's already substantial sense of outrage toward the North. In 1905, former Confederate general Clement A. Evans sputtered about the "tragedy, pathos, corruption . . . and absurdities of the military dictatorship and of reconstruction." The postwar era, thought Evans, had been marked by "topsy-turvy conditions generally, domestic upheaval, negroes voting, Black and Tan Conventions and Legislatures, disorder on plantations, Loyal Leagues and Freedmen's Bureaus, Ku Klux and Red Shirts"—all of which, put simply, meant Evans and those who shared his perspective detested the North's forcing unwelcome changes in the former slaveholding states' racial structures.[35]

Many Union veterans matched Evans's strident sectional rhetoric. A publication of the Grand Army of the Republic, the major Union veterans' organization, worried as late as 1925 about textbooks that included material favorable to the Confederacy. Labeling the war a "Great Pro-Slavery Rebellion," the *Grand Army Record* referred to a "Lost Cause of Historical Truth" in attributing influence to pro-Confederate writings that obfuscated the real history and meaning of the conflict. Public displays of the Rebel flag elicited strident responses among northern veterans. In 1891, the Grand Army's national commander forbade members to participate in events that featured "the emblem of treason." Any veteran who ignored this instruction, he lectured, "violates his obligation 'to maintain true allegiance to the United States of America' . . . and brings disgrace upon the order of which he is a member."[36] For a half-century and more after the war, politicians at the state and national levels often resorted to highly charged language that kept wartime passions alive. Republicans waved the "bloody shirt," former Confederates excoriated scalawags and carpetbaggers, and candidates throughout the nation manipulated race and emancipation to suit their purposes.

Still, reconciliationists carried the day in many public forums. The writings and speeches of Ulysses S. Grant, John Brown Gordon, and Joshua Lawrence Chamberlain offer three variations on the reconciliation theme. Grant's memoirs, which sold in huge numbers following the general's death in 1885, show how the Union and Emancipation Causes could be joined to Reconciliation. Grant left no doubt that southern slaveholders bore responsibility for secession and, by extension, war. The "exact truth" of their attitude after the election of Lincoln, he stated, was: "You have been submissive to our rule heretofore; but it looks now as if you did not intend to continue so, and we will remain in the Union no longer." As for the Confederate cause, Grant pronounced it "one of the worst for which a people ever fought, and for which there was the least excuse." Yet his memoirs took a reconciliationist stance toward Robert E. Lee, the great military pillar of that inexcusable cause. Grant described Lee as a "man of much dignity," whose surrender at Appomattox left the Union commander "sad and depressed," feeling "like anything rather than rejoicing at the downfall of a foe who had fought so long and valiantly." He closed his memoirs with acknowledgment of the "universally kind feeling expressed for me" during a losing fight against cancer. "It is a significant and gratifying fact that Confederates should have joined heartily in this spontaneous move," Grant observed, before closing with a final sentence regarding the possibility of a true reconciliation: "I hope the good feeling inaugurated may continue to the end."[37]

John Brown Gordon of Georgia typified the reconciliationist approach of former Confederates. A gifted soldier who had risen to corps command in Lee's army despite an absence of formal military training, he enjoyed a highly successful postwar career that included stints as Georgia's governor and one of its United States senators. Much sought after as a speaker, he also served as the longtime commander-in-chief of the United Confederate Veterans. Gordon promulgated conventional Lost Cause ideas about most aspects of the war. He praised Lee and Jackson, attacked Longstreet's conduct at Gettysburg, and lavished praise on brave Confederate soldiers battling against long odds and on redoubtable Confederate civilians suffering appalling privations. Recalling Jefferson Davis's postwar arguments, he acknowledged slavery as "the immediate fomenting cause of the woeful American conflict" but insisted that it "was far from being the sole cause of the prolonged conflict." As proof of the latter (and ignoring Lincoln's insistence from 1863 forward that emancipation be part of any plan for reunion), he offered "the undeniable fact that at any period of the war from its beginning to near its close the South could have saved slavery by simply laying down its arms and returning to the Union."[38]

Unlike Jubal Early and other ex-Confederates who nourished undiminished hatred of the North, Gordon preached the need to get beyond sectional animosity as the United States marched toward international greatness. He crafted a classic reconciliationist narrative in his 1903 memoirs. "The unseemly things which occurred in the great conflict between the States should be forgotten, or at least forgiven," he counseled his readers, "and no longer permitted to disturb complete harmony between North and South." All young Americans "should be taught to hold in perpetual remembrance all that was great and good on both sides" and to recognize that both sections had fought "to protect what they conceived to be threatened rights and imperilled liberty." Generals Lee and Grant, admirable and talented rivals whose strengths reflected well on the societies that produced them, should "live in history as an inspiration to coming generations." Looking to the future, Gordon predicted that the conflict's blood and tears would contribute to "the upbuilding of American manhood and . . . the future defence of American freedom." Gordon closed with a paean to the modern nation: "So the Republic, rising from its baptism of blood with a national life more robust, a national union more complete, and a national influence ever widening, shall go forever forward in its benign mission to humanity." President William McKinley, among a multitude of northerners during the late nineteenth century, heard Gordon deliver one of his most requested lectures, titled "The Last Days of the Confederacy." "The lecture was intensely interesting," commented the president in April 1895, "and was permeated by a highly patriotic spirit."[39]

Joshua Lawrence Chamberlain resembled Gordon in many ways. A nonprofessional soldier of much accomplishment, he served three terms as Maine's governor after the war and long held the presidency of Bowdoin College. He also wrote extensively about his wartime activities, pursuing Union Cause and to a lesser extent Emancipation Cause themes. At the dedication of monuments to Maine soldiers at Gettysburg on October 3, 1889, he affirmed that the men of his 20th Maine Infantry had carried into battle "the flag of the Union, the flag of the people, vindicating the right and charged with the duty of preventing any factions, no matter how many nor under what pretense, from breaking up this common Country." Chamberlain believed in Lincoln's mystic connections: "The Union was the body of a spiritual Unity. Of this we were part, —responsible to it and for it, —and our sacrifice was its service." Although most concerned with Union, Chamberlain also touched on emancipation. "The 'lost cause' is not lost liberty and right of self-government," he stated that autumn day in Gettysburg, "What is lost is slavery of men and supremacy of States."[40]

Chamberlain joined Gordon in moving beyond sectional interpretations to embrace reconciliation. He and Gordon had faced each other at Appomattox on April 12, 1865, with Chamberlain commanding Union soldiers who watched Gordon's Confederates trudge up the Richmond Stage Road to lay down their arms. In *The Passing of the Armies*, a long account of the last weeks of the war, Chamberlain paid tribute to both Gordon and the Confederacy's common soldiers, acknowledging a shared valor among combatants on the two sides that served as a leitmotif through much of the reconciliation literature. "Before us in proud humiliation stood the embodiment of manhood: men whom neither toils and sufferings, nor the fact of death, nor disaster, nor hopelessness could bend from their resolve," wrote Chamberlain, "standing before us now, thin, worn, and famished, but erect, and with eyes looking level into ours, waking memories that bound us together as no other bond;—was not such manhood to be welcomed back into a Union so tested and assured?" Lost Cause writers scarcely could have exceeded this

...GEN. JOHN B. GORDON...

Clement Opera House.

To-Night, Tuesday, Nov. 10.

"Last Days of the Confederacy"

"First Days of the Confederacy"
(NEW)

UNDER SOLE MANAGEMENT

Southern Lyceum Bureau,
LOUISVILLE,   ATLANTA,   DALLAS.

FIGURE 3. Advertisement for one of John B. Gordon's lectures. Courtesy of T. Michael Parrish.

portrait of desperate Confederate struggle against the odds. Beyond the soldiers at Appomattox, Chamberlain praised Grant and Lee equally, describing the Rebel chieftain as "a master in military economy, making best use with least waste of material." Overall, Lee "exemplified remarkable ability as a commander. In military sagacity and astuteness we recognized his superiority."[41]

The Reconciliation Cause influenced comments by three United States presidents in the first four decades of the twentieth century. On February 13, 1905, Theodore Roosevelt delivered a speech on "the race problem" that called on Americans to emulate Abraham Lincoln's spirit in his second inaugural address by putting aside sectional animosities to knit the nation together "in the unbreakable bonds of eternal friendship." Mindful of both Union and Emancipation, Roosevelt pronounced it "clear to all that the triumph of the cause of freedom and of the Union was essential to the welfare of mankind." But the president, whose uncle James Dunwoody Bulloch had been the Confederacy's principal naval agent in Europe, also served up some vintage reconciliationist rhetoric. "The great Civil War, in which Lincoln towered as the loftiest figure, left us not only a reunited country," he remarked, "but a country which has the proud right to claim as its own the glory won alike by those who wore the blue and by those who wore the gray, by those who followed Grant and by those who followed Lee." Both sides "fought with equal bravery and with equal sincerity of conviction," added Roosevelt in language similar to that of countless Reconciliation writers and speakers, "each striving for the light as it was given him to see the light." Although Roosevelt did not say so explicitly, his listeners and those who later read his words almost certainly thought his comments about bravery and conviction applied to white soldiers. The rest of the speech, which dealt with how best to handle racial questions, addressed only white Americans, imploring them to be sympathetic and helpful to one another in dealing with "one of the gravest problems before our people."[42]

Myrta Lockett Avary, surely not the only white southerner to embrace Roosevelt's public expressions about the Confederate military resistance and the postwar South, closed her book about Reconstruction with a quotation from a speech the president had delivered in Richmond. "Great though the need of praise which is due the South for the soldierly valor her sons displayed during the four years of war," said Roosevelt with scrupulous attention to both the Lost Cause and Reconciliation, "I think that even greater praise is due for what her people have accomplished in the forty years which have followed. . . . You stand loyally to your traditions and memories; you stand also loyally for our great common country of today and for our common flag."[43]

Woodrow Wilson and Franklin D. Roosevelt also adopted reconciliation themes for their comments at the fiftieth and seventy-fifth commemorations of the battle of Gettysburg. Unlike Theodore Roosevelt, neither of them made even oblique references to emancipation. The stirring rivalry of courageous white soldiers at Gettysburg, together with the formidable nation that emerged from the conflict, dominated both speeches. President Wilson arrived at Gettysburg in 1913 as a reconciliationist with evident Lost Cause sympathies. A native of Virginia who had lived as a boy in Georgia and South Carolina, he treasured a youthful memory of seeing Robert E. Lee, of whom he later wrote: "It is not an exaggeration to say that in all parts of this country the manhood and the self-forgetfulness and the achievements of General Lee are a conscious model to men who would be morally great." At Gettysburg, surrounded by "gallant men in blue and gray," Wilson celebrated the masculine virtues and capacity for forgiveness the aged warriors had exhibited. "We have found one another again as brothers and comrades in arms," said Wilson, "enemies no longer, generous friends rather, our battles long past, the quarrel forgotten — except that we shall not forget the splendid valour, the manly devotion of the men then arrayed against one another, now grasping hands and smiling into each other's eyes."[44]

Franklin Roosevelt chose similar rhetoric at Gettysburg on July 3, 1938. Speaking at the unveiling of the Eternal Light Peace Memorial on Oak Hill, with approximately 1,800 veterans in attendance, Roosevelt remarked, "Men who wore the blue and men who wore the gray . . . are brought here by the memories of old divided loyalties, but they meet here in united loyalty to a united cause which the unfolding years have made it easier to see." Of the veterans present, said Roosevelt to listeners who could read the words "Peace Eternal in a Nation United" on the white stone of the monument, "All of them we honor, not asking under which flag they fought then — thankful that they stand together under one flag now." Iconic photographs from that same anniversary celebration showed old soldiers, decked out in uniforms adorned with reunion ribbons, shaking hands across the stone wall on Cemetery Hill that had sheltered Union troops firing into the ranks of North Carolinians and Virginians in Pickett's Charge. The president's words and the image of former enemies fraternizing on a once bloody field epitomized the Reconciliation Cause.[45]

By the time Roosevelt spoke at Gettysburg, the individuals who had done the most to create the four interpretive traditions were long dead. Had they been alive to witness the shifting landscape of Civil War memory over the succeeding decades of the twentieth century, some would have been encouraged and others left frustrated. Academic historians, popular writers, novelists, artists, and filmmakers, among others, had a hand in shaping perceptions of the conflict. In terms of their opportunity to reach huge audiences, those who made movies held a decided advantage over the others. The work of filmmakers during the past twenty years will be the focus of the next two chapters.

Going but Not Yet Gone : The Confederate War on Film

2

The Lost Cause narrative flourished in films for nearly half a century before losing ground, and eventually supremacy, to the Emancipation and Reconciliation Causes. Much of the Lost Cause success grew from Hollywood's two most popular and influential Civil War–related films — *The Birth of a Nation*, director D. W. Griffith's silent-era blockbuster released in 1915, and *Gone with the Wind*, producer David O. Selznick's 1939 treatment of Margaret Mitchell's best-selling novel of the same name. Between them, the films grossed approximately $2 billion, adjusted for inflation;[1] they also exposed generations of Americans to strongly positive depictions of the Confederacy and the slaveholding South, as well as to hostile treatments of Reconstruction. Even during the Lost Cause heyday, Hollywood typically featured an element of Reconciliation and often at least a tincture of the Union Cause in its Civil War films. The appearance of *Glory* in 1989 ushered Emancipation to center stage. Since the late 1980s, the Lost Cause has steadily receded. Only the appearance of *Gods and Generals* in 2003 suggested that a major Hollywood production could still offer an interpretation of the conflict that embraced much of the Lost Cause tradition.

Hollywood and the Lost Cause before *Glory*

Hollywood produced many short Civil War–related films prior to 1915, but *The Birth of a Nation* represented the first full-scale cinematic exploration of America's great national bloodletting. Prior to its release, producer Thomas Ince's fifty-minute *The Battle of Gettysburg*, which debuted in June 1913 before an enthusiastic audience in New York's Grand Opera House, stood as the longest and most expensive film devoted to the conflict.[2] Griffith's sprawling narrative preeminently idealizes the Old South, the Confederacy, and white southerners during Reconstruction; however, it also contains a reconciliationist theme and more than a perfunctory nod in the direction of the Union Cause (Reconciliation and Union in the film will be discussed in the next chapter). With Thomas F. Dixon's noxiously racist novel *The Clansman* as its guiding text, the film originally carried that title. Dixon watched it for the first time at a private screening in New York City in early 1915. Impressed by the small invited audience's reaction, he suggested a change in the title. *The Clansman* was unsuitable for a film of such power, he told Griffith, "It should be called *The Birth of a Nation*."[3]

In his story of war, reunion, and Reconstruction, Griffith wholeheartedly embraces Lost Cause themes. The Old South, epitomized by the courtly

Dr. Cameron and his family in South Carolina, features a social structure "where life runs in a quaintly way that is to be no more." The "kindly master" of Cameron Hall presides over a world populated by cheerfully loyal slaves and genteel white people. During a prewar visit by members of the Stoneman family, for example, the Camerons take their guests to the slave quarters, where apparently contented slaves perform exaggerated dances. Storm clouds menace what Griffith considers an idyllic land following Lincoln's election. "The power of the sovereign states," viewers learn in language reminiscent of Jefferson Davis's and Alexander H. Stephens's postwar writings, "established when Lord Cornwallis surrendered to the individual colonies in 1781, is threatened by the new administration." Four years later, Appomattox marks the "end of state sovereignty." The intervening period, as imagined by Griffith, features Confederate devotion and sacrifice in pursuit of independence. The Camerons send three sons to war—a "mother's gift to the cause"—and two of them die. They also contribute their material wealth, willingly accepting hardship and proudly wearing old clothes. On the battlefield late in the war, tattered Confederate soldiers find "parched corn their only rations."

Griffith's use of Colonel Ben Cameron, the one son who survives the war, and his soldiers to highlight Confederate privations and sustained courage fits nicely within the Lost Cause framework of honorable struggle against long odds. The film's most impressively staged scene depicts a Confederate offensive during the siege of Petersburg late in the war. Seeking to capture a wagon train filled with food, Colonel Cameron's men mount a desperate charge that carries them across two lines of Union works before finally losing momentum. Cameron himself leads a small group toward a third line, eliciting cheers from admiring Federals when he stops for a moment to succor a fallen foe. At the climax of the attack, he thrusts a flagstaff into the muzzle of a Union cannon and collapses with a serious wound (fig. 4). Resolute despite their rags and empty bellies, Cameron's infantrymen personify devotion to duty uncompromised by eventual defeat.

Additionally, the film portrays a heroic southern home front menaced by hordes of United States soldiers. Anticipating Gone with the Wind's handling of a major Lost Cause villain, Griffith focuses considerable attention on William Tecumseh Sherman's operations in Georgia during 1864. "While women and children weep," proclaims one panel, "a great conqueror marches to the sea." Cutting between scenes of civilians clutching one another and panoramic shots of United States troops amid smoke and battle action, Griffith reaches the moment when the "torch of war" is directed "against the

FIGURE 4. Union soldiers in *The Birth of a Nation* help the wounded Colonel Ben Cameron (Henry B. Walthall) after he has rammed a Confederate flag into the cannon barrel to the viewer's left. Photofest.

breast of Atlanta." United States artillery pounds the city, whose residents find themselves helpless in the face of cruel military power. After watching images of dislocation and loss on the Confederate home front, coupled with those of enormous sacrifice on the battlefield, viewers could understand Griffith's sense of the "agony which the South endured that a nation might be born."

Between 1915 and 1949, *The Birth of a Nation* played to large audiences throughout the United States. A cinematic landmark, it was the first film to cost more than $100,000 to make, the first with a $2.00 admission fee, and the first to have a gala premiere. Its racist message prompted outrage in some places outside the old Confederacy, as when a reviewer in *The New Republic* pronounced it an "aggressively vicious and defamatory" spectacle that amounted to "spiritual assassination. It degrades the censors that passed it and the white race that endures it." Yet the film generated its largest profits in northern and western cities, where patrons likely were dazzled by Griffith's technical skill and masterful staging and little bothered by his racism. Burns Mantle, drama critic for the *New York Daily News*, addressed this phenomenon in noting an "element of excitement that swept a sophisticated audience like a prairie fire in a high wind." The *New York Tribune*'s critic similarly described the film as a "spectacular drama" that served up "thrills piled upon thrills."[4]

Gone with the Wind ended *The Birth of a Nation*'s reign as the most impressive and profitable cinematic expression of the Lost Cause. David O. Selznick's epic almost certainly has been the single most powerful influence on American perceptions of the Civil War. It remains part of the cultural landscape through repeated airings on television, its canonical characters and scenes available for comparison with more recent cinematic treatments.

It initially benefited from a vast potential audience of readers who had devoured Margaret Mitchell's novel. In the midst of the Great Depression, the book sold nearly 1.7 million copies in its first year and won the Pulitzer Prize for literature in 1937. At first reluctant to purchase the rights because *So Red the Rose* (1935) and other recent Civil War films had performed poorly at the box office, Selznick eventually paid Mitchell $50,000 and set about converting the book's 1,037 pages into a movie that ran for three hours and forty-two minutes—a record at the time. Selznick arranged for a lavish premiere in Atlanta on December 15, 1939, complete with a parade past a throng estimated at 300,000 and a costume ball attended by more than 6,000. Hoopskirts, Confederate uniforms, and other period dress were much in evidence in what amounted to a gigantic, nostalgic revisiting of the slaveholding South before and during the Civil War.[5]

Reviews left no doubt about the impact of the film's sweeping narrative. The *New York Times* rhapsodized about the "greatest motion picture mural we have ever seen and the most ambitious film-making venture in Hollywood's spectacular history." *Variety* struck an equally rapt note: "*Gone with the Wind* . . . comes to the screen as one of the truly great films. . . . The lavishness of its production, the consummate care and skill which went into its making, the assemblage of its fine cast and expert technical staff combine in presenting a theatrical attraction justifying the princely investment of $3,900,000." Although most likely alluding to spectacle rather than Lost Cause themes, Hollywood gossip columnist Louella Parsons called *Gone with the Wind* "the best thing since *The Birth of a Nation*." A record-breaking first release, several subsequent re-releases, and a continuing presence on television garnered an unmatched audience among films within the Civil War genre.[6]

Gone with the Wind echoed *The Birth of a Nation* in many ways—though Selznick replaced Griffith's blatant racism with a paternalistic treatment of slavery that would have pleased the original Lost Cause warriors. The film opens with an embellished version of Griffith's tribute to a "quaintly," doomed southern way of life: "There was a land of Cavaliers and Cotton Fields called the Old South. . . . Here in this pretty world Gallantry took its last bow. . . . Here was the last ever to be seen of Knights and their Ladies Fair, of Master and of Slave. . . . Look for it only in books, for it is no more than a dream remembered. A Civilization gone with the wind." The film's heroine, Scarlett O'Hara, and, for most of the Civil War part of the film, its hero, Rhett Butler, admittedly do not fit Lost Cause stereotypes, each being too self-absorbed to care about the fortunes of the Confederacy. Yet the film as a whole adheres closely to the Lost Cause narrative and, unlike *The Birth of a Nation*, virtually ignores both the Reconciliation and Union Causes (never mind Emancipation).

Gone with the Wind's white South strives mightily and suffers enormously in pursuit of Confederate nationhood. These parts of the Lost Cause narrative, it is worth repeating, did not stray far from the historical record. The human toll receives sustained attention. Many of the O'Haras' friends and neighbors die in the war, including the Tarleton twins, Melanie Wilkes's brother—and Scarlett's first husband—Charles, and Dr. Meade's son. Two scenes in Atlanta offer gripping vignettes of Confederate sacrifice. In the first, people jostle for copies of a list of casualties from Gettysburg. Name after name is marked "killed in action," and many grief-stricken relatives and friends console one another. An old couple who have lost a soldier glance at each other briefly before he, putting aside personal tragedy to bolster Confederate spirits, leads a band in playing "Dixie." Perhaps the most memorable scene in the film occurs at Atlanta's railroad depot, where wounded soldiers are brought for medical attention. Fifteen hundred extras fill the screen as the longest and highest tracking shot to that point in film history affords graphic evidence of the war's grisly toll (fig. 5). A flapping Confederate battle flag, dominating the foreground when the camera reaches its highest point, reminds viewers of the cause for which these men risked their lives.[7]

Most of the white civilians in *Gone with the Wind* also express devotion to the Confederacy. Melanie Wilkes exemplifies the Lost Cause model of patriotic womanhood. Impeccably ladylike, she willingly parts with material goods, including her wedding ring, and literally takes up a sword when confronted by one of Sherman's scavenging "bummers" at Tara.[8] At the other end of the social spectrum, whorehouse madam Belle Watling donates money to the soldiers' hospital, observing that she is "a Confederate like everybody else." Even the cynically materialistic Rhett Butler has a conversion experience on the road to Tara after Atlanta falls. "I am going, my dear, to join the army," he tells an incredulous Scarlett after watching exhausted Confederate soldiers trudge by. "I'm a little late, but better late than never." *Why* is he going, she presses. "Maybe it's because I've always had a weakness for lost causes, once they're really lost," he answers. "Or maybe, maybe I'm ashamed of myself. Who knows?"

Ashley Wilkes addresses the Lost Cause preoccupation with Union manpower and resources in a scene with Scarlett at Christmas in 1863. Home from Lee's army on furlough, he observes, "We shall need all our prayers, now the end is coming." "The end?" she asks. "The end of the war, and the end of our world, Scarlett. . . . Oh, Scarlett, my men are barefooted now, and the snow in Virginia is deep. When I see them, and I see the Yankees coming and coming, always more and more . . ." Gettysburg persuaded Wilkes that the Confederacy could not win—another Lost Cause staple. Text accompanying the aforementioned scene featuring casualty lists also suggests the centrality of Gettysburg: "Hushed and grim, Atlanta turned painful eyes towards the far-away little town of Gettysburg . . . and a page of history waited for three days while two nations came to death grips on the farm lands of Pennsylva-

FIGURE 5. The Confederate battle flag against a background of soldiers wounded in fighting at Atlanta. This image from *Gone with the Wind* links the scale of Confederate sacrifice directly to the most famous symbol of the struggle for southern nationhood. Photofest.

nia." News about Gettysburg and reckonings of its dead and wounded would not have reached Atlanta so quickly, but the device works well in reminding audiences about Confederate valor, however hopeless, at Gettysburg.

Sherman and his army reprise their role from *The Birth of a Nation* in *Gone with the Wind*. Griffith's "great conqueror" returns as the "Great Invader," whose legions form an "oncoming juggernaut" that spreads terror and destruction among Confederate noncombatants: "And the wind swept through Georgia . . . SHERMAN! To split the Confederacy, to leave it crippled and forever humbled, the Great Invader marched . . . leaving behind him a path of destruction sixty miles wide, from Atlanta to the sea." A montage of endless lines of Union soldiers set against a background of flames recalls Griffith's long-range shots of Federals amid a smoky Georgia landscape, representing the irresistible, faceless Union power so important to Lost Cause writers. Scarlett's journey from Atlanta to Tara reveals Sherman's impact on the Georgia countryside. She passes ruined farms and plantations littered with military detritus and carcasses of dead animals that invite attention from circling vultures.

As it did in *The Birth of a Nation*, the end of the war brings a new kind of vulture into the ruined South. The "tattered Cavaliers . . . came hobbling back to the desolation that had once been a land of grace and plenty" accompanied by "another invader . . . more cruel and vicious than any they had fought . . . the Carpetbagger." A white man and a black man in a carriage, carpetbag by their side to remind even the dullest theatergoer who they are, sing "Marching through Georgia" as they move along a road filled with ragged Confederate soldiers walking back to their homes. Subsequent scenes leave no doubt that the white South must resist venal Carpetbaggers, offering a few instances of black people forcing white citizens off sidewalks and the like.

The most widely read book on Reconstruction during the preceding decade had anticipated the film's interpretation. Claude Bowers's *The Tragic Era: The Revolution After Lincoln* fit comfortably within the sensational tradition of Thomas Dixon and *The Birth of a Nation*: "Then came the scum of Northern society, emissaries of the politicians, soldiers of fortune, and not a few degenerates, inflaming the negroes' egotism, and soon the lustful assaults began. Rape is the foul daughter of Reconstruction. . . . It was not until the original Klan began to ride that white women felt some sense of security."[9] Yet *Gone with the Wind* never celebrates the Ku Klux Klan or shows violence against freedpeople. An unnamed Klanlike organization does mount a raid outside Atlanta, during which Scarlett's second husband, Frank Kennedy, is killed and Ashley Wilkes wounded, but the event takes place beyond the camera's eye. Overall, the film avoids the more inflammatory racial politics of *The Birth of a Nation*.

Selznick chose to mute the issue of slavery by emphasizing a reciprocal loyalty between the principal black characters and their owners. Mammy, Pork, and Big Sam resemble the *Confederate Veteran*'s "old-time Southern negro." A suggestion that slavery did not form an essential element of southern society comes early in the film. During the barbecue at the Wilkeses' plantation, Twelve Oaks, Ashley confides to Melanie his intention to free all the family's slaves. How he will maintain a lifestyle utterly dependent on them goes unexplored—just as the fact that almost all the slaves at Tara run away when Sherman arrives receives only a casual mention. The black characters the audience has gotten to know best, including Mammy and Pork, remain at Tara to help Scarlett and her sisters cope with their diminished circumstances. Another slave, the house servant named Prissy, stays with Scarlett during the siege of Atlanta, exhibiting an array of cruelly degrading stereotypical traits and behaviors intended as comic relief in the late 1930s.[10]

As the fight for Atlanta enters its last phase, Scarlett engages Big Sam and three other field hands from Tara in a conversation that bristles with Lost Cause meaning. A scene that lasts but a few moments conveys white devotion to the Confederacy, slaves' loyalty to their owners, and slaveholder concern for the bondsmen's welfare. Scarlett hails the slaves, escorted by a mounted Confederate officer, as they march out to dig defensive works. Big Sam reports that Scarlett's father, ever the loyal Confederate, complained because a bad knee prevented his fighting for the Confederacy. Mr. O'Hara's willingness to help the cause weakened a bit when he was faced with the prospect of sending the slaves to Atlanta, "but," Big Sam explains, "your Ma says the Confederacy needs us, so we'se gwine to dig for the South." As the column of laborers begins to move, Big Sam reassures his owner's daughter: "Goodbye, Miss Scarlett. Don't worry, we'll stop them Yankees." "Good-bye, Big Sam," she answers with some feeling. "Good-bye, boys. If any of you get sick or hurt, let me know."[11] The *Confederate Veteran* could not have improved on these tender expressions of affection between slaveholder and slaves. It was perhaps a measure of the racial temper of the times that Eleanor Roosevelt, whose credentials regarding race certainly placed her among the most progressive segment of the populace, pronounced *Gone with the Wind* "an extraordinary movie, beautifully acted."[12]

Although *Gone with the Wind* marked the apogee of Lost Cause influence in Hollywood, the twenty-five succeeding years yielded a number of major films that handled the Old South and the Confederacy gently. Two examples will illustrate this phenomenon. *Santa Fe Trail*, released in 1940 and directed by Michael Curtiz, deals with sectional tensions in the late antebellum years. Laughably inaccurate in terms of historical details, it adopts a staunchly pro-southern stance. Errol Flynn's Jeb Stuart, together with fellow slaveholders Robert E. Lee and Jefferson Davis, appear as reasonable characters set against Raymond Massey's fanatically menacing John Brown. In one scene, Stuart asserts that white southerners can best handle the issue of slavery. "I know the truth of this problem far better than you do," he tells an antislavery character named Rader. "The South will settle it in its own time and in its own way. But not through the propaganda of this John Brown or any of his followers." Black characters never rise above a helpless passivity, even those whom Brown and his supporters strive to liberate. In one scene, Stuart talks with three slaves who followed Brown to free territory in Kansas. They have just witnessed a gun battle between cavalrymen and Brown's followers, and one of the slaves, a woman, dresses a wound on Stuart's arm. "Well, old John Brown said he's gwine give us freedom," she remarks, "but shuckin's, if this here Kansas is freedom, then I ain't got no use for it, no sir." "Me neither," adds one of the two black men, "I just wants to get back home to Texas and set 'til Kingdom come."

Released nineteen years after *Santa Fe Trail*, director John Ford's *The Horse Soldiers* insinuated a number of Lost Cause touches into the story of a Union cavalry operation. Based loosely on Colonel Benjamin F. Grierson's raid through Mississippi during the Vicksburg campaign, the film stars John Wayne as Union colonel John Marlowe. The civil rights ferment of the 1950s apparently had minimal effect on the screenwriters' sensibility.[13] The main black character, a slave named Lukey played by tennis star Althea Gibson, devotedly serves her mistress — even helping her spy on Marlowe's officers as they plan their expedition. Confederate soldiers exhibit bravery throughout the film, most notably a one-armed officer who leads a futile (and ridiculously staged) charge against Marlowe's troopers and a group of teenaged cadets called into service because of the South's lack of manpower. Both of these battle sequences buttress the Lost Cause vision of hopeless southern striving against more powerful northern opponents. They also make the point that the Confederacy had to muster virtually all of its white males, including those already maimed in battle and mere boys, to resist the northern invaders.

Shenandoah marked a watershed in Hollywood's relationship with the Lost

Cause. Released in January 1965, six months after congressional passage of the Civil Rights Act of 1964, it shuns glorification of the plantation South and, most tellingly, places slavery at the center of the Confederate war. The film focuses on the nonslaveholding family of Charlie Anderson (Jimmy Stewart), who live on a prosperous 500-acre farm in Virginia's Shenandoah Valley during the last autumn of the war. Because of the Confederacy's stringent conscription act passed more than two years earlier, approximately 90 percent of Virginia's military-age white males were in the army or engaged in war-related occupations by the period covered in the film.[14] Yet Anderson and his six sons, as well as his daughter and daughter-in-law, have managed to remain aloof from the conflict.

The film's anti–Lost Cause tenor emerges early, when one of the sons remarks that as Virginians the Andersons can no longer ignore the war. Charlie responds by asking if the sons want to own slaves. No, they reply. "Now suppose you had a friend that owned slaves and suppose somebody was going to come and take them away from him," continues Anderson. "Would you help him fight to keep them?" The sons say they would not, with one explaining, "I don't see any reason to fight for something that I don't believe is right, and I don't think that a real friend would ask me to." Later, Anderson rebuffs a Confederate officer seeking recruits and government purchasing agents in search of horses and mules. He built his farm "without the sweat of one slave," he affirms, and when told that Virginia "needs all her sons," replies: "These are *my* sons. They don't belong to the state." Unlike most white southerners in previous films dealing with the Civil War, he consistently refuses to make any sacrifice for either slaveholding Virginia or the Confederacy.

The film similarly abandons the model of black servility in place as recently as Althea Gibson's character in *The Horse Soldiers*. In one scene, a teenaged slave named Gabriel watches a Union patrol capture Boy, Anderson's youngest son. Boy instructs Gabriel to tell Mr. Anderson what happened, whereupon a black Union soldier breaks in: "You don't have to tell his pa nothin'. You're free." Gabriel delivers the bad news about Boy to Anderson's daughter-in-law, after which the two discuss whether Gabriel is indeed free. His owner has left the area, and she tells him that he can go wherever he chooses. He seizes the opportunity, shows up later in the film as a United States soldier, and improbably is thrown together with Boy on a battlefield. While earlier films had grossly exaggerated the degree to which slaves remained loyal to their masters, *Shenandoah* distorts historical reality by showing integrated United States military units—both the one that captures Boy and the one in which Gabriel

FIGURE 6. *Shenandoah*'s Charlie Anderson (James Stewart, second from right) and five of his six sons (left to right: James [Patrick Wayne], Henry [Tim McIntire], John [James McMullan], Jacob [Glenn Corbett], and Nathan [Charles Robinson]). Because they oppose slavery, all of the Anderson men have refused to serve in the Confederate army. In reality, five military-age white men in the Shenandoah Valley would not have been able to avoid Confederate conscription. Photofest.

serves. This shift from loyal or childlike slaves to black and white soldiers in the same regiments suggests how far *Shenandoah* moved beyond Hollywood's well-worn conventions for black characters in Civil War stories.

The few Lost Cause interpretive elements that show up in *Shenandoah* do little to affect the film's overall tone. Most Confederate soldiers are ragged, including Anderson's son-in-law, who undergoes a remarkable transformation, wearing a resplendent uniform at his wedding and a tattered ensemble shortly thereafter. United States forces appear to be far more numerous as well as better fed and clothed than the Confederates. Some of Anderson's neighbors sacrifice sons for the cause, and there is an obligatory shot of a ravaged southern landscape. But these things in no way offset Anderson's antipathy toward slavery, insistence that a southern desire to keep slaves caused the war, and lack of concern about whether the Confederacy wins or loses. Lost Cause adherents would find no comfort in any aspect of Anderson's worldview, nor would they applaud the implications of Gabriel's actions.

Shenandoah stands as more of an Emancipation than a Lost Cause narrative—though it should be considered preeminently an antiwar film. Whatever a character's ideology, the war wreaks its impersonal havoc. Confederate deserters kill one of Anderson's sons and his daughter-in-law, and a nervous young southern soldier accidentally kills a second son (Union soldiers probably would have perpetrated these acts in a Lost Cause treatment). Near the end, Anderson stands at his wife's well-tended grave, now flanked by three fresh ones. "There is nothing much I can tell you about this war," he states sadly. "It is like all wars, I suppose. The undertakers are winning it. The politicians will talk a lot about the glory of it, and the old men will talk about the need of it. The soldiers, they just want to go home."

Shenandoah proved to be the last major Civil War film until *Glory* in 1989. Hollywood, like most of the publishing world, chose to neglect the conflict during what might be called the long Vietnam era between the mid-1960s and the mid-1980s. Several films that superficially fit the genre are really westerns dressed up in ill-fitting Civil War garb. These include *Alvarez Kelly* (1966), a clunky vehicle for William Holden and Richard Widmark inspired by Confederate general Wade Hampton's "Beefsteak Raid" of September 1864, in which Confederate cavalrymen captured 2,500 cattle for Lee's army; *The Good, the Bad, and the Ugly* (1967), the last, longest, and least satisfying of Clint Eastwood's three "spaghetti westerns"; *Journey to Shiloh* (1968), a plodding mess that is all about the Vietnam War; the spectacularly wretched *The Undefeated* (1969), which offers John Wayne as a Union colonel and Rock Hudson as a

Confederate colonel whose southern accent is so bad it must be heard to be believed; and Eastwood's *The Outlaw Josie Wales* (1976), a tough film with a superb opening sequence devoted to the last phase of the guerrilla war in Missouri.[15] Eastwood's quirky *The Beguiled* (1971), though set in Confederate Louisiana, could just as easily have been made as a dark comedy set anywhere at any time.

Hollywood Turns Away from Dixie's Land: The Lost Cause in Crisis

After what could be labeled a "Civil War on the Edge of the Range" period, *Glory* heralded a turn toward films specifically concerned with the conflict. The next fourteen years yielded *Gettysburg*, *Pharaoh's Army*, *Ride with the Devil*, *Andersonville*, *Gods and Generals*, *Cold Mountain*, and *C.S.A.: The Confederate States of America*. *Sommersby*, *Dances with Wolves*, *Little Women*, *Gangs of New York*, *The Last Samurai*, and *Seraphim Falls*, all of which touched on the conflict to a greater or lesser degree, added to a cinematic bounty that coincided with the expansion of general interest in the Civil War.

The years that separated *Glory* from *Gods and Generals* and *Cold Mountain* witnessed a retreat from the Lost Cause that mirrored the national trend regarding public displays of Confederate symbols. Some of the films from this era offer little evidence to gauge how the Lost Cause fared. In *Glory*, Confederates function as a mostly faceless, indistinct foe opposing the 54th Massachusetts Infantry and other United States units. Tension between white and black United States soldiers, not confrontations with the "enemy," dominate the film. One scene, however, would greatly unsettle any Lost Cause advocate. On a rainy night during the initial period of training, Colonel Robert Gould Shaw informs the soldiers of the 54th that if captured they will not be treated as prisoners of war. They will be returned to slavery and their white officers executed—an unequivocal reminder that the Confederacy was determined to preserve slavery and adamantly opposed to any United States policy that promised freedom. In *Dances with Wolves*, Confederates have their only moment as unimaginably inept riflemen who cannot kill Union lieutenant John Dunbar (or even his horse) as he rides the length of their long battle line not once but twice. These Confederates bear no resemblance to the heroes in gray celebrated by the Lost Cause. Set several years after the war, *Seraphim Falls* offers a former Confederate colonel as one of its two main characters. Flashbacks reveal that the colonel's wartime profile goes against the Lost Cause grain; rather than fight to the bitter end, he ordered his men to lay down their arms well ahead of the official Confederate capitulation. He does carry an all-consuming grudge against a Yankee captain who inadvertently presided over the death of his family. *Little Women*, *Gangs of New York*, and *The Last Samurai*, as one would expect, allocate virtually no attention to Confederates.

Beginning with *Gettysburg*, the rest of the films afford a good deal more to discuss in terms of Lost Cause emphasis. Taken in chronological turn, they chart Hollywood's eroding sympathy for Confederates and their war. The screenplay for *Gettysburg* follows Michael Shaara's *The Killer Angels* very closely, serving up a mixture of the Reconciliation Cause, Emancipation Cause, and Lost Cause traditions, as well as a bit of the Union Cause, perfectly calculated to give an array of viewers something to their taste.[16] Several Lost Cause elements stand out, most obviously the idea that Gettysburg represented a dramatic moment when the Confederacy could have established its independence. The opening voice-over says this about Lee and his army as they march toward the United States: "Their main objective is to draw the Union army out into the open where it can be destroyed. . . . General Lee knows that a letter has been prepared by the southern government, a letter which offers peace. It is to be placed on the desk of Abraham Lincoln, president of the United States, the day after Lee has destroyed the Army of the Potomac somewhere north of Washington." Everything about this statement is flawed as history but almost perfect as Lost Cause analysis of what Lee might have accomplished in Pennsylvania.

It falls to Brig. Gen. Lewis A. Armistead, one of Maj. Gen. George E. Pickett's brigade commanders, to establish the battle as the Confederacy's moment of decision. "They are all willing to make the supreme sacrifice to achieve victory here," he remarks about his soldiers just before the Pickett-Pettigrew assault on July 3, "the crowning victory and the end of this war." Joshua Lawrence Chamberlain, the film's Union hero during fighting on Little Round Top on July 2, agrees that Confederate independence hangs in the balance: "I think if we lose this fight," he states before the fighting begins, "we lose the war."[17]

The film also parallels Lost Cause writers in lavishing attention on generalship and questions of responsibility for the Confederate defeat. The roles of Lee, Longstreet, Jeb Stuart, Richard S. Ewell, and others receive full exposition. Stuart and Ewell, the Confederate cavalry commander and chief of the Second Corps, respectively, play their Lost Cause roles as subordinates who frustrate Lee's plans. Lee and Longstreet, in contrast, depart from Lost Cause models. Extensive attention to Lee leaves no doubt about his importance, and in one scene his soldiers erupt in a spontaneous expression of admiration—shaking their weapons, shouting their loyalty, and reaching out to touch him—that Lost Cause adherents would savor.[18] But overall Lee is tired and ill and strangely passive, seemingly resigned to leaving everything to God even before the battle opens. Twice shown in a rocking chair, once with an aide carefully placing a blanket over him as he slumps with fatigue, Lee intones as early as June 30, "All in God's hands now." Longstreet, in contrast, functions as a modern warrior who knows the value of defensive fighting and repeatedly urges Lee to abandon offensive tactics. The sulking subordinate so often sketched in Lost Cause literature makes no appearance. Indeed, most viewers likely would conclude that Longstreet is the better general and Lee a noble anachronism with little understanding of how to fight an enemy whose weaponry renders frontal assaults suicidal.[19]

Scenes involving Confederate motivation relegate the institution of slavery to the margins, allowing characters to voice Lost Cause attitudes. In one, a visual *homage* to Winslow Homer's iconic painting titled *Prisoners from the Front* that does not draw directly on Shaara's text, Tom Chamberlain, a young Union officer, asks three captured Confederates why they fight. A Tennessee yeoman responds: "I don't know about some other folk, but I ain't fightin' for no darkies one way or the other. I'm fightin' for my rights [pronounced "rats"]. All of us here, that's what we're fightin' for." Why can't the North just "live and let live?" wonders the Tennessean.[20] Up the chain of command, Brig. Gen. James L. Kemper, a Virginia politician commanding a brigade in Pickett's division, similarly denies the importance of slavery. "What we are fighting for here," he tells the British observer A. J. L. Fremantle, "is freedom from what we consider to be the rule of a foreign power. . . . That's what this war is all about." The "damn money-grubbing Yankees," adds Kemper fiercely, talk about "the darkies, nothing but the darkies."

In a scene set on the morning of July 2, Lee and Longstreet agree that they resigned their United States commissions only because they could not countenance fighting against their families. On another occasion Longstreet tells Fremantle, "We should have freed the slaves, then fired on Fort Sumter." This last quite astonishing observation has no basis in historical fact but seeks to emphasize Longstreet's modern sensibilities, raising a crucial question: Why fire on Fort Sumter if the slaves are already free?[21]

The absence of African Americans in *Gettysburg* might lend credence to Confederate statements about slavery's tangential role. If moviegoers could see the real armies as they campaigned in Pennsylvania during June and July

1863, however, they would notice several thousand slaves performing non-combatant duties in the Army of Northern Virginia and many black laborers accompanying the Army of the Potomac.[22] The movie's one black character appears to be an escaped slave who has a nonspeaking role in a single scene. The rest of the film pits two all-white armies against one another, a formulation well in line with both Lost Cause and Reconciliation Cause efforts to banish slaves and slavery to the periphery of the conflict—as well as with long-standing conventions in Hollywood that, with few exceptions, left little room for black characters in Civil War armies.

A centerpiece of Lost Cause celebrations of Confederate gallantry and manhood, the Pickett-Pettigrew assault unfolds in a sequence that lasts about as long as it took Lee's infantry to traverse the undulating ground between Seminary Ridge and Cemetery Ridge on July 3. During the massive bombardment preceding the advance, a scene behind General Armistead's line establishes ties between Confederates and their Revolutionary War forebears. Armistead chats with the inquisitive Englishman Fremantle, pointing to officers descended from Patrick Henry and other Revolutionary patriots. Former Confederates who tried hard after the war to portray themselves as the true inheritors of the Revolutionary tradition surely would like this scene. They also would appreciate director Maxwell's detailed treatment of the attack itself, which is reminiscent in scale of the southern assault at Petersburg in The Birth of a Nation. Panoramic shots of attacking formations dotted with battle flags, close-ups of the grisly human toll exacted by Union artillery and musket fire, and a climactic final surge that carries a few hundred Confederates through the northern defensive line create a feeling of desperate courage against intimidating obstacles. General Kemper falls with a ghastly wound and General Armistead with a mortal one, joining masses of their nameless infantrymen sacrificed for the cause.

But precisely what cause is it? Apart from its characterizations of a passive Lee and a highly admirable Longstreet, Gettysburg contradicts Lost Cause tradition in one important way. There are innumerable Confederate flags in evidence but no sense of Confederate nationalism animating soldiers in the Army of Northern Virginia—many of whom in 1863 would have described the army as the embodiment of their nation. Time and again southerners celebrate their states, as when Armistead tells Fremantle on July 3, "We are all sons of Virginia here." Lee and Longstreet address this topic in several scenes. On the morning of July 2, Longstreet remarks that his loyalty lies with his home state and his family—a sentiment with which Lee concurs. That night Longstreet confides to Armistead his suspicion of all political causes: "My only cause is victory." Following the bitter failure on July 3, Lee and Longstreet talk beside a flickering fire. "If this war goes on," Lee mutters, "and it will, it will, what else can we do but go on you and I? Does it matter, after all, who wins? Is that ever really the question? Will Almighty God ask that question in the end?"

Former Confederates certainly asked that question after the war, and the historical Lee cared passionately about Confederate independence. He functioned throughout the war as an ardent nationalist, as did many of his subordinates and men who served in Confederate ranks. *Gettysburg* would have it otherwise. In the foreword to a book published in conjunction with release of the film, actor Martin Sheen, who plays Lee, also neatly separates the general from the Confederacy (and, remarkably, from slavery). "I began to study the man and the period in earnest, to learn what I could to enhance my interpretation of Lee," writes Sheen, "an enigmatic Virginian who favored neither secession nor slavery, but whose sense of honor demanded that allegiance to his native state supersede loyalty to the nation." Sheen probably read traditional accounts of Lee, which highlight his devotion to Virginia during the secession crisis. Anyone who consults Lee's wartime letters, in contrast, cannot miss their undeniable evidence of Lee's nationalist feeling.[23]

Released the same year as *Gettysburg, Sommersby* takes a decidedly less tolerant stance toward the Confederate cause.[24] Set in the early postwar period, it shifts Daniel Vigne's *The Return of Martin Guerre* (1982) from sixteenth-century France to Tennessee in 1865–66. The film contains a few elements that would meet the Lost Cause code of standards—none of them, it is safe to say, so intended by director Jon Amiel. The title character, named Jack Sommersby and as ragged as the "tattered Cavaliers" returning home in *Gone with the Wind*, travels through devastated countryside en route to Tennessee. This opening section of the film echoes Scarlett's journey from Atlanta to Tara. Sommersby gazes at burned houses, a cemetery with numerous fresh graves, and other sights that attest to the heavy hand laid on the area by invading Yankees. Townspeople include veterans maimed at Chickamauga and Vicksburg, alerting viewers to the war's human toll. "Everybody here is missing somebody," Jack hears when he first gets home. Jack's wife, Laurel, recalls the O'Hara women at Tara after Sherman's March; she is reduced to working alongside poorer whites and black people in the shadow of her shabby plantation house. Viewers also learn that Sommersby has spent time in Elmira Prison, the most notorious of the northern camps, where, as he puts it in a line that suggests Union brutality, he "starved [and] froze, like everybody else." All of this sup-

FIGURE 7. Robert E. Lee (left; Martin Sheen) and James Longstreet (right; Tom Berenger) take their ease in *Gettysburg*. Both characters exhibit a devotion to their home states rather than the larger Confederacy in the film. Photofest.

ports the Lost Cause preoccupation with white southern loss and sacrifice in a war against a brutal enemy.

As the story unfolds following Sommersby's return, it takes on a decidedly post–civil rights movement tone. In contrast to *The Birth of a Nation* and *Gone with the Wind*, *Sommersby* presents an interpretation of Reconstruction that features white rather than black villains. African Americans play a major role in the film. They are neither airbrushed out as in *Gettysburg* nor cast as the loyal retainers so dear to Lost Cause hearts. Jack Sommersby manifests implausibly enlightened views about race. Two scenes will serve to convey the positive tenor of his racial attitudes, as well as the very racist attitudes of former Confederates. At a party for Sommersby on his first night home, a group of black people comes to call. "Evening, folks," he says, offering them food. "My daddy paid a hundred dollars for you," a smiling Sommersby tells a man named Joseph. He invites the callers to "come on in," but they, aware of racial proscriptions in a state where United States military power only recently had brought emancipation, know enough not to do so. Joseph explains to Sommersby that they dropped by only to welcome him home. "Jack, let's not get too friendly with the niggers," says one man at the party, adding that Joseph has been squatting on Sommersby land. "Next thing you know they'll be moving up to the big house," says another. A third, seeing Jack's behavior with the black people, asks what is wrong with him: What did the "goddamned Yankees do to you?"

In a second scene, Jack proposes to a mixed crowd of black and white people in a town meeting that they grow tobacco. He will give them a piece of land, tools, and fertilizer, and they will keep half of the profits. When he pays off the mortgage on his farm, moreover, they can buy their plots of land at a fair price. He is a thoroughly sympathetic character who hopes former slaves will participate fully. An incredulous Joseph asks if "coloreds and all" can take part? Jack says yes. The other white people are taken aback, murmuring that they won't work that way. "I ain't livin' next to no niggers," rasps one woman. In these and other scenes dealing with race, Jack and Laurel find themselves opposed by former Confederates.

Jack envisions a biracial community in which shared economic want trumps race. He calls for collective action. In order to purchase seed and other supplies to make the tobacco crop, the community must pool its resources. Black people and white people contribute watches, valuables, or whatever they can muster. An old black man gives a piece of pottery, and Joseph offers some beautiful carved ivory. As Jack leaves to get the seed, Joseph, an old black woman, Laurel, and Laurel's son all wave good-bye. Several community action sequences follow, with black and white people stepping off beds for seedlings while the music swells and their children play together. They eventually harvest the crop and cure the tobacco.

The film closes with a courtroom sequence in which Jack is tried for murder. His black friends join Laurel in rallying around him despite having learned that he is not in fact her husband but rather a man named Horace Townsend, a look-alike who spent time in Yankee prison with the real Jack Sommersby and determined to take his place. Jack confronts one racist neighbor during the trial, insisting that the man agreed to testify only to prevent Sommersby from "selling land to a colored man, who would then be a property owner on a level with citizens like yourself." The neighbor turns to the judge, played by James Earl Jones, calling him a "nappy-headed son-of-a-bitch." "In two years when the Yankees are gone," the witness hisses, "you will be in the field where you belong."

Ex-Confederate racists figure in other scenes as well, most notably when a Ku Klux Klan–type group terrorizes Joseph. Their actions are not grounded in any lingering devotion to the Confederacy. In fact, there is no discussion of the failed slaveholding republic at all, no sense that the white people had been Confederates. At one point, Laurel comments that the Sommersbys used to be "rich and stupid" but now are poor and happy. Is this an oblique jab at the Old South? at the Confederacy? Were they stupid as slaveholders but happy as members of a biracial community? Or is Laurel merely referring to the changed personal relationship between her and Jack? None of this is clear. There is no attempt to explain why the Sommersbys differ so radically from their white neighbors regarding race. Whatever the meaning of Laurel's remark, it reflects the film's post–civil rights movement sensibility. No matter how anachronistic Jack and Laurel's behavior within the context of early postwar Tennessee, its repudiation of the Lost Cause tradition is unequivocal and powerful.[25]

Pharaoh's Army presents more interpretive complexity than *Sommersby*.[26] A small film based on a folklorist's oral history with a Kentucky mountaineer in 1941, it does not engage most Lost Cause conventions. There are no grand mansions or refined slaveholding men and women. The Eastern Theater of war where Robert E. Lee and other Confederate military icons waged their celebrated campaigns is entirely absent. Loyal family slaves, stalwart Confederate soldiers, civilians sacrificing for "the cause," and other staples of the Lost Cause narrative play no part in the film. The story unfolds in 1862

FIGURE 8. *Sommersby*'s protagonist, Jack Sommersby (Richard Gere), works alongside white and black neighbors on his farm in postwar Tennessee. Photofest.

on a hardscrabble farm in the Cumberland Mountains of Kentucky. A Union captain named John Abston, commanding four other United States soldiers, encounters a woman named Sarah Anders. Married to a Confederate soldier, Sarah lives on the farm with her son Boy (like Charlie Anderson with his youngest son in *Shenandoah*, she seems to have drawn a blank when it came to selecting a name for the lad). Her daughter is dead, and Sarah harbors deep bitterness and sorrow because pro-Union sympathizers defiled the young girl's grave. Shortly before the Federals arrive, Sarah and Boy reburied the daughter on their farm. As an old man in voice-over, the son explains what happened to his sister: "Some Yankee bastards dug her up and tossed her out like a rag doll on account of Pap's siding with the South." Neighbor had turned against neighbor, the voice-over continues, in an area evenly divided between Union and Confederate sentiment. "It was rough through here," he says with considerable understatement.[27]

Captain Abston's basic decency stirs feelings of empathy for Sarah. A farmer himself, he watches her struggle on a rocky patch of land. Over the course of two days, he fumbles toward a reconciliationist accommodation with Sarah and Boy. Although ordered to seize goods from pro-Rebel families, he promises not to take her mule. "Ma'am, I apologize for the things this war makes," he tells Sarah. Later he helps plow and chops some wood. She tells him how Unionists refused to allow her daughter's body to rest in a graveyard among the loyal dead and vows to dig up the first Yankee grave she finds near her farm. Sobbing, she recalls that her daughter's body "smelled so bad," adding grimly, "There will be hell to pay." Abston later expresses regret about Sarah's little girl. "Sorry don't do nothin'," she snaps, "Don't stop you from taking our cow or ham or killing our chickens." Sarah shows glimmers of softening toward Abston, wiping his hands blistered by the plowing and putting on a nice dress. She even nurses one of Abston's soldiers named Newt, who falls in her barn. Abston reveals to Sarah that he lost his wife three years earlier and that he misses her, his farm, and their child.

Sarah's loathing for Yankees, including most of Abston's men, trumps the captain's conciliatory gestures and smothers her impulses toward accommodation. She suggests that Abston's plowing represents an effort to ease his guilty conscience and exhibits no regret when an old couple are found murdered and thrown into a well. They were Yankees, she observes callously, who had sent sons into the Union army. When Abston shares the information about his wife and farm, Sarah responds that she and the captain cannot be friends—they must stick to being enemies. Meanwhile, she has sent Boy to get help from pro-Confederates in the vicinity.

The film builds to a bloody climax when smoldering resentments flare into violence and death. One of the Union soldiers is killed by the men Boy summoned. Abston now views Sarah and her son as Rebel enemies. He buries the dead soldier next to Sarah's daughter before taking everything of value—her mule, cow, and wagon. Expressing outrage at the burial, Sarah asks how she and Boy can survive: "What do you expect us to eat?" Bring her husband home from Confederate service, says Abston coldly, or "Maybe the boy can shoot squirrels." Sarah picks up a rifle Abston has left them with the intent to kill him, but he has taken all the powder. Abston and his remaining soldiers depart with the injured Newt in the wagon. Sarah immediately digs up the dead soldier, while Boy chases the Federals and kills Newt.

Intractable enmity pervades the final confrontation between Abston and Sarah. He returns to the farm with the murdered Newt's body, asks Sarah what she knows about it, and forces Boy to look at the corpse. Sarah lays all blame on the Yankees, who provoked the violence by coming to her farm. Abston draws his pistol and points it at Sarah and Boy—then shoots twice in the air. Shaken by his urge to murder them, Abston leaves Newt's body and expresses a hope that whoever killed him will provide a Christian burial. Sarah has no intention of handling Newt's body with decency. Soon after Abston leaves for the last time, she tells Boy, "Get that damn Yankee out of our yard!" The voice-over ties up the story's loose ends. Sarah and Boy threw the first dead Yankee's body into a nearby creek. Then they carried Newt's corpse up the hill, tossed it into a sinkhole, and covered it with dirt. Sarah's husband never came back from the Confederate army. "That war," concludes the voice-over, "was a widow maker."

Although this gritty tale of strife and hatred on the border between the United States and the Confederacy includes strong anti-Union sentiment, it cannot be placed in the Lost Cause tradition. It is true that United States soldiers wreak havoc on the lives of pro-Confederate civilians, descending on their farm out of nowhere and leaving it bereft of food and the means to make a living. Moreover, Sarah is filled with hatred for Yankees and unrepentant in the end. In an odd and unexplained Lost Cause twist, a slave belonging to a Confederate preacher is the person who killed the Union soldier Abston buried next to Sarah's daughter. But Sarah and her son never make any statements about the Confederacy; indeed, as Kentuckians, they live in the United States. Viewers receive no clues about why Sarah's husband joined the Confederate army. Sarah's loathing for Yankees arises from personal and local factors rather than from ideology. The themes that inspired Lost Cause writers, such as constitutional principles and Lee's military victories and honorable struggle against long odds, seem utterly irrelevant to the lives and attitudes of the major characters in *Pharaoh's Army*.

Less complex than *Pharaoh's Army*, *Andersonville* can be placed squarely on the roster of anti–Lost Cause films.[28] A story devoted to the most infamous southern prisoner-of-war camp would trouble anyone with pro-Confederate leanings. Prisons on both sides were the subject of vitriolic writings during the last several decades of the nineteenth century, with partisans North and South accusing each other of atrocities. But Andersonville, a palisade-enclosed installation in the pine woods of south Georgia, stood out as the worst of many hellholes. Nearly 13,000 United States soldiers, roughly 29 percent of the total number of prisoners who passed through its gates, died there. Andersonville's commandant, a Swiss-born officer named Henry Wirz, was executed for war crimes by the United States government in the summer of 1865 — the only Confederate officer to be tried and convicted on that charge. Lost Cause writers labored mightily to play down the horrors at Andersonville and highlight deplorable conditions in northern camps at Elmira, New York, and elsewhere. Shortages of food and medicine at Andersonville approximated those in Confederate society at large, argued ex-Confederates, whereas hunger and illness in northern camps stemmed from deliberate governmental policies. Many thousands of Confederates who perished at Elmira could have been saved, they implied or stated outright; however, the unfortunate United States soldiers at Andersonville, as one Confederate apologist put it, died "from epidemics and chronic diseases which our surgeons had not the means of preventing or arresting." Such arguments had little effect, and the name Andersonville remains synonymous with inhuman conditions in Civil War prison camps.[29]

The film follows the narrative of MacKinlay Kantor's novel titled *Andersonville*, a best-seller that won the Pulitzer Prize for Fiction in 1956.[30] Far more concerned with Federal prisoners than with the Confederates who held them, it gives a mixed treatment of southern officers and soldiers. Henry Wirz and the guards at the prison are brutish and vindictive. As the leading historian of Andersonville remarked in a review of the film, "Confederates are portrayed as the malicious beasts they were accused of being in 1865" by bitter ex-prisoners.[31] In one typical scene, Wirz cuts off bread rations because a bridle and halter have been stolen. He threatens would-be escapees with dogs and employs harsh punishments. Guards entice a prisoner to cross the "dead line," a small fence inside the palisade, and shoot him in cold blood. "You know the rules," an officer yells at the prisoners, and a vicious young guard lies, "I warned them."

Other Confederate characters, especially officers not associated with the prison, are more attractive. Early in the film, Confederates guarding Union soldiers captured in the battle of Cold Harbor allow them to bury slain comrades and retrieve their haversacks. One officer says he would give the prisoners food, "but we don't have anything here." A colonel sent to inspect the camp serves as a positive contrast to Wirz. Learning that one hundred prisoners die each day, the colonel pronounces their medical care "a disgrace to civilization" and labels the water supply, a single fetid stream that runs through the camp, horrible. He also chides Wirz for employing the ball-and-chain and stocks—both violations of the rules of war—to discipline escapees and other prisoners. Wirz pleads that he does his best under horrible conditions. Numbers overwhelm him, he claims, with the population soaring far past the camp's original capacity. He needs more soldiers and staff and, selfishly, more rank for himself. He implores the colonel to make his case to authorities in Richmond. In some ways, the camp seems more an anomaly attributable to Wirz's actions than an indictment of the Confederacy.

A few standard Lost Cause scenes regarding destruction and deprivation crop up. On the train ride from Cold Harbor to the camp, prisoners see ruined cities, barren countryside, and other evidence of economic and social disruption. The officer's comment about lacking food to share with the Union prisoners implies a general shortage of victuals in the Confederacy. Extremely young guards at Andersonville bespeak a lack of Confederate manpower that compels the government to expand the usual definition of "military-age" men. As one character puts it, the South was "robbing the cradle and the grave." All of these things support the idea of sacrifice amid crushing circumstances so important to the Lost Cause tradition. Yet they do not counterbalance the negative images of Andersonville. Snarling dogs, stacks of corpses awaiting burial, the menacing behavior of Wirz and his guards, and emaciated prisoners living amid filthy conditions add up to a powerful indictment of the Confederate prison camp that undercuts Lost Cause attempts to cast Yankees as the barbaric actors in the conflict.[32]

Ride with the Devil deals with another unsavory dimension of the conflict and neatly sidesteps the major pitfalls inherent in making a modern film about

FIGURE 9. A group of Union soldiers in *Andersonville*, illustrating the ragged clothing, insufficient shelter, and crowded conditions that plagued prisoners in the Confederate camp. (From left in the foreground are actors Ted Marcoux, Justin Henry, and Jerrod Emick; Frederic Forrest reclines behind Marcoux.) Photofest.

Confederates.[33] Director Ang Lee shows how to explore a proslavery society that nearly destroyed the United States without alienating critics and much of his potential audience. He adopts a two-part approach: first, show racism and brutality on both sides; and second, create a violent tapestry in which the principal characters stand aloof from politics and ideology, dealing in human terms with disruptive events and manifesting enlightened attitudes about slavery and race. Like *Pharaoh's Army*, Lee's film depicts war on the border. An opening text accurately sets the turbulent stage: "On the western frontier of Missouri, the American Civil War was fought not by armies, but by neighbors. Informal gangs of local southern *bushwhackers* fought a bloody and desperate guerrilla war against the occupying Union army and pro-Union *Jayhawkers*. Allegiance to either side was dangerous. But it was more dangerous still to find oneself caught in the middle." The film includes large doses of vicious behavior by Union and Confederate soldiers, murders of pro-Confederate and pro-Union civilians, and almost casual savagery on both sides (in one scene, Confederate guerrillas playing poker bet scalps they have taken from African Americans and pro-Union Germans).[34]

The protagonists are Confederate guerrillas Jacob "Jake" Roedel, Jack Bull Chiles, George Clyde (who makes "Yankee killing as entertaining as greasing a gander"), and a free black man named Daniel Holt. This diverse quartet departs conspicuously from *Gone with the Wind*'s Lost Cause catalog of Confederate types. No grand planters, cultured ladies, or honor-bound regular army officers populate the film. Jake's parents are Unionist Germans, but his friendship with Jack's family has made him "as southern as they come." Jack's family lives in a comfortable two-story brick house—not a mansion like Tara or Twelve Oaks—and owns some slaves. Clyde and Holt grew up together, with Clyde part of a slaveholding family targeted by Kansas Jayhawkers.

A film charged with racial tensions among both Union and Confederate figures labors to portray a believable bond among the four Confederate guerrillas. The men transcend nineteenth-century racial boundaries in ways that seem highly unlikely but probably are necessary in a film about Confederates released in 1999 and directed by Lee. Early on, viewers learn that Holt killed three Kansas Jayhawkers who came after Clyde. Now other Yankees want to settle accounts with Holt "real bad." Clyde sums up the relationship succinctly: "He's not my nigger. He's just a nigger who I trust with my life every day and every night, that's all." Late in the film, Holt tells Jake that Clyde had bought his freedom. Jake initially voices doubts about Holt, remarking that "a nigger with guns is still a nervous thing to me." The two gradually become close friends and the film's principal male characters. Although they cannot be dismissed as mere action "buddies," they do function in ways typical of that stock Hollywood type.

After the men's relationships have been established, they link up with a young widow named Sue Lee Shelley. A pro-Confederate Missourian, she falls in love with Jack, with whom she has a child, but eventually marries Jake. Sue Lee also must accept Holt, whom she initially identifies as a slave rather than one of the guerrillas. The four men are spending the winter on a farm owned by the family of Sue Lee's dead husband. During her first visit to a small cabin they have built into the side of a hill, Holt walks in. "What's he doing here, inside?" she asks. "Ma'am, this nigger's with me," answers Clyde, "His name is Holt." "Wouldn't he be more useful off in a field plowing?" she responds. No, says Clyde, he is "one nigger I wouldn't try to hitch behind a plow." Sue Lee soon acknowledges Holt as one of the guerrillas, allowing her entry into what has become an ever more implausible group.

Having dealt with the problem of race among his leading characters, Lee carefully defines them as "good" Confederate guerrillas. They all participate in bloody encounters, and the body count of innocent civilians and Union and Confederate guerrillas rapidly mounts. Jack and his father, George Clyde, Jake's Unionist father, and Sue Lee's former father-in-law are among the slain. But the good guerrillas are easily identifiable among more loathsome comrades who exhibit repellent racism and a willingness to kill indiscriminately. One of the bad guerrillas casually mentions that some units are "scalping every nigger they can find," glances at Holt, and adds, "except, of course, our own." A crucial sequence depicts the sack of Lawrence, Kansas, on August 21, 1863, by Confederate guerrillas under William Clarke Quantrill. Quantrill's raid, which left approximately 150 men and boys in Lawrence dead, ranks among the war's notable atrocities, a brutal mission of retribution aimed at punishing the town for its role in the long-standing contest over slavery in the territories. In Lee's rendering of the event, bad guerrillas are personified by a character named Pitt Mackeson, played with cold-eyed menace by Jonathan Rhys Meyers. They kill unarmed men in front of the men's terrified families, burn the school, and ransack businesses and homes. Jake and Holt refuse to participate in the slaughter. Their behavior raises doubts in Mackeson, who threatens Holt and later wounds Jake before leading his own band on a rampage of robbery and plunder.

The guerrillas in Ride with the Devil operate in a world little concerned with national allegiance. Only a few scenes address the Confederacy, most of

FIGURE 10. During the raid on Lawrence, Kansas, in *Ride with the Devil*, Jake Roedel (Tobey Maguire) confronts a racist Confederate guerrilla who threatens Daniel Holt (Jeffrey Wright). The scene fosters a sense of the improbable comradeship that unites Roedel and Holt across racial lines. Photofest.

which question parts of southern culture. In one, Sue Lee's pro-Confederate former father-in-law remarks that the North educates its children without "regard to station, custom, propriety, and that is why they will win. Because they believe everyone should live and think like them." "Are you saying, Sir, that we fight for nothing?" demands Jack. "Far from it, Mr. Chiles," comes the answer. "You fight for everything that we ever had, as did my son. It's just that we don't have it any more." Many of the film's Confederates are illiterate, and Jake often reads to them from captured Union letters. One writer notes that Rebels claim the war is for liberty and rights but wonders what kind of liberty makes slaves of others. Holt hears this, thinks a bit, and for the first time reveals to Jake that his name is Daniel—like the man in the Bible thrown into the lion's den "but never ate." Although viewers know in a general way that the guerrillas favor a southern way of life dependent on slavery, no character takes the time to explain precisely what the Confederacy means to him.

Jake and Holt discuss motivation in a crucial scene toward the end of the film. Why had they fought as Confederate guerrillas? What had been their *cause*? Holt's cause had been his friend George Clyde, with whom he stood when Yankees killed Clyde's family. Jake, similarly, had supported Jack after Yankees brutalized the Chiles family. Thus did a former slave and the son of pro-Union German parents find themselves fighting against the United States. Neither is really a Confederate. They have no sense of a Confederate cause. Their causes are more personal, and when George Clyde and Jack Chiles are killed, Holt and Jake are free to cast off their nominal Confederate association. Holt decides to look for his mother. Considering himself truly free for the first time because Clyde is dead, he vows never again to "be nobody's nigger." Jake wishes Holt well and prepares to strike out on his own new life—married to Sue Lee and shorn of the long hair favored by the Missouri guerrillas. The film ends on a note of racial harmony between men who had been caught up in, but ideologically unconnected with, a bloody war between the Confederacy and the United States.

Sommersby and *Ride with the Devil* strongly suggested that Hollywood would no longer rely on durable Lost Cause themes in exploring the Confederate experience. Perhaps the exploits of Confederate soldiers who fight for their beleaguered cause, attractive white characters who unabashedly embrace and sacrifice for the slaveholding republic, and loyal slaves who help keep the home front functioning had been banished for good. So it seemed until 2003, when *Gods and Generals* highlighted the resiliency of the Lost Cause tradition.[35]

Directed by Ron Maxwell, whose credits included *Gettysburg* a decade earlier, this film served up a hearty helping of Lost Cause fare. It also triggered a contentious debate among reviewers and historians that recalled, in more subdued form, the reactions to *The Birth of a Nation* and *Gone with the Wind*. *Newsday* dismissed the film as a "shameless apologia for the Confederacy as a divinely inspired crusade for faith, home and slave labor." The *Boston Globe* thought "it insults the sensibilities of anyone not clinging to rosy memories of the slave-era South." The *Washington Post* charged that the film was "clearly intended as something of a Confederate Honor Restoration Project, in which the men of the South are cut loose from the weight of slavery's evil and portrayed as God-fearing, patriotic, noble and heroic." Academic critics also weighed in. "*Gods and Generals* brings to the big screen," wrote one, "the major themes of Lost Cause mythology that professional historians have been working for half a century to combat."[36]

Maxwell countered that such criticism amounted to nothing but political correctness. Asked what would entice a multiethnic American audience to a story that "treats Confederate figures with dignity," he remarked: "The truth! . . . Jackson was a Union man. Lee and Jackson were both uncomfortable with slavery. But that is not what their war was about. . . . Virginia was their home. They would fight for their home. . . . There are some things in my picture over which some historians might differ, but there are no lies or outright distortions in it. And 'political correctness'? Never!" Dennis Frye, a historian who worked closely with Maxwell on the film, supported the director. "Making history a reality is Ron Maxwell's passion," wrote Frye. "Generating *good* history from Hollywood is his indefatigable mission." *American Enterprise* seconded Frye's opinion in a staunchly supportive review that declared the film "an American masterpiece about the most myth-laden, destructive, and regenerative episode in American history." This reviewer observed that Maxwell understood "just how startling it will be for an audience to see Southerners presented as men who believe they are fighting a defensive war against Yankee imperialists."[37]

A "prequel" to *Gettysburg* based on Jeff Shaara's novel of the same title, *Gods and Generals* touches almost every Lost Cause base. To a greater degree than the book, Ron Maxwell's screenplay makes Stonewall Jackson the central character, and its handling of slaves and slavery also departs significantly from Shaara's text. It sympathetically explores Confederate motivations for secession and features Lee and Jackson as a brilliant and deeply religious command team. Combat sequences center on the battles of First Bull Run,

Fredericksburg, and Chancellorsville—all Confederate victories and the last two showcases for the talents of Lee and Jackson against much larger United States armies. It links Confederates to the Revolutionary generation and takes pains to explain that Confederates fight to defend home and hearth. Although the film also portrays Union characters, Confederate generals and civilians dominate the narrative. More than forty minutes pass before the first United States soldiers appear to serve as an amorphous foe vanquished by Confederates at First Bull Run. No Federal soldier has a speaking part until Joshua Chamberlain's entrance nearly an hour into the film.[38]

Lee and Jackson shoulder the burden of explaining Confederate motivations. Much of Jackson's explanatory dialogue, it is worth noting, does not come directly from Shaara's novel (Jackson does not have a major part in the book between April 1861 and December 1862). In a scene at the Virginia secession convention, a speaker denounces Abraham Lincoln and evokes the example of George Washington and Lee's father, Revolutionary hero Henry "Light Horse Harry" Lee, in tendering command of the state's forces. "Profoundly impressed," Lee accepts and vows to devote himself to "the service of my native state, in whose behalf alone I will ever again draw my sword." Shortly after Virginia secedes, Jackson tells his brigade of Shenandoah Valley soldiers that the North precipitated the sectional crisis just as Great Britain forced a crisis on their ancestors. "We will never allow the armies of others to march into our state and tyrannize our people," affirms Jackson. In a subsequent conversation with cavalry officer James E. B. Stuart, Jackson refers to Yankees as "violators of our homes and firesides." More than a year later, before the battle of Fredericksburg, Lee makes the same point more fully. "There is something that these Yankees do not understand, will never understand," he says while gazing across the Rappahannock River toward Ferry Farm, where George Washington was born. "You see these rivers and valleys and streams, fields, even towns?" he asks with emotion in his voice. "They are just markings on a map to those people in the War Office in Washington," but for Lee and Confederates they are birthplaces, burial grounds, and battlefields where their ancestors fought: "They are the incarnation of all our memories and all that we are, all that we are."

Most vocal about their loyalty to Virginia at the outset, Lee and Jackson soon become ardent Confederates. Everything they prize about Virginia becomes exemplified by the Confederacy. In this vein, Jackson directly ties the Confederate attempt at nation-building to that of the revolutionary generation when, in taking leave from his first command, he alludes to "this, our second war of

FIGURE 11. Robert E. Lee (right; Robert Duvall) and Thomas J. "Stonewall" Jackson (left; Stephen Lang), the key Confederate characters in *Gods and Generals*. Photofest.

independence." Jackson also lectures a member of his staff about the relative nobility of the Union and Confederate war efforts. "If the Republicans lose their little war" and suffer defeat in the next round of elections, he observes, they will simply return to their homes "fat with war profits." But if Confederates fail to achieve victory, "we lose our country. We lose our independence. We lose it all." Jubal Early and his ex-Confederate comrades could not have offered a more invidious comparison of the two causes. That same winter, Lee toasts southern women, without whose bravery and fortitude southern soldiers would lack the strength to "defend the Confederate cause."

Lee's toast reflects the film's portrayal of Confederate slaveholding women and other civilians as self-sacrificing patriots. In an early scene in Fredericksburg, young men leaving for the army receive a flag and assurances from their mother, Jane Howison Beale, that everyone on the home front will support them. She also remarks with an air of acceptance that many men will fall before true freedom comes to the Confederacy. Another scene suggests support for the Confederacy across class lines. Common soldiers bid their wives goodbye and brothers exchange parting words as mechanics, yeoman farmers, and working-class men hurry to join their units. During the bombardment of Fredericksburg in December 1862, women and children show pluck as they become refugees, trudging across a winter's landscape to the safety of Confederate military lines. Stonewall Jackson commends the courage of women and children left to fend for themselves, calling for the execution of deserters in part because they have betrayed the trust of loyal civilians.

Treatment of African American characters stands as the film's most controversial dimension. One of the Beale family's house slaves named Martha sets the overall tone. Although a bit more complex than Mammy in *Gone with the Wind*, Martha shares a similar bond with her owners. She wishes her young masters well with kisses and a brief embrace when they ride off to war in their new Confederate uniforms. As the Union's Army of the Potomac approaches before the battle of Fredericksburg, Martha thinks primarily of the white family's safety. "We got to get you and dem children out of here in a hurry," she tells her mistress. "We'll all leave together," replies Jane Beale. "I will not leave you to the mercy of those blue devils." "Miss Jane," comes the reply, "you know they are not going to be bothering us colored folks." If she stays, adds Martha, the Yankees likely will not plunder the house. After the Federal shelling on December 11, during which the black and white members of the household seek shelter in the cellar, the Beales leave in an ambulance—after Jane and Martha embrace. Federals arrive soon thereafter and meet Martha in the front yard. "Is this your master's place?" inquires a soldier. "This is my place," she answers. "Sorry to bother you, Ma'am," reply the soldiers, who spare the Beale property without expressing a hint of surprise that a black woman would own such a fine home. After the battle of Fredericksburg, Federals use the Beale house as a hospital, which gives Martha an opportunity to deliver a mixed message of loyalty to the Beales and a yearning to be free: "I love them people you done chased from this house. I'se known them most all of my life. The Beales is good people. Mister General, I'se born a slave, and I wants to die free. Lord knows I wants to die free, and I want my children to be free. Heaven help me. And God bless you all."[39]

Two scenes between Stonewall Jackson and Jim Lewis, his black cook, match *Gone with the Wind* in establishing a sympathetic relationship across racial lines. Both scenes represent departures from Shaara's novel, which does not include the cook. The first occurs when Jackson meets Lewis in 1861. "I understand you are from Lexington," says the general. "You come highly recommended to me, Jim." Lewis replies: "Lexington is my home, General, same as you'rn. If I could do my share in defendin' my home, I'll be doin' the same as you." "If you love your country, fear the Lord, and have no trouble getting up at four in the morning, the job is yours," says Jackson. Lewis takes the assignment—eager, apparently, to help defend his home and his "country" against Federals who pose an unexplained threat to him and other black people in Lexington.

Later in the film, after a long day's march, the two men look forward to a Confederacy without slavery. Under a star-studded night sky, the mounted Jackson asks whether Jim, who stands on the ground, has heard from his family. Then he looks skyward and asks God "to watch over Jim Lewis's family, over his friends, his loved ones wherever they may be." Lewis says, "Lord, I know you sees into the hearts of all men just like you sees into the heart of old Jim Lewis." The camera focuses on Jackson, his eyes closed, as Lewis talks. "And Lord, I know . . . there be no hidin' from your truth and your ever-watchful eye." "Amen," says Jackson. "How is it, Lord," continues Lewis, "a good Christian man like some folks I know can tolerate dey black brothers in bondage? How is it, Lord, you don't just break dem chains? How is it, Lord? My heart is open and achin', and I wants to know." Caught up in Lewis's questions, Jackson takes over: "Lord, speak to us, speak to your children, speak to Jim Lewis and Thomas Jackson, your humble and obedient servants. Speak to all of us. Our hearts *are* open. Lord, you show us the way, we will follow." Lewis and Jackson both say "Amen."

FIGURE 12. Jane Beale (center; Mia Dillon) and her slave Martha
(Donzaleigh Abernathy) in one of the *Gods and Generals* scenes that
depict their reciprocal affection and loyalty. Photofest.

FIGURE 13. Stonewall Jackson offers Jim Lewis (Frankie Faison) the job as his cook in *Gods and Generals*. Photofest.

Jackson next asks about the status of Lewis's family, learning that "about half is free and half slave, counting cousins and such." Then the slaveholding general raises the possibility of freedom: "Jim, you must know that there are some officers in this army who are of the opinion that we should be enlisting Negroes as a condition for freedom. General Lee is among them." Lewis acknowledges rumors about this "'round the camp." "Your people will be free, one way or t'other," asserts Jackson; the "only question is whether the southern government will have the good sense to do it first and soon and in so doing seal a bond of enduring friendship between us." "That what they says, General," allows Lewis without a trace of sarcasm or irony. "God's plan is a great mystery," concludes Jackson. "It will be revealed to us."[40]

As far as testimony from the time reveals, this last episode between Jackson and Lewis has no basis in fact. Nor does the historical record suggest that Jackson manifested any active opposition to slavery. He probably believed that God would settle the question in time and that mortals should refrain from tampering with divine intentions. Why, then, construct the exchange with Jim Lewis? It seems a gratuitous Lost Cause gesture calculated to recast the nineteenth-century Jackson for a modern audience. Maxwell conceded that modern viewers might find it hard to understand the scenes with Lewis and Martha Beale. But Lewis "stayed with Jackson as long as he lived, out of loyalty to him as a man," and Martha Beale, "a real historical figure," is "treated with respect" in the film.[41]

As already noted, Maxwell proudly touted the accuracy of his film. "Perhaps the most powerful aspect of the motion picture *Gods and Generals*," he wrote in a book published as a companion to the film, "is the fact that the story is true."[42] Indeed, apart from the imagined scenes between Jackson and Lewis, the treatment of Confederates generally hews close to the historical record. Maxwell's attention to feelings of Confederate nationalism on the part of Lee and other characters certainly makes sense. Lee and Jackson were very religious men and gifted commanders who won victories against long odds. Although the Confederacy suffered from internal tensions of various kinds, most civilians supported the war despite widespread suffering. Civilian and military leaders often praised the steadfastness of Confederate women, and letters and diaries include myriad references to the war as a fight for home and against northern coercion. Some slaves probably exhibited loyalty, or at least experienced complex emotions, regarding their masters. The problem in *Gods and Generals* is one of balance—what Maxwell left out in creating his tapestry of valiant Confederate officers and citizens at war. What about the thousands of slaves who ran away to Union lines? Or those who sullenly went about their business but hoped for United States success? What about slavery as a precipitant of secession and war? Or the white citizens unhappy with the Confederacy? The list of questions could go on and might include this: Who would guess that a film so celebratory of Confederates at war could be released in 2003?

As if on cue, later in 2003, *Cold Mountain* offered a striking counterpoint to *Gods and Generals*.[43] Based on Charles Frazier's wildly successful novel and directed by Anthony Minghella, it tells the story of a Confederate deserter's Odysseus-like trek home to North Carolina from the Virginia battlefront. Many reviewers praised it, as when *USA Today* gushed: "In its vivid depiction of tragedy, waste and the plundering of a generation, Anthony Minghella's epic . . . is the equal of any Civil War movie ever made." Slightly less enthusiastic, the *Washington Post* lauded the "subtly spectacular craftsman Anthony Minghella" and termed *Cold Mountain* "one of those films that might be called 'complete.'" An academic reviewer noted various factual errors but applauded Minghella's bringing to the screen so "unflinching a portrayal of the bleak and unsettling realities" of a Civil War experienced by "thousands of hardscrabble Southern men and women who lived through it." The *New York Times* liked the film's showing that "the Civil War, like World War II, empowered a generation of women."[44]

Taking a dramatically different position from Maxwell, Minghella stressed that neither historical accuracy nor the Civil War especially concerned him. "The film is not a history lesson," he stated. "It doesn't exist to stand in for a study of a real event. Rather, it tries to cast light on some circumstances which surround any war. . . . If I thought I was making a Civil War film, then I wouldn't have taken this project on." Hoping to explore characters "caught up in tensions they often don't understand," he simply used the Civil War as a setting. Yet he also noted, "I mired myself in Civil War books"—an odd expenditure of time in light of his other comments.[45]

Cold Mountain can best be understood as a feminist antiwar film that turns almost every Lost Cause convention on its head. In the process, it distorts history at least as much as *Gods and Generals*. Virtually all white southern women in the film are either indifferent or deeply opposed to the war. This interpretation fits a modern sensibility, especially prevalent in academia, that embraces the idea of Confederate women as lukewarm or openly hostile toward the war.[46] A few examples will illustrate this point. Just before the war, in a scene much like one at Twelve Oaks in *Gone with the Wind*, a man bursts into church and announces secession. "We got our war!" a young man shouts. Amid much whooping and hollering, other men exclaim: "We got our war! We got it! We got it! It's about time!" Ada Monroe, the film's slaveholding heroine, says derisively to Inman, the nonslaveholding male protagonist, that now he has "his" war. A short time later she asks if Inman is enlisting. "If there is a war, we'll all fight," he answers. Did he get a tintype made, she inquires sarcastically, "With your musket and your courage on display?" In another scene, privation plagues the home front, and Ada wants Inman to stop fighting, leave the army, and return to her. "Come back to me is my request," reads her letter to him. He promptly deserts, affirming women's power to undermine the Confederate war effort. Later in the film, the rough yeoman prototype Ruby Thewes learns that her father, himself a Confederate deserter, has been shot. She pronounces the war "bullshit." Men made the weather, she proclaims in her usual salty manner, and now they stand in the rain and say, "Shit, it's raining!" These and many other moments in the film leave no doubt that Melanie Wilkes and her ilk would find few compatriots among their North Carolina sisters on Cold Mountain.

Few appealing characters in *Cold Mountain* exhibit any pro-Confederate sentiment. The Home Guard, commanded by a simplistically evil officer named Teague, represents the most obvious expression of the Confederate state. Early in the war, Teague announces that the Home Guard will watch over Cold Mountain while the area's men are away fighting with Confederate armies. He later says deserters will be executed and anyone who helps them deemed a traitor to the Confederacy. Teague's men pillage and kill at their whim, presenting an inaccurate portrait of the Home Guard that conflates bushwhackers, deserters, guerrillas, and other irregular units. In one graphic scene, the Home Guard murders a yeoman farmer in cold blood, tortures his wife, and kills two sons who are trying to avoid Confederate service. In another, the Guard enlists what can only be described as white trash to trap southern deserters. A dispirited Inman refers to Confederate soldiers as fools "sent off to fight with a flag and a lie," leaving viewers to conclude that the Confederacy duped the poor fellows into donning gray uniforms. A military surgeon's comments support this idea. Looking out at slaves working in a field, he speaks scornfully about the cause for which wounded men in his hospital are fighting. The fools are dying for rich slaveholders, he says, in a classic example of the "rich man's war, poor man's fight" formulation. It seems that all the nice white folks in the Confederacy are deserters, soldiers suffering from false consciousness, or disgruntled women against the war,

FIGURE 14. Ada Monroe (Nicole Kidman) and Inman (Jude Law) shortly before he leaves to fight for the Confederacy in *Cold Mountain*. In an earlier scene, she had mocked his decision to join the army. Photofest.

while the Home Guard consists of pro-Confederate fiends who wrap themselves in patriotism and torment their neighbors.[47]

As in *Sommersby*, slivers of the Lost Cause narrative crop up in *Cold Mountain*. Hardship on the home front, a dimension of the Confederate experience highlighted in Lost Cause writings, leaves Ada in straitened circumstances. In a scene borrowed directly from Scarlett O'Hara in *Gone with the Wind*, she is reduced to eating roots, although she resists vowing never to be hungry again. Several references to casualties speak to the human toll. By the autumn of 1864, tragedy has touched nearly every home, and people dread each day's news about who has fallen "in this terrible war." Like many Lost Cause writers, Minghella largely removes slaves and slavery from the story. Unlike Frazier's novel, the film version of *Cold Mountain* imagines western North Carolina as very white—almost as white as the *Andy Griffith Show*'s Mayberry, which was set in the same part of the world. Although fewer black people lived in the mountains of North Carolina than in piedmont or tidewater areas, the absence of African Americans rings false.

The director also chose to play down the importance of African American soldiers at the battle of the Crater. Departing from Frazier's novel, he substituted the Crater, fought at Petersburg on July 30, 1864, for the clash at Fredericksburg on December 13, 1862, as Inman's major experience in combat. This makes sense cinematically because the Crater offers singular dramatic elements—a Union tunnel filled with 8,000 pounds of black powder, a massive explosion that wrecked an entire South Carolina regiment, and the debut in Virginia of African American units on a large scale. In the course of an unfolding Union disaster, enraged Confederates summarily executed a number of black soldiers. *Cold Mountain* only hints at the part played by United States Colored Troops at the Crater; indeed, Minghella seems most interested in using their presence to suggest an anachronistic sense of shared subjugation between Native Americans and African Americans. In the midst of hellish hand-to-hand fighting, a Cherokee Confederate and a USCT infantryman briefly lock eyes, alerting modern audiences to the tragedy of their killing one another rather than standing together against the South's slaveholding class.[48]

Slavery and black people serve principally to help leading white characters manifest enlightened attitudes. Ada finds herself in western North Carolina after leaving Charleston, South Carolina. The daughter of a slaveholding clergyman from the birthplace of secession, she nevertheless expresses happiness at escaping "from a world of slaves and corsets and cotton." Following

FIGURE 15. Teague (right; Ray Winstone) and his son Bosie (left; Charlie Hunnam), whose activities with the Home Guard spread terror among residents of Cold Mountain. Photofest.

her father's death, Ada frees the family's slaves. Antislavery sentiment among women from South Carolina's slaveholding class was not unknown, as abolitionists Sarah and Angelina Grimké most famously demonstrated, but Ada would have belonged to a statistically insignificant minority. The film offers no explanation for her actions, which imply covert abolitionism and support the reassuring, if almost entirely false, notion that women of the slaveholding class secretly hated the peculiar institution.[49] Inman also distances himself from proslavery Confederates. One night he stumbles upon a preacher carrying a black woman's limp body. The man had gotten her pregnant and, having drugged her, is on his way to drown the unfortunate soul. Inman saves the woman, ties the preacher to a post, and continues his journey back to Cold Mountain. Along the way he encounters a group of African Americans running toward freedom. "I've got no quarrel with you," he tells them, inviting further conversation, but they, understandably wary of a white man, move on past. Soon the Home Guard arrives, dogs in tow, to chase Inman and the African Americans, who join one another as victims of predatory Confederate oppression.

Anyone watching Cold Mountain might wonder how the Confederacy lasted four years. What regime would not collapse quickly under the weight of women unhappy with the war, yeomen duped into fighting for slaveholders, and a Home Guard deployed to terrorize citizens? As with Gods and Generals, the problem lies in the film's emphases. Cold Mountain usefully portrays aspects of conflict on the home front seldom captured on film. Many men and women in the Confederacy opposed the war, and desertion plagued every southern army. Parts of mountainous North Carolina experienced lethal internal tensions, sometimes tied to heavy-handed actions by Confederate conscription officers in the state. Guerrillas, bushwhackers, and local troops often preyed on civilians. But the large majority of white southern women—especially slaveholding women like Ada Monroe—resolutely supported the Confederate nation until very late in the conflict. An equally large proportion of Confederate soldiers, most of them nonslaveholders, remained in the ranks. Nothing like Minghella's Home Guard existed, and Ada's stance regarding slavery can be dismissed as profoundly anachronistic. Minghella's anti–Lost Cause version of the Confederacy, though more appealing to most modern audiences than the version in Gods and Generals, continues a long Hollywood tradition of ignoring historical facts in favor of good storytelling.[50]

Lost Cause enthusiasts put off by Cold Mountain would find no comfort in C.S.A.: The Confederate States of America. Kevin Willmott wrote and directed this mock documentary,[51] first shown at the Sundance Film Festival in January 2004 and released on a limited basis in the United States two years later. Framed as a British Broadcasting Service production, it examines the history of a Confederacy that won the Civil War, annexed the northern states, and remained a viable slaveholding nation through the twentieth century. "If you're going to tell the truth," reads an opening quotation from George Bernard Shaw, "you better make them laugh; otherwise they'll kill you." Ninety minutes of dark satire ensue, with canonical images from American history featuring Confederate flags—Teddy Roosevelt and his Rough Riders in the Spanish-American War, the flag-raising on Iwo Jima (fig. 16), and astronauts walking on the moon in the 1960s—and disturbing advertisements, interspersed between segments of the documentary, for such things as "Sambo X-15" engine additive and a Slave Shopping Network selling black people as individuals or as families.[52]

Willmott's script places slavery at the heart of secession and all of Confederate history. Scene after scene would trigger winces from anyone hoping to separate the Confederate story from slavery. In one, a grade-school teacher in the late 1950s explains to an attentive white student that prime field hands cost as much in 1860 as new luxury cars in the modern Confederacy. The North threatened that property, he tells the obviously impressed boy, and thereby forced the slaveholding South to fight. Mimicking Ken Burns's style in The Civil War, the film uses a pair of historians—one a white Confederate and the other a black woman—to offer different explanations for historic events. Near the film's end, the white historian echoes Alexander H. Stephens's "Cornerstone Speech": "Slavery, like nothing else, is what defines us, shapes us—as a people, as a nation. Owning a slave is a constant reminder of who you are." The explanation for long-term Confederate success lies partially in Jefferson Davis's ability to reintroduce slavery to the northern states—a plan first suggested to him by one of his loyal slaves. Later, the Confederacy conquers Latin America, establishes apartheid in Mexico, reopens the international slave trade during the Great Depression, and approves of Nazi Germany's celebration of Aryan superiority (though urging Hitler to enslave Jews rather than waste labor by killing them). The film's last scene depicts schoolchildren reciting the Confederate Pledge of Allegiance, ending with a promise of "liberty and justice for all white people."

The power of Robert E. Lee's legend oddly affects Willmott's otherwise scathing depiction. Much like Lost Cause writers, he separates Lee from the mass of white southerners who sought to safeguard slavery. After the war, Lee

FIGURE 16. Soldiers raise the Confederacy's St. Andrew's Cross flag on Iwo Jima in *C.S.A.: The Confederate States of America*. Photofest.

calls for emancipation and the removal of freed slaves. A proslavery character named John Ambrose Fauntroy, who spearheads Davis's plan to transform the North into a slaveholding society, remarks condescendingly: "We have always known that the honorable General Lee was a secret emancipationist; however, the noble gentleman knows more of military matters than civil affairs." The film also credits Lee with the quotation "War is hell"—which neither he nor William Tecumseh Sherman, to whom it has always been attributed, ever said or wrote as far as historical sources show. This implication of antiwar sentiment on Lee's part overlooks the Virginian's preternatural aggressiveness on the battlefield and willingness to absorb frightful casualties in pursuit of success.

This somewhat gentle treatment of Lee in no way vitiates the larger anti–Lost Cause interpretation in C.S.A. The drumbeat of slavery's importance, cruel television advertisements, casually profound racism of modern Confederate citizens, and links between the Confederacy and Nazi Germany create a grim picture of the slaveholding republic's impact on the world. Neo-Confederates sometimes equate Lincoln's actions with those of Hitler—as when, to protest a statue of Lincoln at the Tredegar Iron Works in Richmond in 2003, they held up a sign that read "Hitler/Paris 1940. Lincoln/Richmond 1865."[53] Such people would find Willmott's treatment of Confederate relations with the Thousand-Year Reich most troubling. Their one bright moment in C.S.A. would come when the white historian dismisses Lincoln as a historical footnote remembered only as "the man who lost the war of northern aggression."

The Lost Cause tradition may have enjoyed its last hurrah in Gods and Generals. Residual influence likely will rest with television, where Gone with the Wind and other films with Lost Cause themes are always available, and in the availability of older films in other formats. What about the traditions that dealt with the northern side of the conflict? The next chapter will consider how Hollywood has presented the victors' war.

Emancipation and Reconciliation but Not the Union : Hollywood and the North's Civil War

3

Hollywood's recent Civil War films fail almost completely to convey any sense of what the Union Cause meant to millions of northern citizens. More than that, they often cast the United States Army, a military force that saved the republic and destroyed slavery, in a decidedly negative, post-Vietnam light. The Emancipation and Reconciliation Causes, both of which strike modern Americans as more meaningful than the Union Cause, have fared much better. Ironically, the Union Cause received more attention during the era when the Lost Cause dominated Civil War films, in large measure because some notable movies featured Abraham Lincoln. Reconciliation also flourished during the period 1915–65, easily outstripping Emancipation. As already noted, *Shenandoah* heralded a turn toward Emancipation that accelerated dramatically with *Glory* as the 1980s came to a close. Throughout the 1990s and beyond, Emancipation has achieved cinematic dominance, with Reconciliation maintaining a steady but secondary presence in a number of films.

Historians often place freedom alongside Union as an equivalent northern war aim, and of the two, Americans more easily grasp freedom as a noble goal worth great sacrifice.[1] The concept of Union is much more nebulous; indeed, it is almost impossible to convey to a modern audience why the Union meant so much to so many millions of northerners. Americans can readily conclude, as historian Barbara J. Fields has argued, that preservation of the Union was "a goal too shallow to be worth the sacrifice of a single life." Fields's memorable commentary in Ken Burns's documentary gave her views far wider circulation than those of most academic historians. In several parts of the series, she maintains that only the addition of freedom to the North's strategic goals elevated the cause in a way that justified the awful human and material cost. This statement recalls Frederick Douglass's speech at Arlington that celebrated Union success but pronounced the war's greatest outcome the death of "the hell-black system of human bondage." Fields's statements about the North's war effort make sense in terms of issues important to modern Americans. For anyone in search of what led white northerners of the 1860s to commit human and material treasure in profusion, however, dismissal of the Union Cause poses serious problems. The assertion that Union was unworthy of a single life's sacrifice trivializes the deaths of roughly a third of a million United States soldiers, while also promoting a flawed conception of the North's Civil War.[2]

~~ "To Free the Slaves, of Course"

Since the late 1980s, Hollywood has produced films strongly supportive of Fields's view. To their credit, these films have brought emancipation and black people to the forefront in ways virtually unknown in earlier generations. Before the 1980s, moviegoers could find only sporadic hints of the emancipation narrative. John Ford's *Young Mr. Lincoln* (1940) closes with a stirring rendition of "The Battle Hymn of the Republic," playing while the camera frames Daniel Chester French's statue of the seated president in the Lincoln Memorial. That combination of music and image surely encouraged thoughts of Lincoln as the Great Emancipator. In *Seven Angry Men* (1955), Raymond Massey reprises his role as John Brown in an interpretation that, while deeply flawed, treats abolitionism more sympathetically than had *Santa Fe Trail* fifteen years earlier. *Band of Angels* (1956), a melodramatic stew of racial hedging, presents a very young Sidney Poitier as a slave who joins the Union army.[3]

Director William Wyler's *Friendly Persuasion* (1956) merits more serious consideration. Set among Indiana's Quakers in 1863, it stars Gary Cooper and Dorothy McGuire as Jess and Eliza Birdwell and locates emancipation at the core of the northern war effort. The Birdwells and their family confront the dilemma of how to react to Brig. Gen. John Hunt Morgan's invading Confederate cavalrymen. As the Rebels approach, a United States officer interrupts a Quaker meeting. "I have had the duty placed upon me of speaking to you Quakers about the war," he explains. "The Union has endured two years of bloody civil war. Thousands have given their lives in battle to free our country from slavery." Eliza Birdwell responds that Quakers concur with the North's goal but not its means: "We are opposed to slavery, but we do not believe it right to kill one man to free another." A black man who works for the Birdwells reinforces the theme of a war to end slavery. As a runaway, he knows he will not stand a chance with the Confederates. "So if they're going to catch me," he says after announcing his intention to take the field against the Rebels, "I'm going down fighting."

Released a year after *Friendly Persuasion* and also set in Indiana, the self-conscious epic *Raintree County* tepidly embraces the emancipation narrative.[4] A convoluted tale scarcely worth recounting, it relies on John Wickliff Shawnessy, a sensitive student and later teacher, to make the case against slavery. Married early in the film to a beautiful southern belle named Susanna Drake,

FIGURE 17. Jess Birdwell (left; Gary Cooper) and sons Little Jess (center; Richard Eyer) and Josh (right; Anthony Perkins) in the Quaker meetinghouse where a Union officer asks for volunteers to fight a war against slavery in *Friendly Persuasion*. Josh eventually joins neighbors who take up arms to resist Confederate raiders. Photofest.

he clashes with her about slavery. "Well, to us Yankees," he says just after their wedding on the eve of the election of 1860, "the South is not too easy to understand. Have you ever read *Uncle Tom's Cabin*?" Taken aback, she exclaims: "*Uncle Tom's Cabin*! I haven't married an abolitionist, have I?" "That is the skeleton in my closet," he confesses. Back in Raintree County after a brief sojourn in the South, they quarrel on Election Day in 1860. She has brought two slaves with her, and Shawnessy, a Lincoln man, castigates her: "Susanna, you're not south now! You can't have your slaves here. . . . I'm not picking on you. I just don't want slaves in my house."

Emancipation disappears once the war begins, however, and Shawnessy adopts a friendly stance toward former Confederates after Appomattox. When an opportunist declares his intention to run for Congress so he can "see that the rebellious South gets its just deserts," Shawnessy says forcefully, "It's no longer rebellious. . . . It's beaten, and it's bleeding." Overall, *Raintree County* steers a careful course regarding slavery and emancipation. It avoids stereotypical black characters but also shies away from overt criticism of the white South.

Shenandoah's emancipationist elements built on these insubstantial precedents, but it remained for *Glory* to thrust the Emancipation Cause into heroic cinematic relief.[5] Prior to its release, black men in the Union army had been largely absent from American conceptions of the Civil War. Sixteen students at Ohio State University played black soldiers in the film, and one of them spoke of the experience as a revelation. "There is this whole world that I had no idea about," remarked Vince Mason. "This information wasn't in the history books. It's like an unquenchable thirst. The history is so rich—you want to jump right in with both feet." Denzel Washington, whose performance as the embittered Trip earned him an Oscar for best supporting actor, reacted much like Mason. "I knew absolutely nothing," he confessed. "I didn't even know that blacks fought in the Civil War. The American history classes that I took didn't seem to dwell on that at all. It was inspiring for me; it gave me a lot of energy to continue research and get further and further into it." Moviegoers across the United States left screenings with a similar realization that the military struggle between 1861 and 1865 had not been a lily-white affair. In that respect, *Glory* worked a sea change in popular perceptions about the conflict.[6]

Glory narrates the gripping story of Col. Robert Gould Shaw and the black soldiers in the 54th Massachusetts Infantry Regiment. Shaw's voice-over from a letter written early in the war when he served with a white regiment from

Massachusetts sets the tone (and also eliminates the complexity and racial ambiguity present in Shaw's correspondence). The young officer expresses pride at serving alongside men from all over the nation who are "ready to fight for their country, as the old fellows did in the Revolution. But this time we must make it a whole country, for all who live here." Before the war, many in his regiment had never seen a black person, but now northern soldiers traveled roads choked with the dispossessed. "We fight for men and women whose poetry is not yet written," observes Shaw, "but which will presently be as enviable and as renowned as any." Later, in conversation with a white officer who doubts the military ability of black enlistees, Shaw vows to get the men ready for combat. "They have risked their lives to be here," he explains; they "have given up their freedom." Shaw promises to match their sacrifice: "I owe them *my* freedom, my life if necessary."

The black characters in *Glory* unsurprisingly consider their military service to be primarily in the cause of emancipation. This treatment aligns perfectly with testimony from soldiers who served in black regiments.[7] As in most war movies, the men of the 54th represent a variety of types: Trip is the rebel, Thomas Searles the bookworm, John Rawlins the steady older man, and Jupiter Sharts the former slave who cannot read or write. Deployment of the 54th to South Carolina brings the men, and the viewer, face-to-face with slavery. As the soldiers float along a river and gaze at a plantation house near Beaufort, Rawlins and Sharts predict that the slaveholding South will soon be gone. "Take a good look," says Rawlins. "It's all a memory now that the North man come." "Now that *we* come," adds Sharts. Soon after the soldiers leave their boats, they see a number of local black children. Rawlins urges them to tell their parents that the appearance of the 54th means the year of jubilee has come. Here again, the film presents moviegoers with an interpretation that meets high standards of both drama and historical evidence. On June 8, 1863, Corporal James Henry Gooding of the 54th wrote about recently liberated black residents in Beaufort: "The contrabands did not believe we were coming; one of them said, 'I nebber bleeve black Yankee comee here help culer men.' They think now the kingdom is coming sure enough."[8]

Glory's most powerful scene takes place on the night before the regiment's famous assault against Fort Wagner on July 18, 1863. Gathered around a campfire, the men take turns singing, speaking about what it means to be part of the 54th, and explaining their motivations for fighting. Rawlins ran off and left his family in bondage, and now he has a chance to prove his manhood and strike a blow at slavery. "Heavenly Father, we want you to let our

FIGURE 18. Col. Robert Gould Shaw (Matthew Broderick) in the early stage of his service with the 54th Massachusetts in *Glory*. Photofest.

folks know that we died facing the enemy," he says in the rhythmic cadence of a church service: "We want them to know that we went down standing up. Amongst those that are fighting against our oppression, we want them to know, Heavenly Father, that we died for freedom. We ask these blessings in Jesus' name, Amen." The least religious of the speakers, Trip announces, "I loves the 54th." He fights for his comrades and echoes Rawlins in wanting to hold his head up like a man: "It ain't much a matter what happens tomorrow, cause we men, ain't we?"

Union has no place in the black soldiers' calculus of motivations. At the first mustering of the regiment, Shaw addresses them: "It is my hope that the same courage, spirit, and honor which has brought us together, will one day restore the Union. May God bless us all." The men cheer, but subsequent scenes indicate that their response has nothing to do with conceptions of Union (interestingly, the recruiting poster for the 54th has "Bounty" in larger and bolder letters than "Freedom"). During a tense confrontation after the regiment reaches South Carolina, Trip taunts Searles, who had been a friend of Colonel Shaw's in Boston before the war, by insisting he will never be anything but "an ugly-ass chimp in a blue suit" to white people. Rawlins steps in and slaps Trip. White boys have been dying for going on three years, he says to Trip, "dyin' by the thousands, dyin' for you, fool." Rawlins knows this because he dug graves for Union dead at Antietam. While he dug, he wondered when his time would come. Now he is in uniform, and the time will come for the 54th "to ante up and kick in like men. Like men!" Notably missing in Rawlins's speech is any reference to Union, and he incorrectly suggests most United States soldiers would have said in June 1863 that they had been dying for black men when in fact they would have identified Union as their primary goal. As for himself, the twin themes of freedom and manhood, both of which permeate wartime letters from African American soldiers, persuasively stand out.

Colonel Shaw and Trip also have an intense discussion about motivation. When it seems clear the 54th will soon be committed to combat, Shaw asks Trip to carry the flag. Trip declines what typically would be considered an honor. "I ain't fightin' this war for you, Sir," he remarks, adding: "I mean, what's the point? Ain't nobody gonna win. Its just gonna go on and on." Shaw counters that somebody will win, to which Trip replies that Shaw will go back to Boston and his big house. "What about us?" he wonders. "What do we get?" "Well, you won't get anything if we lose," says Shaw pointedly. "It stinks, I suppose," the colonel muses. "Yes, stinks bad, and we all covered

FIGURE 19. Thomas Searles (far left in front row; Andre Braugher), Trip (second from left in front row; Denzel Washington), and Jupiter Sharts (third from left in front row; Jihmi Kennedy) in line just prior to the attack by the 54th Massachusetts against Fort Wagner in *Glory*. Photofest.

up in it, too," agrees Trip. "I mean ain't nobody clean. Be nice to get clean though." "How do we do that?" asks Shaw. "We ante up and kick in, Sir," says Trip, carrying forward the theme of manhood among the black soldiers. "But I still don't want to carry your flag." Like Rawlins and Sharts, Trip has no commitment to a Union that has condoned slavery. Unlike them, he also seems to have no sense of participation in a historic struggle for emancipation. It is all about his comrades. Perhaps the most "modern" of *Glory's* black characters, Trip exhibits a post-Vietnam attitude that envisions no long-term good coming out of war. In the final attack, after Shaw falls while climbing the earthen parapet of Fort Wagner, Trip does pick up the flag before being killed himself. His act, unrelated to any grand cause, cements his bond with comrades suffering under heavy Confederate fire.[9]

Although markedly different from *Glory* in tone and subject, *Gettysburg* also embraces the Emancipation Cause. Early in the film, Col. Joshua Lawrence Chamberlain of the 20th Maine Infantry offers the film's major rumination about northern motivation. "All of us volunteered to fight for the Union," he remarks. Some joined the army out of boredom, others because it looked like fun or they were ashamed not to join up. "Many of us came because it was the right thing to do," he declares, and "all of us have seen men die." The war soon demonstrated that the Union army holds a special place in history. Men in the past had fought for pay, women, loot, land, and power. Some had fought just because they liked killing. "But we are here for something new," argues Chamberlain: "This has not happened much in the history of the world. We are an army out to set other men free. America should be free ground, all of it, not divided by a line between slave state and free, all the way from here to the Pacific Ocean." Chamberlain's younger brother Tom later reinforces the concept of a war for emancipation. In the scene, mentioned in the preceding chapter, where a Confederate yeoman talks about fighting for his "rats," Tom remarks that men in the Army of the Potomac fight "to free the slaves, of course, and to preserve the Union." Exactly the reverse of what most soldiers in the Army of the Potomac would have said (if they mentioned emancipation at all), Tom Chamberlain's comment strongly suggests that Union soldiers saw freedom as the great goal of the conflict.[10]

A scene between Joshua Chamberlain and Sergeant Buster Kilrain further elaborates northern war aims. Chamberlain asks Kilrain what he thinks of black people. The Irish-born Kilrain, who speaks in a brogue and probably would have shared the intense racism typical of Irish Americans of the mid-nineteenth century, confesses uncertainty but affirms that only a "pea wit" would judge a whole race. "You take men one at a time," he insists. Chamberlain claims never to have seen any difference between the races, though admitting he has not known many free black people. He did see some in Maine, looked them in the eye, and "there was a man" with "a divine spark." Kilrain brushes the comment aside to stress he does not fight for Chamberlain's idealism. He detects no divine spark in men and fights not for equality but to prove his superiority to other men. Kilrain wonders where Chamberlain has seen this divine spark. Where has he noted equality? Race and country do not matter a damn to Kilrain. "What matters, Colonel, is justice, which is why I'm here. I'll be treated as I deserve, not as my father deserved." In fine Irish fashion, he damns all gentlemen and, tapping his temple, calls for an aristocracy of intellect. "And that's why we've got to win this war," he concludes.[11]

Set on the New England home front whence men such as the Chamberlains went off to war, Little Women is a third example of a film that makes the case for slavery and emancipation as the basis of northern war-making.[12] Most useful to illustrate how northern civilians often experienced the conflict less directly than those in the Confederacy, Little Women nonetheless offers snippets of discussion about motivation. The March girls miss their father, who is serving in Virginia. "I rather crave violence," announces Jo March, clearly with emancipation in mind: "If only I could be like father and go to war and stand up to the lions of injustice." Later, a group of girls alludes to the March family as abolitionists who "haven't bought silk in years" because "they have views on slavery." When Mr. March returns home in uniform with his wounded arm in a sling, the family engages in a discussion around a welcoming fire. The March daughters' friend Laurie is present, along with an adult tutor and two of Laurie's Harvard classmates—four military-age men who have avoided service. Apparently not interested enough to enlist themselves, the men nevertheless discuss what should happen to slaves liberated by the war. "Perhaps the freedmen should be given land," remarks one of the Harvard men, a sentiment with which Mr. March agrees.[13]

If anything, the film and Louisa May Alcott's novel on which it is based play down the emancipationist sentiments prevalent in Alcott's family. The real Alcott joined Jo March, her character in the novel, in seeing the conflict as an opportunity to confront the slaveholding "lions of injustice." Her account of nursing wounded Union soldiers in Washington, D.C., titled Hospital Sketches and published in 1863, includes several references to emancipation. Describing herself as "a red-hot Abolitionist," she observes that Lincoln "immortalized himself" by issuing the Emancipation Proclamation. Her ideal

FIGURE 20. Col. Joshua Lawrence Chamberlain (left; Jeff Daniels) and Sgt. Buster Kilrain (right; Kevin Conway) discuss their motivations and the meaning of the Union's war effort early in *Gettysburg*. Photofest.

Union volunteers would be "earnest, brave, and faithful; fighting for liberty and justice with both heart and hand, true soldiers of the Lord." Although forced by ill health to return home to Concord after a few weeks, she says that she hopes to re-enter service in a hospital for one of "the colored regiments, as they seem to be proving their right to the admiration and kind offices of their white relations, who owe them so large a debt, a little part of which I shall be proud to pay."[14]

Although it contains no characters who are such thoroughgoing abolitionists as Louisa May Alcott, *Pharaoh's Army* engages the Emancipation Cause a bit more directly than *Little Women*. The film's Union soldiers devote minimal attention to discussing why they enlisted and what they hope their time in uniform will accomplish, but by far the most attractive of them, Captain John Abston, aligns himself with emancipationists. The captain and a foreign-born soldier nicknamed Chicago take a few minutes to address the subject in a scene that illustrates the complexity of soldiers' motivations. Why would a damned foreigner join the army? inquires Abston. To see new places and because he was tired of making sausage, comes Chicago's hardly uplifting reply. Abston pronounces those poor reasons to risk death. Does the captain have a better one, wonders Chicago, who then scorns all sense of righteous purpose in the war: "I have heard your big reasons. To save the Union? This is what the general says. To free the slaves? Nobody that I know wants to get killed to free a bunch of nigs." "It's a mess," allows Abston in language similar to that of Colonel Shaw and Trip during their key discussion, "ain't it?" "Why did you sign up?" asks Chicago. A minister brought a runaway slave to Abston's church, had the man show the scars on his back, and from the pulpit asked for volunteers. "I stood up," says Abston with considerable sarcasm, "and here I am, stealing chickens." Is he disillusioned about the original promise of the war as a struggle for freedom? Or is he just feeling trapped in a backwater where his contribution seems minimal? Viewers get no clear answer, though Abston's story imparts a sense that the most thoughtful United States soldiers embrace emancipation.

Gods and Generals communicates a similar idea. Mostly concerned with Confederate determination to defend hearth and home, the prequel to *Gettysburg* also allocates a few minutes to Union motivation. Once again the Chamberlain brothers assume the burden of explaining why the North fights. In one prewar scene, Joshua is teaching at Bowdoin College. He tells a group of students that freedom can exist only as part of law. One young man asks why slavery protected by law is tolerated—a question that sets up the possibility a war will be necessary to kill the hateful institution. The principal discussion of emancipation focuses on Lincoln's proclamation. Tom remarks that many of the men oppose risking their lives to free slaves. Joshua says he signed up to save the Union, but the war has taken on a more revolutionary cast. "What's the use of uniting the country by force and leaving slavery in place?" Tom persists, remarking that not "everybody thinks the way we do about the darkies, especially when it comes to fighting and dying." "Don't call Negroes darkies," Joshua patiently instructs his younger brother in a line tailor-made for a modern audience, "That's a patronizing expression from which we must free ourselves."

As the pair strolls to a place that affords a view of their encampment, Joshua tells Tom that the army is about power. The point of raising armies is to coerce. "This kind of power cannot be used carelessly or recklessly," he says. "This kind of power can do great harm. . . . We have seen more suffering than any men should ever see, and if there is going to be an end to it, it must be an end that justifies the cost." The Confederates believe they fight for freedom and independence, concedes Joshua: "I believe they are wrong, but I cannot question it. But I do question the system that defends its own freedom while it denies it to others, an entire race of men." Describing war as a scourge, he labels slavery a bigger one. Its existence in much of the world is no reason to tolerate slavery in the United States. "As God is my witness," he concludes in good Scarlett O'Hara style, "there is no one I hold in my heart dearer than you. But if your life, or mine, is part of the price to end this curse and free the Negro, then let God's will be done."

C.S.A.: The Confederate States of America makes the point that not enough white northerners stepped forward to pay Chamberlain's requisite price. Very negative toward Lincoln, who cares little about slaves and slavery, the film voices the common, and misleading, assertion that the president's "proclamation did not free a single slave." "So-called emancipation" stood as a "purely symbolic" gesture that allows Lincoln callously to frame the war in moral terms. When fleeing from Confederates late in the war, Lincoln relies on the aid of Harriet Tubman to reach safety in Canada. She disguises him in blackface; when he protests, she snaps, "We're both niggers now, Mr. President." The pair fall into Confederate hands just short of Canada (Lincoln's disguise in blackface recalling Jefferson Davis's alleged donning of women's clothes to fool Union pursuers in May 1865), and Confederates execute the heroic Tubman. Although tried and found guilty of war crimes, Lincoln receives a pardon and takes up exile in Canada. A filmed interview with an aged Lincoln

FIGURE 21. Joshua Chamberlain (right; Jeff Daniels) and younger brother Tom
(left; C. Thomas Howell) in *Gods and Generals*. Photofest.

in 1905 (Willmott presents him as a spry-looking ninety-six-year-old) under-scores his weak commitment to black people during the war. "I failed to see it," Lincoln confesses: "The abolitionists understood what the consequences would be. They knew it was always about the Negro, but I was blind. . . . I only wish that I had truly cared for the Negro, truly cared for his freedom, for his equality. I used him. Now I am used. Now I, too, am a Negro, without a country. I pray that some day the colored people of Confederate America will be free."[15]

Abolitionists serve as C.S.A.'s northern heroes, resisting the Confeder-acy's postwar efforts to reintroduce slavery above the Potomac River. Most northerners quickly give in to Confederate blandishments and economic in-centives, prompting William Lloyd Garrison to lead an exodus to Canada. The 20,000 emigrants include Mark Twain, Henry David Thoreau (who must have joined the group in spirit, inasmuch as he died in 1862), Harriet Beecher Stowe, and Susan B. Anthony. With the abolitionist influence gone, racism blossoms among white people in the North and South—helping set the stage for a reconciliationist rewriting of the war's history in which "northerners are presented as a valiant people who once ruled a mighty land that simply lost its way." The emancipationist spirit lives on in Canada, where the exiles urge their adopted country not to deport black people who had escaped from slavery. A modern Confederate spokesman demands reparations for lost slave property, but the Canadian government, in heartening contrast to the North both during and after the war, holds firm.

"Almost Brothers"

While the Emancipation Cause has become increasingly popular as an interpretive theme, northern soldiers who evoke the Reconciliationist Cause remain a part of Hollywood's understanding of the Civil War. Films thus buttress a widespread disposition to conceive of the conflict as a tragic example of one brave people somehow coming to a bloody impasse. Anyone seeking evidence of this phenomenon will find it in many quarters. For ex-ample, reconciliation thrives among the community of Civil War reenactors, which has flourished since the mid-1980s. In his perceptive *Confederates in the Attic*, Tony Horwitz observes that "ideology rarely intruded on the hobby. If re-enactors had a mission beyond having fun, or raising money for battle-field preservation, it was educational and nonpartisan." They admired the bravery of soldiers on both sides but shunned talk of slavery or the political divisions that led to the war. Although *Glory* prompted the organization of black reenacting units, Horwitz found the seven reenactments he attended "blindingly white affairs." Honoring soldiers from both sides also was long a staple at Civil War battlefields administered by the National Park Service. Over the past decade, critics have asked whether the Park Service should pay more attention to slavery and other political issues. Or should the battlefields primarily serve as monuments to the courage of soldiers in blue and gray? The Park Service recently has taken steps to provide more information about political and social topics at the sites; however, most visitors to battlefields almost certainly would echo Woodrow Wilson's call to celebrate the "splendid valour, the manly devotion of the men . . . arrayed against one another" at Gettysburg and other famous killing grounds.[16]

The United States Postal Service adopted a classic reconciliation posture with its set of sixteen commemorative stamps issued in 1995. A booklet accompanying the sheet of stamps, which honored eight Union and eight Confederate personalities and four battles, called the war "an agonizing milestone in American history—a composite of grief and glory, heartbreak and heroism. It was a test of fortitude that crumbled a young country, while providing the foundation for a new, united America whose growth continues today." Did combatants on either side have the more virtuous cause? "In 1861 . . . both sides were resolute in their own objectives," read the scrupulously nonpolitical text: "independence and self-reliance for the South and preservation of an ethical Union for the North." As for the soldiers, those "who survived did so due to determination and an idealistic belief in their cause. . . . Both North and South shared responsibility for the conflict, just as they shared their heartache." Only the presence of stamps honoring Harriet Tubman and Frederick Douglass departed from a model that would have pleased many original reconciliationists in the late nineteenth and early twentieth centuries.[17]

The impulse toward the reconciliation narrative always has been evident in films. *The Birth of a Nation* includes a reconciliation theme, as do almost all subsequent Civil War films (the Civil War portion of *Gone with the Wind* is the most notable exception). D. W. Griffith approaches the topic most obviously through the marriage of a northern heroine named Elsie Stoneman to former Confederate colonel Ben Cameron. For Griffith, reconciliation brings together white people across sectional lines to oppose black southerners and their political allies, the carpetbaggers. "The former enemies of North and South," explains one of the film's text panels, "are united again in common defence of their Aryan birthright." Abraham Lincoln, portrayed as the "Great Heart" who pardons Ben Cameron and would have spared the white South the trauma of Reconstruction, affords further evidence of Griffith's reconciliation sentiment. News of Lincoln's assassination saddens the white South. "Our best friend is gone," observes the elder Cameron. "What is to become of us now!"

Innumerable examples of reconciliation in later films could be mustered, but three will suffice. In *Santa Fe Trail*, the friendship between Virginian Jeb Stuart and Ohioan George Armstrong Custer dominates the screenplay and shows the possibility of sectional accord. Similarly, the film uses West Point experience and subsequent antebellum service as unifying factors for United States officers. In addition to Stuart and Custer, Civil War notables such as James Longstreet and Philip H. Sheridan are shown to have cordial ties that establish a "band of brothers" motif. Only the abolitionist cadet Rader falls outside this circle of comrades—a fine example of how reconciliation cast the war as a crucible of American manhood and courage largely divorced from emancipation and African American participation.

Director John Huston's adaptation in 1951 of Stephen Crane's *The Red Badge of Courage* offers a pair of classic reconciliationist moments. The first comes when Henry Fleming, the young northern protagonist, goes on picket duty along a river. A noise disturbs the moonlit night, and Fleming shouts, "Who goes there?" "Me, Yank," answers a southern voice from across the river. "Just Me. Move back into the shaders, Yank, unless you want one of them little red badges. I couldn't miss you standing there in the moonlight." "Are you a Reb?" asks a rather befuddled Fleming. "That's right," comes the friendly response, and "I don't see much point in us sentries shootin' each other. Especially when we ain't fighting no battles. So if you'll just get out of the moonlight, I'll be a much obliged to you." "Thanks, Reb," says an appreciative Fleming. "Now that's mighty polite of you, Yank, to thank me," replies the Rebel, who closes with a mild jape. "I take it most kindly. You're a right dumb good feller. So take care of yourself, and don't go a gettin' one of them little red badges pinned on you." The scene presents two men divided by sectional caprice for whom postwar reconciliation is easy to imagine. It also hews close to historical fact; sentries often observed unofficial truces despite the disapprobation of their officers.[18]

After the battle that forms the centerpiece of the film, Federals talk to a number of Confederate prisoners. Bitter emotions are evident, but a firm reconciliationist tone predominates among the Yankees. "Don't take it too hard, old boy," a northern man says to a sobbing Confederate. "I wish I was dead," the prisoner moans, "I just wish I was dead, that's all. I'd a heap rather be dead." The camera shifts to another pair of soldiers, one a resentful Rebel who laments, "I run out of powder. I'd a killed another Yankee if'n I'd a had powder." "Lucky you weren't kilt' yourself," says a Yankee, who asks, "Want a drink of water?" "Not Yankee water," says the Rebel. "Its Reb water," retorts the Federal testily, "my canteen, but its Reb water." The Rebel, still scowling, takes the proffered canteen. Other soldiers exhibit less rancor. "What state are you fellers from?" inquires a Yankee. "We all are from Tennessee," the Confederates reveal, "How 'bout you all?" Fleming's comrades are Ohioans, news that prompts a Confederate to say, "I ain't never spoke to nobody from Ohio before." The Yankees likewise "never spoke to nobody from Tennessee." The scene closes with the combatants moving to a personal level. A northern soldier inquires, "What's your name?" "Lucius M. Pettigrew," answers the Rebel. "I'm Bill Porter," the Federal replies, establishing for viewers a human connection that renders all the more heartbreaking a war that would set Americans against one another.

Huston's two reconciliationist scenes greatly embellish Crane's text. The exchange between the pickets takes up just thirteen lines in the novel and includes a single sentence of dialogue. Henry Fleming's encounter with the Rebel across the river makes him "temporarily regret war." Crane's passage concerning the prisoners offers four words of dialogue and far less personal revelation than the film's screenplay. No mention of home states or sharing of names draws victor and vanquished together. As in the film, some Confederates react to their capture with anger, others with shame or casual acceptance. After a few minutes of examining their prisoners, whom they consider "trapped strange birds," the Federals lose interest, casually settle "down behind an old rail fence," and shoot "perfunctorily at distant marks."[19]

The Civil War section of How the West Was Won (1962), directed by John Ford, gives a different slant on reconciliation. After the first day's fighting at Shiloh, an Ohio soldier named Zeb Rawlings finds himself by a pond with a Confederate. The two talk, and Zeb reveals that he has not killed anyone. "Well, I ain't killed nobody neither, and I don't want to," says the Rebel, adding, "Hey, where you from?" "Ohio," says Zeb, fulfilling his part of the ritualistic identification common to Hollywood's reconciliationist moments. Soon an antiwar theme takes over. "This fool war started in the East," remarks the Rebel. "What's us westerners doin' in it?" A dazed Zeb mutters, "I don't rightly know any more. It ain't quite what I expected. There ain't much glory in looking at a man with his guts hanging out." When Zeb learns the man is from Texas, he asks, "You ain't a Reb, are you?" Masking any doubts about the intelligence of a Yankee unable to discern that he is a Rebel, the Texan betrays a shaky Confederate allegiance: "Well, I was this morning. Tonight I ain't so sure." The two agree not to shoot each other, and the Rebel suggests they "just leave this here war to the folks who want it." Zeb seems to like the idea, responding that "there ain't no war in California." Plans to desert go awry when the two see Ulysses S. Grant and William Tecumseh Sherman talking. The Rebel tries to shoot Grant, prompting Zeb to bayonet him. Immediately distraught, Zeb kneels over the dying man and demands, "Why'd you make me do that?" Although an unusual variety of reconciliation, this scene underscores the similarity of two antagonists disgusted by the war and unconcerned with national causes.

Gettysburg and God and Generals unfurl a far more conventional reconciliation banner in scenes involving both officers and common soldiers. The absence of any black characters with speaking parts in Gettysburg sets a reconciliationist tone, and the idea of shared heritage and essential American qualities among Federals and Confederates forms a leitmotif in the film. Union general Winfield Scott Hancock and Confederate general Lewis A. Armistead, whose soldiers face one another during the southern assault on July 3, dwell at length on their friendship forged in the prewar United States Army. Hancock's affection for Armistead emerges during a conversation with Joshua Chamberlain on the morning of July 3. Aware that Chamberlain taught at a college, Hancock wonders if he recalls a story from antiquity of two best friends—"almost brothers"—who "find themselves, by a trick of fate, on opposing sides in a great war" and eventually meet on a storied battlefield. Chamberlain thinks the story must have come from the Bible. "There isn't an officer on either side who hasn't known someone wearing the other uniform," says Hancock, drifting into a reverie about his friend: "This morning, when I looked through my glass and saw the fluttering colors of the 9th and 14th Virginia Regiments on those ridges before us, directly facing us, right over there, it was as if I could hear his voice and see his old rumpled hat. Lewis Armistead commands one of Pickett's brigades, and he is out there for sure. I somehow thought this day would never come." Hancock asks what Chamberlain would do in his place—what books would tell a man to do.

The previous evening, viewers know, Armistead talked with Longstreet about Hancock. Outside Longstreet's tent during their conversation a voice sings "Kathleen Mavourneen," a sad Irish song of parting that summons in Armistead bittersweet memories of Hancock. "What do you hear about Hancock?" he asks Longstreet. "Ran into him today," the corps commander re-

FIGURE 22. Zeb Rawlings (right; George Peppard) and the Texas Rebel (left; Russ Tamblyn) in *How the West Was Won*. Photofest.

plies in reference to hard fighting that afternoon. "He's out there about a mile or so, just a mile or so. And he was tough, very tough today." An anguished Armistead pronounces Hancock "the best they got. God don't make 'em any better, and that's a fact. Well, I'd like to go over and see him as soon as I can." He ruminates about the spring of 1861, when he and Hancock took leave from one another in California. A number of blue-uniformed officers in the Old Army had gathered around a piano while Hancock's wife Almira played "Kathleen Mavourneen." The song's lyric "It may be for years, and it may be forever" haunts Armistead. The officers had said "the soldier's farewell" that night. "Win was like a brother to me, remember?" "Towards the end of the evening," continues Armistead haltingly, "things got a little rough. We all began to . . . well, there were a lot of tears. I went over to Hancock, and I took him by the shoulder. I said, 'Win, so help me, if I ever raise my hand against you, may God strike me dead.'" The next afternoon a mortally wounded Armistead, having briefly breached his old friend's battle line, takes one more opportunity to express his affection for Win.[20]

Well before Armistead receives his mortal wound, Longstreet experiences reconciliationist moments. He confesses to General Lee on July 2 that the Federals never quite seem to be the enemy. After all, Longstreet fought with many of them in Mexico as part of Winfield Scott's invading United States Army. Lee agrees, remembering good times in the Old Army, but urges Longstreet to do his duty—that is "God's will." Longstreet also evokes the shared nationality of all Americans in good-naturedly pointing out to Arthur Fremantle that North and South had shouldered arms together in defeating the British during the Revolution and again in the War of 1812.[21]

Lower-ranking Union officers and common soldiers similarly manifest reconciliationist attitudes in both *Gettysburg* and *Gods and Generals*. In *Gettysburg*'s scene involving Tom Chamberlain and the Confederate prisoners, the men share a wish for the war to end before taking leave of one another with a gruffly affectionate exchange. "See you in hell, Billy Yank," the Tennessean tells Chamberlain. "See you in hell, Johnny Reb," replies the Union lieutenant. *Gods and Generals* dusts off the convention of chatting pickets along a river that John Huston employed in *The Red Badge of Courage*. The setting is the Rappahannock River in the aftermath of the battle of Fredericksburg during the winter of 1862–63. Somber soldiers from each side observe an informal truce, conversing and trading southern tobacco for northern coffee. They meet in the middle of the river, which seems to be about a foot deep (surely a record low level in light of the Rappahannock's being navigable by large vessels to

FIGURE 23. Brig. Gen. Lewis A. Armistead (Richard Jordan) leans against a cannon
after the repulse of his brigade in Pickett's Charge in *Gettysburg*. Fighting back the pain
of a mortal wound, he summons the strength to make a reconciliationist speech about
his affection for Winfield Scott Hancock. Photofest.

the fall line just above Fredericksburg). Based on well-documented instances of fraternization at Fredericksburg, this scene renders in cinematic form one of the most ubiquitous episodes in the written reconciliationist narrative. "A truce was speedily declared by Billy Yank and Johnny Reb on the picket line," wrote a memoirist who had served in a North Carolina regiment, "friendly intercourse prevailed, trading in coffee, tobacco, sugar, etc., and even exchanging of newspapers were of daily occurrence. 'The brave always respect the brave.'"[22]

The Real Lost Cause

What about the Union Cause? Of the four main interpretive traditions, it is Hollywood's real lost cause. Lincoln's vision of a democratic nation devoted to economic opportunity would seem to be an attractive theme, but it remains largely unexplored in the Civil War genre. Close analysis of recent films yields no explanation of what Union meant to a mass of northern men who enlisted in the pre-conscription years of 1861 and 1862. Numbering at least 750,000, these men composed the sturdy backbone of the United States war effort. Ideology did not drive the actions of all northerners, but it loomed large for many of them—an overwhelming majority of whom would have talked about Union rather than emancipation. The films suggest various motives for their joining the United States Army; however, devotion to the Union is not one of them. Yet something very like Lincoln's conception of Union as put forth in his message to Congress on July 4, 1861, surely motivated a large proportion of the first flood of volunteers who rushed to the national colors. "This is essentially a People's contest," affirmed Lincoln: "On the side of the Union, it is a struggle for maintaining in the world, that form, and substance of government, whose leading object is, to elevate the condition of men—to lift artificial weights from all shoulders—to clear the paths of laudable pursuit for all—to afford all, an unfettered start, and a fair chance, in the race of life."[23]

The war's length and severity wrought changes in how soldiers and civilians thought about Union. Many accepted, or even championed, emancipation as a means to undermine the Confederacy. Moreover, the human butcher's bill and vast expenditure of national treasure stimulated increasing support for any policy calculated to harm the slaveholding class responsible for secession. How better to strike at slaveholders than to put an end to slavery? Citizens who never would have mentioned emancipation as a war aim in 1861 or the first several months of 1862 came to accept, perhaps even embrace, a postwar Union without black people in bondage. But Union, and not emancipation, remained the key for most of them, and they celebrated its restoration as the war's great outcome. Union remained very much the symbol of what Lincoln had mentioned in his message of July 4, 1861, confirming American nationality for all who cherished ideas of democratic exceptionalism.[24]

A fascinating glimpse into what northern veterans most valued about the war lies in regimental histories published in 1865–66. They seldom referred to the conflict as the Civil War, opting instead for some form of "the war of the Rebellion." This choice of terms revealed a belief that the contest had been preeminently about restoring the Union and the need to safeguard progress toward a free-labor, democratic future. Three examples reflect common arguments. "Remove one block from the arch of liberty, and is it not insecure?" asked the historian of a Delaware unit. "Will it not yield to the rude storm, and be thrown to the ground? . . . Take from the monument to Washington, on the bank of the Potomac, one of those granite blocks which the States have furnished, of which it is constructed, and how long will it be before the whole superstructure will topple and fall?" Unchallenged secession, this man concluded, would ruin forever "the hopes of the world for a free republican form of government." An Ohioan believed "citizen soldiers of the army of the Republic" had affirmed the "great experiment of self government"; after Confederate surrender, "liberty and popular institutions every where [are] recognized as a permanent outgrowth of American destiny." A third author, from an Illinois regiment, prophesied that the war "will descend to posterity as a fearful warning against future attempts to dissolve and destroy the perpetual Union of the States established by the fathers."[25]

Although Hollywood presented many Union characters before the 1980s, none sought to explain the war in language reminiscent of Lincoln's message. The Birth of a Nation acknowledges the Union Cause through an admiring portrait of Abraham Lincoln, cast as a staunch friend of the white South, and by quoting Daniel Webster's stirring reply to Senator Robert Y. Hayne of South Carolina on the Senate floor in 1830. Completely mangling historical chronology, Griffith describes how a post-Appomattox "South under Lincoln's fostering hand goes to work to rebuild itself." Ben Cameron labors alongside a supportive former slave in this fantasy, which ends with Lincoln's assassination: "'And then, when the terrible days were over and a healing time of peace was at hand,'" one text panel declared, "came the fated night of April 14, 1865." Did moviegoers in 1915 wonder how much rebuilding could have taken place between April 12, when Robert E. Lee's soldiers stacked their muskets at Appomattox, and April 14, when John Wilkes Booth shot Lincoln and thousands of Confederates remained under arms across the South? Whatever the answer to that question, they watched as Radical Republicans personified by Elsie's father, Austin Stoneman, a character based on Congressman Thaddeus Stevens of Pennsylvania, sought to force racial equality on an emerging white republic. Griffith quotes Woodrow Wilson regarding Radical Reconstruction: "The policy of the congressional leaders wrought . . . a veritable overthrow of civilization in the South . . . in their determination to 'put the white South under the heel of the black South.'"[26]

The film directly connects the Ku Klux Klan to the triumph of Union. Quite remarkably to twenty-first-century sensibilities (as well as to those of many Americans, black and white, in 1915), Klansmen ride onto center stage late in the film as noble opponents of carpetbaggers and their African American followers. Here Griffith could look for support not only to Thomas Dixon's fictional accounts but also to the era's leading scholar of Reconstruction. William A. Dunning's *Reconstruction Political and Economic, 1865–1877*, published in 1907 as part of Harper & Brothers popular The American Nation series, explained the growth of the Klan as an understandable phenomenon: "The deep dread of negro domination under the auspices of invincible national power impelled thousands of serious and respectable whites to look for some means of mitigation, if not complete salvation, in the methods of the secret societies. . . . The explicit purpose of these organizations was to preserve the social and political ascendancy of the white race."[27] The Klan, contends Griffith's didactic text in language taken from Woodrow Wilson's *A History of the American People*, arose out of the white South's "mere instinct of self-preservation" and through force of arms guaranteed white supremacy in a restored Union. That is the kind of Union Griffith could celebrate, and the film closes with the most famous passage from Webster's response to Hayne: "Liberty and Union, one and inseparable, *now and forever!*"

Fifteen years after *The Birth of a Nation*, Griffith revisited the theme of Union in *Abraham Lincoln*. His first venture into films with sound, it moves woodenly along an interpretive path sometimes dominated by references to Union. Near the end of the Civil War, Lincoln says, "The Union, we've saved it at last. The Union, we'll have them all back." But reconciliation soon takes over with Lincoln's affirmation that "We are going to take them back as if they've never been away." A tribute to Lee during the Appomattox campaign reinforces the reconciliation theme, which pushes Union aside by the end of the film.[28]

Later filmmakers alluded fleetingly to Union. Grant and Sherman appear in *Raintree County* and *How the West was Won*, but unlike Lee and Jackson in *Gods and Generals*, they say nothing about what the war means. In *Raintree County*, Sherman charges his soldiers with making hard war against the Rebels in Georgia: "Now your job is to knock the stomach out of this war. You're gonna travel on the army's front and on its flanks, and you're gonna point the way to provisions and supplies. You're gonna have to live off of the fat and the lean of the land, but you're gonna be on your own, free of brigade command." In *How the West Was Won*, the two generals discuss Grant's future. Worried about negative newspaper coverage, Grant seems poised to resign. Sherman objects, cutting to the chase: "The army is better off with you. That's the test." "All right," Grant answers, "Thanks." Similarly, John Shawnessy in *Raintree County*, Zeb Rawlings in *How the West Was Won*, and various Federals in *The Horse Soldiers*, to name but three examples, join Henry Fleming and all his northern comrades in *The Red Badge of Courage* in avoiding any discussion of the Union Cause. Alert viewers could catch a hint of the Union Cause in the opening to *Young Mr. Lincoln*, which anachronistically features the stirring lyrics of "The Battle Cry of Freedom," composed long after the period covered by the film: "The Union forever, hurrah, boys, hurrah! Down with the traitors, up with the star!" The more casual filmgoer, however, surely would miss this subtle reference.[29]

Glory, *Gettysburg*, and *Gods and Generals*, all of which deal extensively with United States soldiers, contribute almost nothing to an understanding of the Union Cause. Apart from Colonel Shaw's brief mention of Union in his mustering-in speech in *Glory*, Joshua Chamberlain's remarks about enlisting to save the Union before realizing the conflict had meaning only as an effort to abolish slavery in both *Gettysburg* and *Gods and Generals*, and Tom Chamberlain's casting Union as a secondary goal of the war in *Gettysburg*, these three mainline Civil War films remain silent on the topic. Buster Kilrain's search for justice, to "be treated as I deserve, not as my father deserved," comes closest to Lincoln's call "to lift artificial weights from all shoulders—to clear the paths of laudable pursuit for all." Yet Kilrain specifically states that he does not think "country matters a damn"—a sentiment thoroughly at odds with Lincoln's conception of Union and typical of filmmakers' failure to engage the importance of nation among northern soldiers and civilians.

Little Women and *Pharaoh's Army* do no better by the Union. The former mentions it a single time, when Mrs. March tells daughter Meg that before she can get married her intended "must secure a house . . . and must do his service to the Union." This statement identifies her future son-in-law's obligation to

FIGURE 24. In *How the West Was Won*, William Tecumseh Sherman (left; John Wayne) and Ulysses S. Grant (right; Harry Morgan) talk after the first day's fighting at Shiloh. At the upper left, Zeb Rawlings and the Texas Rebel watch the Union commanders. Photofest.

the nation, the precise meaning of which is not defined, as little more than a hurdle to be cleared. In Alcott's novel, Mrs. March betrays more pro-Union sentiment. She relates a touching story to her daughters about encountering an old man. "Have you sons in the army?" she had asked him politely, little expecting his answer. "Yes, ma'am," he said quietly, "I had four, but two were killed; one is a prisoner, and I'm going to the other, who is very sick in a Washington hospital." Respectful of the man, Mrs. March told him he had "done a great deal for your country." "Not a mite more than I ought, ma'am," he affirmed. "I'd go myself, if I was any use; as I ain't, I give my boys, and give 'em free." Mrs. March felt shame at his comments, thinking of her reluctance to see her husband volunteer as a chaplain in the army. "I'd given one man, and thought it too much," she confesses, "while he gave four, without grudging them." Feeling blessed in comparison to the old man, Mrs. March thanked him "heartily for the lesson he had taught me." That lesson could be personal or patriotic or perhaps both, but the film contains nothing equivalent regarding the theme of sacrifice in support of the Union.[30]

As for *Pharaoh's Army*, the foreign-born Chicago and two other enlisted men named Neely and Rodie discuss motivation in an exchange that lacks any ideological dimension. As already noted, Chicago dismisses Union as important only to generals. Neely plucks a chicken as he speaks, observing that he "joined up to fight"—though for what remains unclear. Chicago interjects that they are all chicken thieves. Rodie seems most concerned with proving himself in combat, quoting a brother who describes battle as a crucible that makes men. He consistently pushes for an opportunity to face the Rebels and mocks the masculinity and fighting ability of his captain. The army would not have sent a real fighting man to rob widows and orphans, he tells Abston, adding dismissively: "You can't even do that." At one point, Rodie mentions that Confederate guerrillas are killing Unionists near Cumberland Gap. His desire to smite the enemy, however, springs more from personal demons than from a commitment to saving or restoring the Union.

Many northern soldiers in *Andersonville* demonstrate but do not explain loyalty to the United States. In one scene, a Confederate colonel attempts to entice prisoners to join the Confederate army. General Grant has abandoned them, he argues, by stopping the system of prisoner exchanges that would give them a better chance of going home. Moreover, Lincoln's government knows they suffer at Andersonville, apparently willing to have them "thrown aside to starve and die" (an unintended admission of Confederate cruelty on the colonel's part). They can join the southern army and reap all the rewards

FIGURE 25. "Marmee" March (second from right; Susan Sarandon) and her daughters (left to right), Jo (Winona Ryder), Meg (Trini Alvarado), Amy (Kirsten Dunst), and Beth (Claire Danes) read a letter from Mr. March, who is serving with the Union army in Virginia, in *Little Women*. Photofest.

that go to regular Confederate soldiers—fresh clothes, food, and bounties. No prisoner steps forward to accept the offer. A Union sergeant turns his back on the Rebel colonel and walks away. Others follow suit, including a small group of black prisoners from United States Colored Troops units. But why are they loyal to their nation? Earlier, a white prisoner had expressed disgust at the thought that "we're to die here for niggers." Comradeship seems the most likely factor that binds the men together. No one ever utters the words "Union" or "country" or "nation."[31]

If possible, the Union Cause means even less to characters in *Dances with Wolves* and *Gangs of New York*. The former features John Dunbar, a United States officer whose supposed bravery on a battlefield in Tennessee (really an attempted suicide—viewers later learn he would never risk his life for Union or emancipation) wins the offer of any posting he chooses. Dunbar selects the West, where he bonds with a group of Native Americans and receives the Sioux name Dances With Wolves. In one crucial sequence, he procures firearms for the Sioux and helps defend their village against marauding Pawnees. The victory transforms Dunbar, who fights with his face painted and garbed in Native American dress. "It was hard to know how to feel," he remarks in a voice-over that interprets the war for Union as a pointless exercise in carnage: "I had never been in a battle like this one. There was no dark political objective. This was not a fight for territory or riches, or to make men free." The fight saved the winter's food and protected women and children only a few feet removed from the combat. "I felt a pride I had never felt before," he continues. "I had never really known who John Dunbar was. Perhaps the name itself had no meaning. But as I heard my Sioux name being called over and over, I knew for the first time who I really was." The film's message could not be more unequivocal. Only escape to the West, far from the fight for the "dark" political goal of Union, liberates Dunbar to find himself and a purpose in life.

Gangs of New York portrays a group of northerners as disaffected as Dunbar. Set in New York City during the turbulent period of the draft riots in July 1863, it seethes with cynicism, class conflict, and opposition to the war. No sense of Union characterizes the people who inhabit Martin Scorsese's version of the city. To be sure, New York's Democratic politics and huge foreign-born population spawned a volatile mixture of attitudes toward the war. But the city sent thousands of soldiers into the Union army, including several regiments of Irish volunteers who performed well and suffered terribly on many battlefields. New Yorkers dominated the renowned Irish Brigade, and the 69th New

FIGURE 26. Lt. John Dunbar (right; Kevin Costner) and Kicking Bear
(Graham Greene) in *Dances with Wolves*. At this point in the movie, Dunbar
has not yet fully embraced Sioux culture. Photofest.

York Infantry ranked among the ten northern regiments that suffered the most combat deaths during the war. Because the film acknowledges no pro-Union element in the city, viewers likely would be taken aback to learn that so many of its residents had acted from patriotic impulses.

Scorsese's Irish function as bovine victims of heartless recruiters. One scene shows a civilian brokering immigrants into the army. Greeting them at the wharf, the broker shouts, "Now go fight for your country!" The men literally go from the boat into United States service, donning blue uniforms while a woman's Irish voice sings: "The Yankee man shoved a gun into our hand, saying paddy you must go and fight for Lincoln." An Irish soldier asks, "Where are we going?" "They say to Tennessee," answers another. "Where's that?" comes the reply. "Do they feed us now, do you think?" The poor men obviously have little idea about their circumstances beyond a need for sustenance. The camera pans to a shot of coffins being stacked on the docks, and the woman's song continues, assuring viewers that the Irish men would rather "be in Dublin."[32]

In addition to the wretched Irish, the film highlights poor native New Yorkers subject to an array of material blandishments. Recruitment posters entice them: "Volunteer! Volunteer! Avoid the Draft!" "30,000 Volunteers Wanted." A uniformed officer promises a $677.00 bounty. Poor men wait in line, listening to the officer. "Enlist to serve your country," he tells them, offering "three square meals a day" to any recruit. Ideology, whether pro-Union or antislavery, has no place here. Union military service comes down to a search for food and clothing by the city's cast-off population. A young Irish character named Amsterdam, whose activities form the narrative thread of the film, supplies a voice-over about the draft riots that underscores the absence of Union sentiment: "When the sun rose next, the city had split in half. From all over New York they came, ironworkers, factory boys, street cleaners, Irish, Polish, Germans—anyone who never cared about slavery or the Union, anyone who couldn't buy his way out. 'Let the sons of the rich go and die,' they cried, 'Let the sons of the poor stay home.'"[33]

"And Now I'll Have to Burn This Town"

Recent films not only fail to explain the Union Cause; they also depict United States military forces in strikingly negative ways. In reality, United States soldiers destroyed civilian property, engaged in some atrocities, and otherwise behaved badly—much like their Confederate counterparts. The scholarly literature, however, makes clear that most of them avoided such activities. Despite vicious guerrilla operations along the margins, callous treatment of prisoners of war, and refusal to grant quarter in some instances, the conflict unfolded in remarkably restrained fashion considering its scope.[34] Hollywood's collective portrait departs radically from the scholarly consensus. Except in *Gettysburg* and *Gods and Generals*, white soldiers in blue fare poorly. Hollywood serves up a post-Vietnam vision of the Union army as a cruel, racist juggernaut that wreaks havoc and stands for nothing admirable. It looks remarkably like United States military forces in Vietnam as imagined by Francis Ford Coppola's *Apocalypse Now* (1979), Oliver Stone's *Platoon* (1986), Stanley Kubrick's *Full Metal Jacket* (1987), Brian De Palma's *Casualties of War* (1989), and other such films. These movies offer harsh images of American soldiers in Southeast Asia. Rape of Vietnamese women, indiscriminate murder of some civilians and callous brutality toward others, application of massively superior firepower, and gleeful destruction of noncombatants' property create a collective portrait of unrestrained warriors—a portrait utterly at odds with the uncritically celebratory tone Hollywood adopted for most films about World War II in the 1940s and 1950s.[35]

Before the Vietnam War, movies typically treated Union soldiers as quite admirable (*Gone with the Wind* was an exception, with its thieving, leering, potential rapist whom Scarlett and Melanie confront at Tara). Three examples suggest the tenor of many films. *The Red Badge of Courage* features a confrontation between a column of Union troops and a southern woman on a small farm. A soldier tries to steal a pig, whereupon the woman chases him to retrieve the swine. Several soldiers laugh and call out as she hits their comrade: "Come on, Miss, whack him! Hit him with your stick!" Lighthearted in tone, the scene conveys no sense of menace. In *The Horse Soldiers*, Union cavalrymen come under attack by young cadets from a military school. Rather than shoot them, as Federals did with cadets from the Virginia Military Institute at the battle of New Market in May 1864, the troopers treat them as children. "Hey, Colonel, I've got me a prisoner here," yells a Federal who has collared one of the boys, "What do you want me to do with him?" "Spank him!" replies Colonel Marlowe, mounting to ride off as the trooper bends the cadet over his knee. *Shenandoah* continued this tradition. When Charlie Anderson seeks his youngest son, who has been captured by northern soldiers, an empathetic Union colonel offers to help: "If you happen to find the boy, give this slip to the officer in charge. . . . It's just a statement from me that your son was taken by mistake—that it would be considered a personal favor to me if he is released to you." "I do wish you good luck, Mr. Anderson," the colonel concludes with honest emotion, "I have a sixteen-year-old son, too. He's in school in Boston, thank God."[36]

The prevailing interpretation has been far different since the late 1980s. In *Glory*, only the black soldiers of the 54th Massachusetts and their colonel are admirable. Racism among white soldiers, which certainly would have been repellent by modern standards, meets the men of the 54th at every turn. "I'd rather have a hog than a nigger," bellows one white soldier when recruits of the 54th march into camp. "At least you can eat the hog." Elsewhere, white soldiers pronounce their black comrades better suited for manual labor than for fighting, and a racist quartermaster, sneering that "the nigs never had it so good," denies the 54th shoes and other basic supplies. The negative portrait extends beyond men in the ranks. In South Carolina, white officers plunder plantations for their own enrichment. Colonel James Montgomery, a veteran of the Kansas/Missouri border wars, orders the burning of Darien, Georgia. "You see," he says to a horrified Colonel Shaw, "Secesh has got to be swept away by the hand of God like the Jews of old. And now I'll have to burn this town." A vile racist who shoots one of his own black infantrymen, Montgomery personifies much of what Hollywood ascribes to Union soldiers.[37] A few white soldiers do achieve modest redemption as the 54th prepares to attack Fort Wagner. One shouts, "Give 'em hell, 54th!" Others cheer as the African Americans file into formation on the beach.[38]

Dances with Wolves creates a caricature of northern soldiers that strongly resembles portrayals of United States forces in Vietnam. Union soldiers slaughter Native Americans, show no respect for nature, and even shoot Captain Dunbar's pet wolf. Examples of unsavory Federals abound. The film opens with a badly wounded Dunbar seeking medical aid. Callous Union physicians ignore his intense pain to take a break and "coffee up," as they put it. The first officer Dunbar meets in the West, obese and mentally unbalanced, asks why he has come. Dunbar says he wants to see the frontier before it is gone (in the midst of a seismic conflict, he must have been among the few Americans who worried that the pristine West would soon disappear). As Dunbar leaves, the officer announces he "has just pissed in my pants, and no one can do anything about it." He then commits suicide as Dunbar rides off. Late in the film, after Dunbar has embraced Sioux culture, a party of cavalrymen locates him, kills his beloved horse (filmed in close-up—a slow, wrenching death), and beats him mercilessly. "Turned Injun didn't you?" one of Dunbar's captors asks. "Do we salute him or shoot him?" laughs another. A third soldier, illiterate and loutish, wipes himself with pages from a journal in which Dunbar has

FIGURE 27. Union soldiers on the march in *The Red Badge of Courage* (far left, Bill Mauldin as Tom Wilson; second from right, Audie Murphy as Henry Fleming; far right, John Dierkes as Jim Conklin). In director John Huston's treatment, Union soldiers manifest none of the menacing qualities common in more recent films. Photofest.

described his metamorphosis from Union soldier to Sioux warrior. Beaten again as he is escorted to be hanged at Fort Hays, Dunbar gains freedom when Sioux friends attack and kill all the Union soldiers. A wise native leader summarizes the point of the film, observing that John Dunbar has ceased to exist—replaced by Dances With Wolves.

Pharaoh's Army combines images of unlikable and inept Union soldiers. The film's title tells a great deal: Does anyone have a favorable image of the biblical armies of the pharaohs? In sharp contrast to the behavior of Union soldiers at the yeoman farmstead in *The Red Badge of Courage*, Captain Abston's soldiers plunder Sarah Anders's hardscrabble farm, threatening both her and Boy. The Federals kill all Sarah's chickens—one grinning soldier hollers "Take no prisoners!" as they pursue the birds—and ransack the cabin. Rodie relieves himself on a tree, prompting Captain Abston to order him to use the outhouse because "there is a woman about." The men ridicule Abston for helping Sarah plow. "He ain't much of a soldier," remarks Rodie, who suggests the captain hopes his assistance will "get a little poke" from Sarah. Embittered because a Rebel sniper killed his brother, Rodie also spits on Sarah's son and calls him "Johnnie [Reb]." Already cast as coarse bullies, the Union soldiers prove themselves cowards when fired upon by a lone gunman who kills Rodie. They run around, shooting wildly in every direction and into the air. The scene plays out as pathetic farce, contributing to the rich catalog of Hollywood's negative treatments of the Union army.

The worst component of that army plays a leading role in *Andersonville*. Thoroughly repellent Union soldiers known as the "Raiders," who hail from the "sewers of New York," dominate the crowded interior of the camp and prey on unfortunate comrades. "Nice fresh fish," snarls one of their leaders when some new Union captives arrive. A skeletal prisoner with wild hair warns the newcomers to watch out for the Raiders. Their ominous authority, sustained by savage beatings of other prisoners, casts a further pall over the already forbidding stockade. Rebels give the Raiders a free hand, allowing them to live well on their plunder from Union soldiers. Accelerating tensions eventually lead to an uprising by the good prisoners, displacement of the Raiders, and hangings of their ringleaders. Although vanquished and punished, the Raiders represent an especially repulsive example of unpleasant Union military characters. The film, it is important to acknowledge, neither exaggerates the violent activities of Andersonville's Raiders nor departs from the historical record regarding punishment of their leaders.

Gangs of New York takes viewers into the "sewers" whence *Andersonville's* raiders originated, juxtaposing the city's working poor against pitiless United States military power. An unidentified major general sent to quell rioting in New York vows to take no prisoners because the mob is taking none. Union infantry moves into position and shoots into the mob without provocation, cutting down women as well as men. Blood flows in the streets. Naval vessels open fire as well, sending explosive shells into the poor Five Points neighborhood where rival gangs prepare to clash. More infantry enters Five Points. An officer shoots a man in the head, execution-style, while blue-clad soldiers kick and pummel another civilian. Here is the naked force of the Union army waging war on civilians—though some of the civilians admittedly are gang members. The violent harvest, as presented by Scorsese, lines streets with hundreds of corpses laid out for burial. The actual death toll fell between 105 and 119, a dozen women and several soldiers and policemen among them. More than 175 soldiers and policemen and nearly 130 civilians also were wounded. Union troops killed some civilians, though probably not in the gratuitous manner the film depicts. Tellingly, the film favors the rioters over the soldiers summoned to restore order to the city.[39]

Far removed from Scorsese's roiling streets, Cold Mountain's pastoral setting nonetheless affords an opportunity for Union soldiers to exhibit gratuitous cruelty. The key scene, reminiscent of events in Pharaoh's Army, involves three Federals who visit a poor widow's farm. The deserter Inman has spent the night, learning that her husband died from a mortal wound at Gettysburg. "Man dead, woman left," she explains succinctly. Inman hides on a hillside as the Federals approach. "We're looking for food!" the soldiers shout, pounding on her door. The commanding officer drags the woman out of the cabin, ties her up, and calls her "lying southern trash" when she claims to own nothing but a few chickens. Soldiers place her infant on the cold, bare ground. She begs them to cover the child, who lies completely exposed to a chilly wind that rustles fallen leaves. The officer cares nothing about the infant and begins to rape the woman. Inman steps in to kill the rapist and another of the soldiers. He tells the third, who had tried to cover the baby, to get out of his boots and clothes and run away. But the woman emerges from the cabin and shoots him in the back, setting up a camera shot of the three dead soldiers. These Federals play much the same role as the thief/rapist from Sherman's army whom Scarlett kills at Tara.

No individual United States soldiers stand out in The Last Samurai, but the army as a whole plays a sinister role. The film could be titled Dances with Wolves Goes to Japan because of the similarity of their story lines. In The Last Samurai the Union officer is Captain Nathan Algren, who fought at Gettysburg and remained in the army during the Indian wars. A disillusioned, thoroughly unattractive alcoholic who presumably served with George A. Custer's 7th Cavalry, Algren experiences several flashbacks to the Washita massacre of November 27, 1868. At no point does he suggest that his Civil War service was honorable. In 1876, he finds himself in Japan as a military adviser charged with modernizing the Japanese army. Would powerful Japanese business and governmental figures choose a drunken former captain who performs at sleazy sideshows to train their national forces? Viewers not reduced to stupefaction by this notion soon face even more improbable scenarios. Captured by a group of samurai, Algren embraces their pastoral, honor-centered culture and quite ridiculously transforms himself into a formidable samurai warrior. His new comrades eventually succumb to the modern Japanese army, but Algren survives to lecture the emperor about what it means to be Japanese (a charitable interpretation of such scenes suggests the director considered his film a comedy).

Like Dunbar in *Dances with Wolves*, Algren discovers meaning in life only after repudiating the army, the United States, and his past. The films employ samurai and Native Americans as romanticized foils for evil Americans and their powerful military forces. The United States Army, as an extension of the nation, functions as a corrosive agent in both films—killing mercilessly and possessing material and technological advantages the premodern peoples can match with nothing but determination and honor. Director Edward Zwick seems unaware that his samurai share characteristics with the South's slaveholding class as represented in Lost Cause films. The honor-bound Ashley Wilkes facing irresistible Union military strength fits comfortably alongside warrior-aristocrats of *The Last Samurai* confronting an American-trained war machine. Inferior classes, whether slaves or Japanese peasants, defer to and support the aristocrats, apparently satisfied with their positions in highly stratified social structures. A review in the *Washington Post* usefully addressed this aspect of the film. For Zwick, wrote Stephen Hunter, "the way of the samurai is akin to the way of purity: It stands for nobility, service, self-sacrifice, denial of ego, tradition. It did, of course, but only for . . . the elite who enjoyed its fruits." For the masses, "it was a simple, brutal system of exploitation, in which the anonymous millions lived and died to provide sustenance for a few." Hunter likely would agree that Zwick's samurai Eden might be labeled a civilization "Gone With the Western Wind."[40]

Although far less antagonistic toward the Union army, *Gods and Generals* unsparingly depicts the sack of Fredericksburg by northern soldiers on December 12, 1862. Civilians stream out of the town as refugees, trudging up the heights held by the Army of Northern Virginia. This scene showing Union soldiers at their worst certainly belongs in the film—though one wonders why Ron Maxwell elected not to show how Lee's army appropriated foodstuffs and livestock from Pennsylvania's farms in *Gettysburg*. More problematical in *Gods and Generals*, Joshua Chamberlain alludes to Julius Caesar as he gazes across the Rappahannock toward Fredericksburg. A bit later, just before the 20th Maine goes into battle, Sergeant Kilrain says, "Those who are about to die salute you"—another reference to Rome. In *Gods and Generals*, the Rebels constantly talk about God, while the Yankees refer to ancient Rome. The United States as Rome—huge, dominating, wielding inexorable power—offers quite a contrast to a Confederacy struggling for home and freedom from northern interference.

Seraphim Falls contributes a final example of United States soldiers tormenting Confederate civilians.[41] Most of the action consists of a prolonged pursuit set in the West during 1868, with a former Confederate colonel named Carver seeking retribution against a former Union captain named Gideon. As the action shifts from snow-covered mountains to sere plateaus to New Mexico's alkali desert, flashbacks suggest that something terrible happened to Carver's family during the Civil War. Fleeting images show Union cavalry on the attack, a woman running, and a burning building. One scene alerts viewers that the captain had compiled an improbably bloody wartime record and also experienced great personal loss. Gideon encounters a group of men, one of whom recognizes him. As Gideon walks away, the man says, "I'll be damned. That's one of McClellan's boys up at Antietam. Lost both his sons in one day at that god-damned bridge. I seen it myself. But nothin' touched him. Not a scratch. Not a splinter. They say he kilt over a hundred men that day alone."

Near the end of the film, Carver and Gideon confront one another. In an earlier encounter, Gideon had identified Carver as the husband of a woman who died at the hands of his Union troopers at Seraphim Falls. Now he explains, "It was war." "War is men fightin', you son-of-a-bitch," replies Carver with a less impressive command of the language than most colonels would have mustered: "That weren't war what you did." "That was orders," says Gideon. "Orders you gave, Captain," Carver responds. A long flashback reveals what happened at Seraphim Falls. Carver and his son are working in the field on a golden autumn day. Union cavalry pounds toward the farm, and the camera cuts back and forth between father and son and Gideon and his Federals. When the troopers ride into Carver's yard, his wife emerges from the house and yells at Gideon: "Get off this land!" "Ma'am, we have it on good information that this is the house of Colonel Morsman Carver," the captain states politely but firmly. She identifies herself as the colonel's wife but insists he is not on the farm. Gideon orders his men to search the yard and house. There is a baby upstairs. A Union trooper inadvertently knocks over an oil lamp while leaving a room and goes downstairs without realizing what he has done.

Back outside, with the fire started by the oil lamp as yet undiscovered, tensions escalate. "Where's the colonel, Ma'am?" demands Gideon. Mrs. Carver spits on him, and a Union lieutenant immediately strikes her. "Mind yourself, Lieutenant," snaps Gideon. He then issues orders to "Fire the barns, leave the house" just as Carver arrives from the field. "Where are your men, Colonel?" demands Gideon. Restrained and beaten by several northern troopers, Carver responds: "The war's over. You know the war's over." He does not mean the conflict has officially ended—just that he decided it was pointless to continue the fight and released his soldiers months ago. Fire and smoke soon gain everyone's attention, prompting Mrs. Carver to run into the house to save her baby. "Rose!" calls Carver. "Let go of me!" he yells at Gideon's troopers. Soon Mrs. Carver and the child are trapped upstairs at a window. Everyone in the yard can see them, but Federals prevent Carver from going to his wife and child's aid. A close-up shows the woman and child engulfed by flames. Gideon mutters that he thought the house was empty. "You son-of-a-bitch," shouts Carver, "God damn you to hell!" Turning to one of his lieutenants, the captain grabs him: "You said the house was empty!" The man replies coldly, "They're Rebs, Captain." The only Union soldier who seems disgusted by what has transpired, Gideon walks away, unbuckling the belt that holds his sword and side arm. Fire rages in the background, and Union troopers, once again cast as cruel and willing agents of destruction, ride back and forth around the yard.

The film returns to 1868, with Carver aiming a pistol at Gideon as he declares, "You burned that house with them in it. Your turn now." Gideon replies wearily, "All they that take the sword shall perish with the sword." A long final fight ensues, during which Gideon shoots Carver and then gives him a pistol and invites him to fire back. Carver cannot do it. He mutters,

FIGURE 28. In *Seraphim Falls*, Captain Gideon (left, with back to viewer; Pierce Brosnan) watches his Union troopers restrain Colonel Carver (Liam Neeson), who struggles to follow his wife into their burning house to save their baby. Photofest.

"Rose." Gideon says "Forgive me," gives Carver water, and helps him up. The two, hardened by a war that had claimed the lives of their loved ones, start to walk out of the desert. Reconciled in accepting the need to let go of the past, they stagger forward a few paces before angling off in different directions as the action fades.

Anyone knowing little about the conflict would come away from recent films with strong impressions about the North's Civil War. Almost all of the admirable characters wage a war for emancipation. The United States Army harbors many white soldiers capable of great brutality toward civilians and Native Americans. These men express profoundly racist views and often appear to be inept, cowardly, or even deranged. Apart from those devoted to emancipation, Federals subscribe to no guiding set of principles—certainly nothing connected to the Union. In some cases, northern soldiers manifest a sense of comradeship with their Confederate foes, touching on points of commonality between North and South and seemingly trapped in a conflict not of their choosing. In sum, viewers will find strong echoes of the Emancipation Cause and to a lesser extent of the Reconciliation Cause. They will not form any appreciation for the Union Cause.

This absence of a strong Union theme must be read on one level as a triumph for the Lost Cause. Many former Confederates of the nineteenth and early twentieth centuries surely would have rejoiced at images of pillaging, unattractive Union soldiers. Modern neo-Confederates have offered a portrait very similar to that in many recent movies (most filmmakers would be horrified to know they had such allies). In 1968, Richard M. Weaver, a self-styled member of the Southern Agrarian school of thought who trumpeted the antebellum South as "the last non-materialist civilization in the Western world," turned his attention to Union war-making: "It scarcely needs pointing out that from the military policies of Sherman and Sheridan there lies but an easy step to the modern conception of total war, the greatest threat to our civilization since its founding." The author of a volume published in 2007 took an equally negative stance, asserting that "the kind of warfare practiced by the Federal military during 1861–65 turned America—and arguably the whole world—back to a darker age." A blurb on this volume's dust jacket echoed the most vitriolic, and statistically misleading, anti-Yankee rhetoric of the Lost Cause generation: "Of all the enormities committed by Americans in the nineteenth century—including slavery and the Indian wars—the worst was the invasion of the South, which destroyed some twenty billion dollars of private and public property and resulted in the deaths of some two million people, most of whom were civilians—both black and white."[42]

Would friends of the Union, who seem irretrievably to have lost the war on film, find much to like about how recent artists have treated their side of the war? Or would admirers of the Lost Cause find modern artworks more to their taste? The next chapter will attempt to answer those questions.

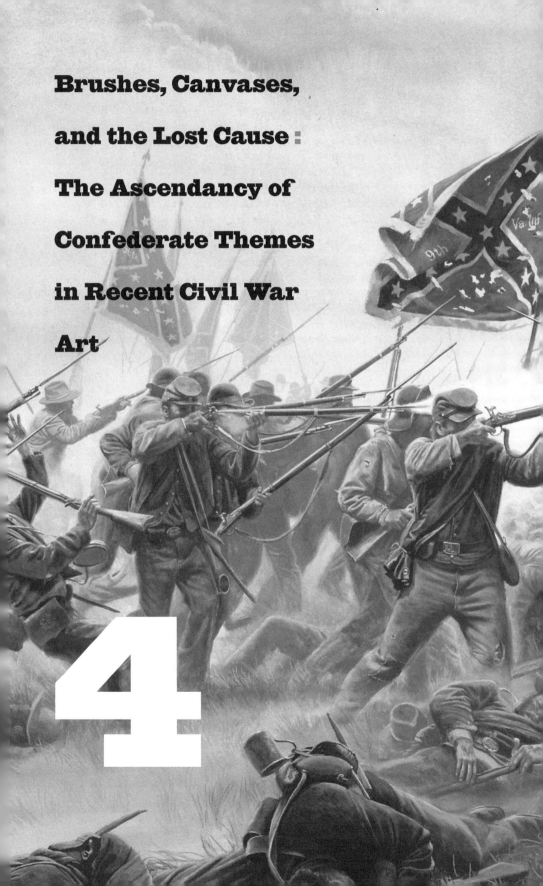

Brushes, Canvases, and the Lost Cause :
The Ascendancy of
Confederate Themes
in Recent Civil War
Art

4

orks of art produced for the Civil War market in the past twenty-five years would warm the hearts of former Confederates who laid the groundwork for the Lost Cause tradition. To a quite astonishing degree, Robert E. Lee, Stonewall Jackson, and the soldiers they commanded have emerged triumphant in the world of contemporary painters and sculptors. The subjects the artists select, as well as many of the interpretive materials that describe their pieces, mirror the original Lost Cause art of the late nineteenth and early twentieth centuries. In some ways, recent artworks have gone beyond those of the Lost Cause era by emphasizing the religious devotion of southern leaders and, in a few disturbing cases, placing black soldiers in the Confederate ranks. The St. Andrew's Cross battle flag also appears more prominently and frequently, rendering current art more readily identifiable as Confederate than many paintings and prints of the immediate postwar decades. Largely absent are important elements of late-nineteenth-century artworks devoted to the triumphant Union. Most obviously, Ulysses S. Grant, William Tecumseh Sherman, and Philip H. Sheridan, together with their victories, occupy a decidedly secondary position that belies their importance in northern conceptions of national triumph.

This art also reflects the power of films and television to shape the marketplace. Events and characters prominent in Ken Burns's series and Ron Maxwell's adaptations of *The Killer Angels* and *Gods and Generals* have received considerable attention from artists since the early 1990s. Joshua Lawrence Chamberlain's popularity provides the best example of this trend. A subject of no importance in Civil War artworks produced in the nineteenth century, Chamberlain has become the most-painted United States military officer; he and other Union commanders at Gettysburg account for a significant proportion of all artworks on Union topics. In a few fascinating instances, figures in paintings resemble the actors in Maxwell's *Gettysburg* as much as the historical figures they represent.

"Chivalry, Bravery, Duty, and Honor Were Paramount"—for Confederates

Confederate ascendancy in recent art rivals that in Hollywood during the period bracketed by *The Birth of a Nation* and *Gone with the Wind*. One way to measure this phenomenon is through more than 2,750 advertisements for prints of paintings and other artworks that ran between 1962 and 2006 in *Civil War Times Illustrated*, *Blue & Gray Magazine*, and *North & South*. None of these publications can be labeled pro-Confederate in its editorial stance. All three reach a national audience, with more than two-thirds of their subscribers living outside the states of the Confederacy.[1] Yet advertisements suggest that the art-buying Civil War public, wherever they live, overwhelmingly prefer Confederate leaders and themes. Information about individual purchasers is not available, which prevents definitive conclusions about why certain topics sell better than others. But the disjunction between Lost Cause supremacy in the art world, which parallels the preference for the Confederacy among reenactors,[2] and its retreat in both Hollywood and the public sphere is conspicuous. Many collectors with no ancestral ties to the Confederacy may simply find Lee, Jackson, and other Confederates more appealing or interesting than their Union counterparts. Some may display Lost Cause artworks in their homes as a way to express admiration for Confederate generals or soldiers free of the acrimonious public debates about the St. Andrew's Cross battle flag or the Confederacy as a slave-based republic. A desire to assert regional pride or honor Confederate ancestors—two parts of the Sons of Confederate Veterans' "heritage not hate" campaign—almost certainly plays a role, as does the romantic underdog aura of the Confederate war that transcends geography.

For some purchasers, artworks that prominently feature the battle flag almost certainly serve a purpose related to current political debates about affirmative action and other race-based issues, secularism, and the size and reach of the federal government. An issue of the modern incarnation of *Confederate Veteran* magazine, published in the spring of 1988, provides several clues to the connections between politics and the most obvious symbol of the Confederacy. One column in the magazine claimed that "a look at the daily newspapers or television 'news'" revealed "not merely an effort to do away with a battleflag; it is an effort to revise or delete the truths about the Confederacy." Such was to be expected from "professional black racists," believed the author, who also contended that the problem ran deeper in American public life. Another columnist, in a piece titled "Attacks on the Colors," argued that "reverence for the beloved battle flag of the Confederate States of America is a continued adherence, not to a lost cause, but to an abiding faith in the freedom of mankind everywhere." That freedom, like the St. Andrew's Cross flag, was under siege from those "who care little for the past because they are only interested in the progressive (i.e., more authoritarian) future." This second columnist highlighted religion and race in his interpretation of the battle flag: "In few other national banners is so closely linked the spiritual and national aspirations of a people. More thoroughly 'English' than any other region of the United States, the Confederacy brings together in . . . the battle flag, the abstract design of the Union Jack with the Christian religious fervor that has been the primary missionary impulse among Anglo-Saxons for several hundred years."[3]

Whatever the reasons for Lost Cause dominance, statistics leave no doubt about its extent. Between 1962 and 2006, nearly 1,700 advertisements in the three periodicals surveyed featured artworks with Confederate subjects compared to approximately 600 devoted to the Union. Another 450, mostly battle scenes, included both Confederates and Federals. Military events and personalities account for the overwhelming majority of subjects throughout the period. By decade, the totals break down as follows:

1960s	10 Confederate, 4 Union
1970s	59 Confederate, 12 Union
1980s	408 Confederate, 81 Union
1990s	919 Confederate, 379 Union
2000–2005	300 Confederate, 118 Union

Since 1990, the ratio has remained at about 2.5 to 1 in favor of the Confederacy, with the Union percentage rising slowly over the past two years. In terms of famous leaders, Lost Cause idols Robert E. Lee and Stonewall Jackson rank first and second; Lee's subordinates Jeb Stuart, James Longstreet, and George E. Pickett also make the top ten at numbers five, eight, and ten respectively. Lee and Ulysses S. Grant paired at Appomattox rank seventh (Lee and Jackson together, most often at Chancellorsville, place eleventh). Nathan Bedford Forrest, the sole Confederate from the Western Theater in the top ten, trails just behind Stuart at sixth. Maj. Gen. Patrick R. Cleburne, an Irish-born division commander in the Army of Tennessee known as the "Stonewall Jackson of the West," ranks twelfth. Despite his Irish connection (a strong point in selling prints) and fine combat record, the Western Theater's version of Lee's great lieutenant appears in roughly one-thirteenth as many advertisements as Jackson.[4]

What about United States leaders? Abraham Lincoln stands third for the entire period, after holding the top position during the 1960s and 1970s when few artworks were advertised. Invisible in the 1960s and 1970s and tied for ninth with George A. Custer in the 1980s, Joshua Chamberlain reaches the fourth position with a 1990s surge due to his prominence in Ken Burns's documentary and Ron Maxwell's *Gettysburg*. Poor Grant, a hero of the Republic second only to Lincoln, languishes in ninth place. That he barely edges out Pickett, a historical gnat to Grant's elephant, underscores the cockeyed nature of the coverage. Someone seeking images of Grant can select from fewer than 40 advertised works—those enamored of Lee from more than 300. If Grant's admirers will accept their hero alongside Lee at Appomattox, they can choose from another 65. Custer, a cavalryman who led a division in the war's final year, ranks fourth behind Lincoln, Chamberlain, and Grant among all United States figures—a showing almost certainly explained by his postwar notoriety. Had his campaigns against Native Americans not ended dramatically at the Little Bighorn in June 1876, he likely would be much farther down on the list. As a quintet, Grant's great friend and lieutenant William Tecumseh Sherman and fellow army commanders Philip H. Sheridan, George G. Meade, George B. McClellan, and George H. Thomas have attracted less artistic attention than Lt. Gen. Ambrose Powell Hill, who compiled a decidedly mixed record as a corps commander in the Army of Northern Virginia but is featured in nearly two dozen advertisements.[5]

Lee's battles similarly overshadow those of the Western Theater, and artists have shown the same fascination with Gettysburg as Lost Cause writers who endlessly dissected its various episodes. This departs from trends in Union-centered art of the late nineteenth century, when Gettysburg, though painted many times and offered in a number of prints, did not tower above all other battles. The work of Ken Burns and Ron Maxwell transmitted the Lost Cause emphasis on Gettysburg to vast modern audiences, which in turn fed an appetite for artworks devoted to the battle's famous incidents and personalities. More than 400 advertisements reach out to collectors eager for pieces on Gettysburg, roughly 250 from the 1990s alone. Lee and Jackson participated in the five battles that follow Gettysburg in the number of works devoted to them (in descending order): Antietam, the 1862 Shenandoah Valley campaign, Manassas, Fredericksburg, and Chancellorsville—which together appear in fewer than half as many advertisements as the Pennsylvania battle. Appomattox, Petersburg, and the Wilderness, three more of Lee's campaigns, occupy the seventh, ninth, and tenth positions. Only Grant's victory at Shiloh, in eighth place, adds a western touch to the roster.[6]

What of the Atlanta campaign, Sherman's seismic victory that virtually guaranteed Lincoln's reelection in 1864? Or Chattanooga, which served as the capstone for Grant's dazzling service in the Western Theater? Or, most obviously, Vicksburg, the showcase for Grant's strategic talents that established United States control of the Mississippi River? None makes the top ten, a fact that probably would not surprise viewers of Ken Burns's series. Burns allocated forty-five minutes to Gettysburg and only a little more than ten to Vicksburg. Moreover, Hollywood offered no film titled *Vicksburg* to compete for viewers with Maxwell's *Gettysburg*. Vicksburg certainly poses no challenge to its more famous eastern counterpart in the world of art, barely reaching double digits in contrast to Gettysburg's hundreds of pieces. Should Hollywood feature Atlanta again, as it did in both *The Birth of a Nation* and *Gone with the Wind*, Sherman's triumph might attract artists in pursuit of dramatic subjects.[7]

Within the universe of Gettysburg artworks, the influence of Maxwell's film (and by extension of Shaara's novel) stands out. James Longstreet, George E. Pickett, and Lewis A. Armistead, each a major character in *Gettysburg*, appear repeatedly in paintings. "Pickett's Charge" on the battle's third day, which cost Armistead his life and conferred on Pickett undeserved fame, became an artistic staple. This emphasis on the grand assault enhances the Confederate advantage; however, Longstreet's treatment departs from the Lost Cause narrative. A prime villain at Gettysburg to Lost Cause warriors such as Jubal Early, Longstreet has been reinterpreted as a prescient, enormously attractive soldier in the work of Shaara, Maxwell, and a number of artists.

Maxwell's film surely spurred support for the General Longstreet Memorial Fund. Founded in 1991, this group labored through the 1990s to raise money for an equestrian statue of Lee's "Old War Horse" at Gettysburg. Longstreet's admirers hoped the statue would help undo the effects of "a campaign of slander and ridicule perpetuated by a handful of his so-called comrades" during the late nineteenth century. Artist Gary Casteel produced the sculpture (fig. 29), which was dedicated on Seminary Ridge in July 1998. Casteel's statue bears more than a passing resemblance to actor Tom Berenger's Longstreet in *Gettysburg*. The greater-than-life-size figure of Longstreet, turning in the saddle to look over his left shoulder, sports a huge beard and a wide-brimmed hat (the beard looks more like Berenger's than Longstreet's in any of the general's wartime photographs). The oddest feature of the statue is "Hero," Longstreet's horse. The animal's hindquarters are on a smaller scale than its forequarters, giving the statue the rather odd appearance of an outsized Berenger/Longstreet on a carousel horse.[8]

Artists Don Troiani, Dale Gallon, and Mort Künstler confirm Hollywood's role in molding public taste in Civil War art.[9] Troiani estimates that 60 percent of his prints go to buyers in the South and attributes Confederate domination to various factors, including "the stronger interest among Southerners in the

FIGURE 29. Equestrian Statue of James Longstreet by artist Gary Casteel.
Photograph © Chris Heisey, reproduced with his permission.

Civil War in general." Recent films "have been a great influence" because they affect "what battles and generals people will see." Maxwell's two films, as well as Burns's documentary, have framed the war for untold Americans: "In the eyes of the public the 3 main figures of the war were Lee, Jackson and Chamberlain." Shelby Foote's praise for Forrest in Burns's series, which features the mind-boggling observation that Lincoln and Forrest were the two "authentic geniuses" of the conflict, thrust that unstable warrior to the forefront of western Confederate leaders. As for battles, Gettysburg heads the field, followed by Antietam, Fredericksburg, and First Manassas. Sherman and Grant, neither of whom appears in *Gettysburg* or *Gods and Generals*, "lag far behind Lee and Jackson." Without Maxwell and Burns, suggests Troiani, "Chamberlain and Little Round Top would be minor footnotes in the eyes of the public."[10]

Gallon and Künstler express similar opinions. Gallon believes that *Gettysburg* and Burns's series had a "major impact" on the art market, bringing in many new customers who wanted scenes and characters they first saw in the film or the PBS broadcasts. Künstler had the most direct connection to *Gettysburg*. Commissioned by Ted Turner to illustrate a book published in conjunction with the release of the film, he featured Lee, Longstreet, and Chamberlain in many of his paintings. *Gettysburg: The Paintings of Mort Künstler*, with sales of nearly 200,000 copies, reached far more readers than most nonfiction titles devoted to the battle and gave further evidence of Hollywood's ability to shape perceptions of historical events. Like Troiani, Künstler identifies Lee, Jackson, and Chamberlain as the most popular subjects for paintings and finds that, for Civil War art as a whole, "there is much more interest in the South than in the North." He attributes the latter phenomenon, at least in part, to his sense that people in states such as Virginia and South Carolina "seem to connect better with their ancestors."

Books by the five artists whose paintings most often appear in advertisements further buttress Lost Cause artistic supremacy. A native of New York City trained at the Pennsylvania Academy of Art, Don Troiani has established a reputation for scrupulous attention to the war's military material culture. His *Don Troiani's Civil War* offers slightly more Confederate than Union paintings, with Gettysburg the most frequent subject. Other topics include Lee and his major lieutenants (Jackson, Longstreet, and Stuart) as well as Armistead and Pickett's Charge. Although the book contains no image of Grant or Sherman, a few paintings depict western battles. Keith Rocco's *The Soldier's View: The Civil War Art of Keith Rocco* accords Confederate and Union subjects almost equal treatment. An admirer of N. C. Wyeth and Howard Pyle, Rocco focuses on common soldiers more than on famous generals and shows a special affinity for regiments of Zouaves, whose members wore colorful uniforms patterned on those adopted by some French units in North Africa. As in Troiani's book, Gettysburg is Rocco's most painted battle.[11]

The same is true in *Dale Gallon Historical Art: Collectors Edition*, which features three dozen paintings of Gettysburg. A native of southern California trained at the Art Center College of Design in Los Angeles, Gallon moved to Gettysburg in 1984. "I happen to live within a mile or two of where General Robert E. Lee led the Army of Northern Virginia into the pivotal battle of the War," he observes. "The battlefield is my office. I don't need much more inspiration. I suspect people who collect my paintings feel that on the canvas." Gallon's overall body of work divides almost equally between Union and Confederate topics. Longstreet is the most-painted figure in the book (six images), followed by Lee and Joshua Lawrence Chamberlain (four each) and Stonewall Jackson, Jeb Stuart, John F. Reynolds, and John Buford (three each). No painting in the volume focuses on U. S. Grant or William Tecumseh Sherman, though one depicts Maj. Gen. George H. Thomas and his Union soldiers at the battle of Chickamauga. Pickett's Charge, with nine images, and Little Round Top, with four, head the list of Gallon's battlefield scenes.[12]

The prolific Mort Künstler defines Lost Cause orthodoxy. The most widely collected Civil War artist, he came to the subject relatively late in a career that included training at Brooklyn College, the University of California at Los Angeles, and the Pratt Institute. Gettysburg's 125th anniversary in 1988 inspired his first major Civil War–related piece, a treatment of Pickett's Charge titled *The High Water Mark*. Prior to 1988, Künstler readily concedes, he had so little knowledge of the Civil War that he did not "know Sherman from Jackson, literally." Along with Troiani, he stands atop the field of Civil War prints—though according far less attention than Troiani to material culture and historical accuracy. Confederate subjects hold a 4-to-1 edge over their Union counterparts in *Künstler: The Civil War Art of Mort Künstler*. Lee and Jackson account for more than thirty-five images each (Grant and Sherman have two apiece). Jeb Stuart, James Longstreet, and Lewis Armistead are all well represented; the last two, together with Lee, inhabit a number of Gettysburg scenes. Künstler's penchant for Lost Cause themes stands out even more clearly in an earlier book titled *Jackson and Lee: Legends in Gray* (a photograph on the back flap of the dust jacket shows the artist with a Confederate flag prominently displayed in the background). "Sometimes there is honor in tragedy and inspiration in defeat," reads historian James I. Robertson Jr.'s text to accompany the paintings. "Lee and Jackson most seem to embody those truths in the American pantheon. That explains why tens of thousands of people with a respect for history look back on 'Marse Robert' and 'Old Jack' in wonder and with esteem. Those feelings characterize the work of Mort Künstler."[13]

A blending of Hollywood and history also characterizes some of Künstler's work. Anyone leafing through *Künstler: The Civil War Art of Mort Künstler* or *Gettysburg: The Paintings of Mort Künstler* (the companion to Maxwell's film) might conclude that Martin Sheen, who played Lee in the film, must be at least distantly related to the general. *Lee's Old War Horse* (fig. 30), which portrays Lee and Longstreet on the morning of July 3, illustrates this crossover effect. Longstreet gazes toward the Union position, field glasses in his right hand and a cigar in his mouth, as a Sheenlike Lee listens to him talk. "General Longstreet has his doubts," reads the text accompanying the painting, "but he cannot talk Lee out of his plan to charge the center of the Union line." An alternate interpretation of Longstreet's doubt in this painting seems possible. Perhaps it is not Lee's plan that troubles Old Pete, but rather that the gray-bearded officer on Traveller looks so little like the real commander of the Army of Northern Virginia. Other Confederate characters also seem to gallop out of Maxwell's film into some of Künstler's Gettysburg paintings, among them Berenger's Longstreet, Stephen Lang's George E. Pickett, James Patrick Stuart's Col. Edward Porter Alexander, and Ivan Kane's Capt. Thomas J. Goree. Martin Sheen should have the final word on this blurring of history and cinema. His foreword to the companion book describes it as "a permanent and accurate record of the fighters in their battle regalia, precisely executed and flawlessly executed. . . . I can only hope that it will prove to be as momentous an experience for the viewer and reader as it was for me and an extraordinary army of fellow players."[14]

John Paul Strain matches Künstler in his enthusiasm for Confederate subjects. A native of Nashville who sometimes poses in Confederate reenactor garb, he most often paints Lee and Jackson but also depicts western generals such as Nathan Bedford Forrest, John C. Breckinridge, and John Hunt Morgan. The published collection of his Civil War paintings, titled *Witness to the Civil War: The Art of John Paul Strain*, favors Confederate topics by a ratio of more than 5 to 1, with Jackson the most painted subject, followed by Lee, Forrest, Stuart, and Morgan. The handful of Federal subjects includes Grant with Lee at Appomattox and studies of Joshua Chamberlain and Winfield Scott Han-

FIGURE 30. *Lee's Old War Horse* by Mort Künstler. From the original painting by Mort Künstler, "Lee's Old War Horse," © 1992 Mort Künstler, Inc., www.mkunstler.com.

cock at Gettysburg. The dust jacket copy describes Strain as "a historian who wants to convey to others his insight into and affinity for the drama of the War Between the States." Like the choice of "War Between the States," the prose in the book recalls Lost Cause writings. "It was a time," reads the text, "when chivalry, bravery, duty, and honor were paramount in a man's character." Such a man was Lee, who "guided by his sense of duty and honor . . . would prove to be one of the greatest military leaders of all time." Jeb Stuart "personified the ideal chivalrous 19th century leader and cavalryman" and "would become a legend." As for Jackson, he stood among the "noble men, who had a strong sense of honor and duty, and a belief in a supreme being that would help and guide their actions." Jackson's feats on the battlefield made him "a hero on the pages of history."[15]

Evidence from galleries that sell Civil War art lends credence to Strain's comments about the importance of the romantic Lost Cause tradition. According to a gallery owner from California, much of the Confederate art "adds to Lost Cause Mythology by making their [the Confederacy's] leaders gentle Christians who were perfect gentlemen and kind to animals." A print seller from Virginia stressed the romance and ideals of the Confederacy, dusting off a vintage Lost Cause image in likening Grant's aggressive tactics during the Overland campaign to "smashing a fly with a sledgehammer." Galleries in Gettysburg cater to the vast number of tourists who visit the battlefield. Located on northern soil where United States soldiers won a great victory, many of these businesses nonetheless sell far more Confederate than Union items. At one, a salesperson noted that prints highlighting cavalier or romantic images sell briskly—especially with Lee, Jackson, Stuart, Longstreet, Forrest, and John Hunt Morgan as the subject. Jackson leads in sales by "a fairly wide margin," largely because of the romantic, tragic elements of his Confederate career. Prints devoted to the religiosity of Lee and Jackson also do well, along with those depicting soldiers taking leave of their wives. Another gallery in Gettysburg reported similar trends, highlighting the popularity of Lee, Jackson, Stuart, Forrest and Morgan—as well as the leave-taking genre. The popularity of prints featuring couples, whether unnamed soldiers and their sweethearts or Stonewall Jackson with his wife Mary Anna, has risen with the increase of women in the pool of purchasers (more than 50 percent in at least one of the galleries).

Galleries report sales figures even more one-sided than the number of advertisements in Civil War magazines. One in Gettysburg estimated 15 to 1 in favor of Confederate pieces; another, without giving a ratio, described sales as "overwhelmingly Confederate." The proprietor of a gallery in Fredericksburg, Virginia, put the ratio at 3 to 1. "It is part of the romance of the South," he remarked concerning the Confederate advantage, "and Americans normally root for the underdog." A print dealer from near Richmond, Virginia, stated his policy bluntly: "I prefer not to even receive the Union prints because I know they are hard to sell."[16]

The secondary market for Civil War prints provides a final indication of Confederate supremacy. This market recycles pieces that sell out in their original limited editions. "Demand for a sold out print" establishes the price, explains one of Don Troiani's mailings. "Our intent is to report an average of recent verifiable selling prices." Using this formula, Troiani has tracked values over many years, finding that Confederate prints almost always command higher prices. Among Union subjects, only the Irish Brigade, Joshua Lawrence Chamberlain on Little Round Top, and other Union commanders and units at Gettysburg appreciated dramatically. Troiani's studies of Confederate and Union color bearers illustrate the point. *The Confederate Standard Bearer*, issued in an edition of 600 in 1982, had an estimated value of $2,600 on Troiani's Winter 1997 secondary market list; *The Union Standard Bearer*, issued in an identical edition one year later, appears on the same list for $750. Of seventy items on the 1997 list, eleven carried values of more than $1,000. Eight featured Confederates, including one each of Lee, Jackson, and Forrest and two of Armistead in Pickett's Charge; two depicted soldiers of both sides at Gettysburg; and one showed the Irish Brigade at Fredericksburg. Similar price sheets in 2003 and 2007 for Dale Gallon's prints listed five with an estimated value of more than $900—one each of Lee, Stuart, and Forrest and two of Chamberlain at Gettysburg.[17]

In terms of market size, Civil War prints command a far smaller niche than that of the saccharine cottage, lighthouse, and garden scenes produced by Thomas Kinkade, the self-styled "painter of light" whose work has sold in the millions (because of his output and marketing, Mort Künstler has been called the "Kinkade of Civil War art"). Compared to other historical genres, however, the Civil War stands out. Aviation prints, especially those signed by combat pilots, also have been popular, and smaller markets have developed for pieces devoted to the Revolutionary War, the Indian wars, and some other western subjects. Black officers in the United States Army, for example, have shown considerable interest in pieces devoted to the African American regiments of "Buffalo Soldiers" who served in the West during the postwar decades.[18]

Various factors contribute to choices of subject. Most obviously, artists seek to produce work that will sell. To this end, they place well-known generals from both armies at famous parts of the field at Gettysburg (characters and moments from Maxwell's film have the advantage of a larger ready-made audience), lavish attention on Lee and Jackson and their storied operations, and create pieces aimed at people interested in Irish participation in the war — whether the Union's Irish Brigade or the Confederacy's Pat Cleburne. "I try to do a Lee picture once a year," states Mort Künstler, "and a Jackson picture once a year." Dale Gallon attributes the demand for Irish-themed prints to a "cultural influence" that affects the crucial markets in New York City and Boston. Don Troiani agrees that the Irish constituency is important but believes the Irish Brigade's green flags, which stand out as unusual, may be most important. Künstler adds that "flags are a wonderful element in painting" Civil War subjects because they add color to otherwise quite drab depictions of combat. Some artists opt for scenic landscapes, often snow-covered, populated by leading generals — a strategy that gives both women and men something they can appreciate. Künstler and John Paul Strain paint snowscapes most among Civil War artists. The artists sometimes depart from proven formulas to indulge their own artistic or historical interests, a strategy that yields uneven financial results. For example, Dale Gallon was attracted to Army of the Potomac commander George G. Meade and Third Corps chief Daniel E. Sickles at Gettysburg on July 2, painted the scene, and found out, in his words, that "no one wanted it." Many pieces are commissioned by groups or individuals, a process that promotes a strong sale of the resulting prints.[19]

Whatever their reasons for selecting a subject, artists identify two groups of prospective buyers: (1) serious students of the Civil War, and (2) a much larger group whose taste is shaped by Maxwell's films, television documentaries, or the novels of Michael and Jeff Shaara. In marketing works, artists exercise close control over the texts that accompany advertisements in magazines and in flyers mailed to prospective customers. The artists often enlist historians to help with factual details about scenes, as well as to write narratives on which texts for advertisements are based.[20]

 ### *The Last Meeting, The Burial of Latané,* and *Lee and His Generals*: Landmarks of Original Lost Cause Art

The Lost Cause antecedents of modern artworks confirm that Lee and Jackson always stood above other Confederate heroes. Although Jefferson Davis received respectful attention as a patriot or martyr who had suffered postwar imprisonment, he inspired a less adulatory response than the two Virginia generals. Army commanders Joseph E. Johnston and P. G. T. Beauregard occupied a second-tier position behind Lee and Jackson, and various other generals also showed up in prints. Battles, groupings of leaders, scenes of soldier life, and tributes to Confederate women rounded out the roster of subjects in Lost Cause iconography. Most often produced by northern publishers, these works supplied a tangible connection to the Confederate experiment as white southerners pursued lives increasingly distanced from the turbulent days of their slaveholding republic. The prints nourished the sense of collective identity exhibited by Confederates in and out of uniform during the conflict, promoting a continuing sense of separation from the white North that proved to be remarkably resilient.[21]

Three of the most famous images deserve special mention. Taken together, they reflect the Lost Cause preoccupation with Confederate military leaders while also portraying a home front populated by resolute women and loyal slaves. Everett B. D. Julio's *The Heroes of Chancellorsville*, a massive oil completed in 1869 and subsequently retitled *The Last Meeting of Lee and Jackson* (fig. 31), places the two men at the scene of their most celebrated triumph.[22] The image captures Confederate hopes at flood tide, with Gettysburg, never mind Appomattox, still in the future. The brilliant commanders, Lee obviously the superior and Jackson the attentive subordinate, confer on the morning of May 2, 1863, as the latter prepares to maneuver his corps into position opposite the right flank of Joseph Hooker's Army of the Potomac.[23] The viewer's knowledge of Jackson's wounding that evening, the amputation of his left arm, and his death eight days later adds special poignancy to the scene. Julio saw no need to add battle flags or other trappings of Confederate patriotism. The double portrait, with staff officers unobtrusively tucked into the shadowy right background, reminded viewers that their failed nation had been blessed with two grand warriors. Neither did the artist worry about getting details correct: Jackson wore a far less impressive uniform during the battle, for example, and the rolling, heavily wooded terrain near Chancellorsville boasts nothing like the imposing ridge behind Lee and Traveller.

Admirers of Julio's work craved a heroic reminder of Lee and Jackson rather than artistic realism. Abundant testimony leaves no doubt about postwar adulation of the two men. A young Marylander who encountered Lee in the summer of 1867 later recalled that he "looked very tall and majestic." She thought the "man who stood before us, the embodiment of a Lost Cause, was

FIGURE 31. *The Last Meeting of Lee and Jackson* by Everett B. D. Julio. Author's collection.

the realized King Arthur. . . . The years which have passed since that time have dimmed many enthusiasms and destroyed many illusions, but have caused no blush at the memory of the swift thrill of recognition and reverence which ran like an electric flash through one's whole body." Field Marshal Garnet Wolseley, a distinguished British soldier who had visited the Confederacy, wrote almost as effusively about Stonewall Jackson. Calling Jackson "a great soldier" and "a Christian hero," Wolseley claimed that even former enemies held "a feeling of love and reverence for the memory of this great and true-hearted man of war, who fell in what he firmly believed to be a sacred cause." Jackson's fame no longer belonged only to Virginia and the South, thought Wolseley, "it has become the birthright of every man privileged to call himself an American." Such attitudes explain why numerous engravings of Julio's painting were issued over a period of several decades. The most careful students of Confederate prints call Julio's effort "one of the most enduring of all Confederate images" — a judgment born out by advertisements for reproductions between the mid-1980s and 2005.[24]

Five years before Julio completed *The Last Meeting*, a young artist named William DeHartburn Washington exhibited *The Burial of Latané* (fig. 32) at the Virginia state capitol. Viewers responded emotionally to the painting, which amid a brutal war touched on themes of loss and patriotic devotion. A powerful reminder of connections between home front and battlefront, it shows the burial of Capt. William D. Latané, who was killed during Jeb Stuart's first "Ride Around McClellan" in June 1862. Confederate mobilization had stripped white men from the area, so local women, assisted by slaves who dug the grave, took the lead in caring for Latané's remains. One of Washington's inspirations likely had been a eulogy for Latané written in verse by John R. Thompson. The eulogy lauds women who "in accents soft and low / Trembling with pity, touched with pathos, read / Over this hallowed dust the ritual for the dead." In future days for Virginia, it continues, "No prouder memory her breast shall sway / Than thine, our dearly lost, lamented / LATANE." Like the eulogy, Washington's composition most obviously pays homage to Confederate mothers, wives, and sisters; it also imparts value to every life lost in pursuit of independence and reassures white people about slaves' loyalty in a war that had played havoc with the peculiar institution.[25]

An 1868 engraving of Washington's painting quickly gained popularity and remained a Lost Cause staple for many decades. More than sixty years after its publication, the engraving appeared on the cover of *Confederate Veteran*. "In many homes of the South," reads the caption, "may still be found this hand-

FIGURE 32. *The Burial of Latané* by William DeHartburn Washington. Author's collection.

FIGURE 33. *Lee and His Generals* by G. B. Matthews. Author's collection.

some old picture, which tells the story of the burial of a gallant Confederate soldier . . . and which also depicts the spirit of the women of the South, who here are shown officiating in the burial." Fifteen years earlier, a veteran of Stuart's ride fondly remembered Latané, observing that Washington's tribute and Thompson's poem had "so enshrined the name of Latane in the hearts of the people of our Southland that it will endure as long as men are admired for the devotion to duty and for risking their lives upon the perilous edge of battle in defense of homes and country." This man's musings about a long-dead comrade highlight the link between art such as The Burial of Latané and lingering devotion to a Confederate "country."[26]

The third famous Lost Cause era print, while less ubiquitous than Julio's or Washington's, represents a genre devoted to groups of Confederate generals who never actually gathered in one place. Publication of G. B. Matthews's Lee and His Generals (fig. 33) in photogravure coincided with the centennial of Lee's birth in 1907, and the image achieved wide circulation. An article in Confederate Veteran assured readers the "great painting of 'Lee and His Generals' is considered one of the finest of group portraiture doubtless ever produced in America. The great figures stand forth from the canvas with startling resemblance of life, General Lee occupying his rightful place at the center front." An advertisement that ran for several years in the magazine quoted former general Marcus J. Wright, who stated, "The truthfulness of features of these great generals is most remarkable. . . . I hope all Confederates will procure copies." Lest Wright's admonition alone fail to inspire sales, the advertisement closed with a double pitch: "Every home should have a picture. It will make a nice Christmas gift."[27]

Like The Last Meeting, Matthews's painting keeps the historical focus directly on the Confederacy's military leadership. Lee stands just a bit taller than twenty-five fellow generals, all of whom, remarkably, appear to be the same height. Booted and spurred, with swords much in evidence, many of the generals evoke the chivalric tradition. Lee's figure, from a photograph taken just after Appomattox, requires neither saber nor boots to dominate the assemblage. Again like Julio, Matthews decided against adding battle flags. The faces and uniforms of men who led Confederate armies sufficed to stir memories of a struggle for nationhood. Artistically, Lee and His Generals lags far behind the other two iconic prints. Indeed, Albert Sidney Johnston, the South's ranking field commander, who is fourth from the left, seems to have put his left boot on his right foot (historians seeking explanations for Confederate defeat have overlooked this as possible evidence of ineptitude on

Johnston's, rather than Matthews's, part). Such quibbles aside, *Lee and His Generals* remains available in reprint for anyone who favors classic treatments of the Confederacy's military leadership.[28]

The Lost Cause Continued and Embellished

The officers in *Lee and His Generals* received considerable attention in Jubal Early's stem-winding speech delivered at Lexington, Virginia, on January 19, 1872. Early lauded Lee and Jackson as "illustrious men, and congenial Christian heroes." "Let us be thankful that our cause had two such champions," said Early, "and that, in their characters, we can furnish the world at large with the best assurance of the rightfulness of the principles for which they and we fought." Surviving Confederate generals "were worthy defenders of our cause, and not unfit comrades of Lee, Sidney Johnston, and Stonewall Jackson." Against the longest of odds, and with support from their "fair countrywomen," the officers and soldiers of the South had fought honorably. Early hoped future generations would "venerate the memory, emulate the virtues, and cherish the principles" of the Confederate dead.[29]

Early's comments align almost perfectly with much recent Civil War art, which promotes the kind of veneration Old Jube proposed. Virtually all of the Lost Cause interpretive emphases apply: the preeminence of Lee and Jackson and their Eastern Theater campaigns, the absence of attention to the war's causes and political conflicts, and, to a lesser degree, loyal support on the Confederate home front. Recent artworks often go beyond Lost Cause antecedents in ways calculated to celebrate the Confederacy's war. Three examples will illuminate this trend. First, Confederate flags often occupy more prominent positions than in late-nineteenth- and early-twentieth-century artworks. Some customers may like the flags because, in one artist's words, they suggest the "romance" of a "glorious" war. Another artist mentions their value in adding vital color to "the dull, earthy tones of Confederate uniforms."[30] For many purchasers, however, the flags undoubtedly convey a sense of unabashed Confederate patriotism in a modern world where that sentiment increasingly comes under fire. Second, far more pieces focus on the religious devotion of Lee, Jackson, and other southern leaders. Finally, a few prints break troubling new ground regarding African Americans in the Confederacy. Original Lost Cause artists, if they included black people at all, went no further in their propagandistic effort than insisting that slaves remained loyal to Confederate masters. Black men in Confederate uniforms, as well as loyal slaves, have found their way into recent art. This new dimension surely relies on the pseudo-historical literature that claims tens of thousands of black men "served" as Confederate soldiers and seeks retrospectively to get the Confederacy right on race.

Comparisons of representative works will demonstrate how closely current art mirrors Lost Cause themes and subjects. Five treatments of Lee, selected from hundreds of examples, are a good place to begin. Edward Caledon Bruce's somewhat romantic *General Robert E. Lee*, painted from life in the winter of 1864–65 and later published as a black-and-white print (fig. 34), was exhibited in the Virginia capitol in early 1865. Bruce's composition drew heavily on Charles Willson Peale's full-length portrait of George Washington after the battle of Trenton, reinforcing the common belief among Confederates that Lee functioned as their Washington. Anticipating Julio and Matthews, Bruce elected to leave Confederate flags out of his painting. *Robert Edward Lee 1807–1870* (fig. 35), a popular etching issued for the Confederate Memorial Literary Society in 1907, went through a number of printings. Based on a Mathew Brady photograph from 1865, it features a pair of small flags under Lee's image.[31]

In Dale Gallon's *For the Cause* (1986; fig. 36), Lee rallies his soldiers at Sayler's Creek, on April 6, 1865. The flag dramatically captures the viewer's eye, and Gallon's accompanying text in an advertisement fits the Lost Cause template: "Lee picks up a battleflag and holds it, finally revealing what the true heart and soul of this Confederate Army, for four long years, has been. . . . Lee becomes the symbol he never sought to be: the embodiment of the cause soon to be lost, of courage in the face of overwhelming odds, never to be forgotten." Michael Gnatek's *Robert E. Lee* (1994; fig. 37), the first offering in the Hamilton Mint's "Civil War Generals" plate collection, surrounds the general with vivid flag imagery. A flyer for the piece employs language a Lost Cause writer could not have improved: "A Legendary General . . . A Masterful Salute. From the trials of a war that tested our nation's most fundamental ideals, a great leader emerged. He was Robert E. Lee . . . a master of military strategy . . . a man of great loyalty and faith. He was, in the words of Churchill, 'one of the noblest Americans who ever lived,' and today his accomplishments remain a testament to the powers of courage and conviction."[32]

Specific episodes of Lee's Confederate career have proved irresistible to artists of the Lost Cause and modern eras. On May 6, 1864, Lee rode into fierce action on the Widow Tapp's farm during the battle of the Wilderness, prompting soldiers to grab Traveller's bridle and beseech Lee to go toward safety in the rear. Alfred R. Waud, an Englishman who worked as a sketch artist during the war, portrayed the incident for John Esten Cooke's biography of Lee published in 1871. In Waud's *The Wilderness*. "Lee to the Rear" (fig. 38), a dashing Lee, astride a black horse and wearing a cape, gestures toward the enemy while a battle flag flutters to his right front. Don Troiani painted the same scene in *Lee's Texans* (1984; fig. 39), giving a Confederate flag only slightly more prominence. Numerous artists have emulated Julio in painting or sculpting Lee's and Jackson's last conference at Chancellorsville. Robert K. Abbett painted the moment in a work titled *Morning Orders* (1984). "No one knew it then, but it was to be their last meeting," states the advertising text. "Lee and Jackson made the bold and brilliant plans which gave victory to the South. But it was a hollow victory, for at day's end, Stonewall Jackson lay mortally wounded." In sculptor Ron Tunison's *The Last Meeting* (fig. 40), Lee pulls Traveller's head back while Jackson casually allows his horse, Little Sorrel, to nibble on some grass.[33]

Lee's and Jackson's penultimate conversation, held on the night of May 1, 1863, attracted William Ludwell Sheppard's attention in the 1880s for the Century Company's Battles and Leaders of the Civil War series. One of Lee's veterans, Sheppard framed *Lee and Jackson in Council on the Night of May 1* (fig. 41) to suggest an intimate meeting in a heavily wooded setting. A flickering fire between the seated generals breaks the darkness, lighting their faces and revealing barely discernible figures in the right background. Mort Künstler's *The Last Council* (1990; fig. 42) opens up the scene, adding Jeb Stuart to the primary group. A number of soldiers inhabit the background, including a mounted man holding a Confederate flag (that a battle flag would be unfurled at night seems unlikely). "With equal admiration born of battle, Lee and Jackson were the perfect team," states the text in a flyer for Künstler's piece. "Long before dawn, Lee and Jackson sat on a broken cracker box at the same fire and finalized their plan. . . . It would be a Confederate avalanche into the Union lines!"[34]

Stonewall Jackson has been painted and sculpted in battle, in camp, and in domestic scenes with his wife. His entry into Winchester, Virginia, on May 25, 1862, during his storied Shenandoah Valley campaign marked a key moment in his rise to fame. *Jackson Entering Winchester* (fig. 43), painted by William DeHartburn Washington either during or just after the war, captures the moment, with Jackson raising his hat to acknowledge cheering civilians. Two black women, standing to the right and right rear of Jackson, take in the scene with no evident feeling. A tribute to emotional Confederate loyalty, Washington's painting contains no battle flags. Jackson's well-known figure would have sufficed to evoke pro-Confederate sentiment among the wartime generation. Mort Künstler's *General Thomas J. "Stonewall" Jackson, Winchester, Virginia, May 25, 1862* (1988; fig. 44) addresses the same incident but with key differences. Unlike Washington, Künstler insinuated no black figures into his welcoming throng and, most obviously, created a downtown Winchester awash in Confederate flags. "The flags are based on the flags of the Confederacy in 1862," the artist explains in a flyer. "You can see the National flag as well as copies of the battle flag, similar to the style used in the field by the army. I tried to impart as much excitement and joy as possible since this was the first time that Winchester had been liberated from a long, and reportedly harsh period of Union control, with the Confederates being welcomed as conquering heroes." Federal forces would soon return to Winchester, but the moment caught in the painting, reads another advertisement for the print, "will live forever as a part of the fame of Lee's 'right arm.'"[35]

Jackson's devout Christianity occasioned extensive comment during and after the Civil War, often with reference to Joshua or to Oliver Cromwell as models for his behavior. The most famous nineteenth-century print on this theme is John Chester Buttre's *Prayer in Stonewall Jackson's Camp* (1866; fig. 45). Closely patterned on Adalbert J. Volck's wartime etching titled *Scene in Stonewall Jackson's Camp*, it brings together several of the general's subordinates and staff members. The composition approximates a religious service, with Jackson in the preacher's role and his soldiers variously kneeling, bowing their heads, or simply listening. Only General A. P. Hill, sitting in the left foreground, seems utterly unengaged with Jackson's words. Jackson as a pious warrior has gained increasing visibility in recent artworks, the number of which far exceeds that of the Lost Cause years. Typical is *The Prayer Warrior* (1991) by William L. Maughan, an artist who specializes in Confederate paintings with religious themes. A somewhat overwrought treatment of a kneeling Jackson, *The Prayer Warrior* affords what the artist terms "a dramatic glimpse of Jackson's spiritual devotion." Always ready to profess his faith in public, Jackson "never failed to find time to be alone with his Lord." Dale Gallon painted a commissioned piece similar in content for the U.S. Army's Chaplain Corps Museum Association. Titled *The General and His Chaplain* (1994; fig. 46), it shows Jackson and a Presbyterian clergyman named Beverly Tucker Lacy in prayer during the winter of 1862. A steady seller over the years, it ranks among Gallon's most successful pieces.[36]

Lee's piety rivaled that of Jackson, a fact not lost on modern artists seeking religious themes. Maughan's *The Christian General* (1989; fig. 47) shows

Lee reading from the Bible to a child. With an expression best termed other-worldly, Lee appears unaware that the youngster has fallen asleep on his shoulder. "Virtually hundreds of paintings and sketches have been done on the great leader of the Army of Northern Virginia," reads the promotional flyer, "but few, if any, have ever depicted him as one of the greatest spiritual men of the 19th century." Sculptor Gary Casteel created a piece in which Lee bows his head slightly with eyes closed. One advertisement placed a quotation from Lee above an image of the sculpture: "I have fought against the people of the North because I believe they were seeking to wrest from the South its dearest rights. But I have never seen the day when I did not pray for them." Lee and Jackson also appear together in religious settings. For example, Mort Künstler's *The Generals Were Brought To Tears* (1992; fig. 48) situates the commanders and two well-scrubbed children in front of a huge Confederate flag. The Danbury Mint used the image on a "limited-edition collector plate," inviting prospective buyers to share the artist's "extraordinary vision of two great generals reflecting on their faith in God."[37]

Jefferson Davis joins Lee and Jackson in Maughan's *Christian Patriots, C.S.A.* (1990s; fig. 49), which imagines the trio in conference. Lee holds the primary position, addressing Jackson and pointing toward a map while a somewhat bewildered-looking Jefferson Davis gazes into space. "To our knowledge," reads accompanying copy, "a painting showing these great patriots together has never been done." In fact, other paintings and engravings have depicted the three men together, though usually with more generals present—as in, most famously, F. Gutekunst's *Jefferson Davis and the Confederate Generals* (1890; fig. 50), one of the dozen most popular Lost Cause images. All three of Maughan's images and texts exemplify the continuing representation of Lee and Jackson as, in Jubal Early's words, "illustrious men, and congenial Christian heroes."[38]

Portrayals of Confederates as Christian heroes may appeal most directly to people unhappy with what they consider the increasing secularization of American government and life. In the case of Lee and Jackson, however, artists such as Maughan draw on a long-standing tradition. Franklin D. Roosevelt contributed to this tradition in 1936 when he delivered remarks at the dedication of an equestrian statue to Lee in Dallas, Texas. "All over the United States we recognize him as a great leader of men, as a great general," Roosevelt told the crowd in language that anticipated Maughan's advertisements. "But, also, all over the United States I believe that we recognize him as something much more important than that. We recognize Robert E. Lee as one of our greatest American Christians and one of our greatest American gentle-men."[39]

However evident Lee's piety, his military exploits always have been a more attractive subject for artists. Many paintings depict him in the field with vari-ous lieutenants, a subgenre that includes Henry A. Ogden's *Gen. Robert E. Lee at Fredericksburg, December 13, 1862* (1900; fig. 51). This well-known piece from the postwar era shows the Confederate high command on Lee's Hill, where Generals Pickett, Jackson, and Longstreet (from left to right behind Lee) join their chief to observe the fighting. The absence of flags and Lee's rather be-nign expression, which accords with conceptions of him as a reluctant Chris-tian warrior, creates a subdued mood. It was from this high ground that Lee, watching Confederate infantry repulse a Union attack and then pursue the enemy, turned to Longstreet and said in low tones, "It is well this is so ter-rible! We should grow too fond of it!"[40]

Nearly four months before Fredericksburg, the eastern armies clashed at Second Bull Run. Mort Künstler's *"I Will Be Moving Within the Hour"* (1993; fig. 52) unites Lee and his three most famous subordinates—Jackson, Long-street, and Jeb Stuart—on that battlefield. Unlike Ogden, Künstler uses flags to frame the principals. "A council of war was held at the General's head-quarters that afternoon," notes the artist. "Nearby, above General Lee's head-quarters tent, the first national flag of the Confederacy is ruffled by a breeze, alongside the Confederate battle flag. The elevated viewpoint provides the opportunity to depict Lee's great Army of Northern Virginia—troops, tents, wagons, etc.—sprawled across the scenic Virginia countryside." Don Stivers's *Council of War—July 2, 1863* (1985; fig. 53), a study of Lee and Longstreet in tense discussion at Gettysburg, relies less on flags but presents Lee in stirring Lost Cause fashion: "With his fighting-blood up, he was, perhaps, the con-summate commander, the gentleman-warrior with that great flame of genius within . . . loved by his troops to the point of blind adoration; respected by his enemies to the point of blind, debilitating fear." Anyone even casually ac-quainted with the battle knows that the soldiers of the Army of the Potomac overcame their "debilitating fear" over the next two days to win the battle.[41]

Battles fought in Virginia and the rest of the Eastern Theater beckon mod-ern artists just as they did those of the Lost Cause era, and Pickett's Charge wins the palm for most-painted episode on any battlefield. In Charles Prosper Sainton's often-reprinted *Pickett's Charge, Battle of Gettysburg* (fig. 54), Lewis A. Armistead and a fragment of his brigade breach the Union line on Cemetery Ridge. A single Confederate flag, folded and tattered, contends for attention

[COPYRIGHT SECURED ACCORDING TO LAW.]

General Robert E. Lee,

From the Life-sized Portrait by E. C. BRUCE, Painted at Richmond in 1864.

FIGURE 34. *General Robert E. Lee* by Edward Caledon Bruce. Author's collection.

FIGURE 35. *Robert Edward Lee 1807–1870*, etching commissioned by the Confederate Memorial Literary Society in 1907 to mark the centennial of Lee's birth. Author's collection.

FIGURE 36. *For the Cause* by Dale Gallon. Image courtesy of Gallon Historical Art, Gettysburg, Pa., www.gallon.com.

FIGURE 37. Plate featuring *Robert E. Lee* by Michael Gnatek, as shown in a promotional flyer. Author's collection.

FIGURE 38. *The Wilderness.* "*Lee to the Rear*" by Alfred R. Waud. From John Esten Cooke, *A Life of Gen. Robert E. Lee* (New York: Appleton, 1871), opposite p. 398.

FIGURE 39. *Lee's Texans* by Don Troiani. Paintings by Don Troiani, www.historicalimagebank.com.

FIGURE 40. *The Last Meeting* by Ron Tunison, as shown in a promotional flyer.
Author's collection.

FIGURE 41. *Lee and Jackson in Council on the Night of May 1* by William Ludwell Sheppard. From Robert Underwood Johnson and Clarence Clough Buel, eds., *Battles and Leaders of the Civil War*, 4 vols. (New York: Century, 1887–88), 3:204.

FIGURE 42. *The Last Council* by Mort Künstler. From the original painting by Mort Künstler, "The Last Council," © 1990 Mort Künstler, Inc., www.mkunstler.com.

FIGURE 43. *Jackson Entering Winchester* by William DeHartburn Washington. Valentine Richmond History Center.

FIGURE 44. *General Thomas J. "Stonewall" Jackson, Winchester, Virginia, May 25, 1862* by Mort Künstler. From the original painting by Mort Künstler, "General Thomas J. 'Stonewall' Jackson," © 1988 Mort Künstler, Inc., www.mkunstler.com.

FIGURE 45. *Prayer in Stonewall Jackson's Camp* by John Chester Buttre. Author's collection.

FIGURE 46. *The General and His Chaplain* by Dale Gallon. Image courtesy of Gallon Historical Art, Gettysburg, Pa., www.gallon.com.

FIGURE 47. *The Christian General* by William L. Maughan, as shown in a promotional flyer. Author's collection.

FIGURE 48. *The Generals Were Brought To Tears* by Mort Künstler.
From the original painting by Mort Künstler, "The Generals Were Brought
To Tears," © 1992 Mort Künstler, Inc., www.mkunstler.com.

FIGURE 49. *Christian Patriots, C.S.A.* by William L. Maughan, as shown in a promotional flyer.
Author's collection.

FIGURE 50. *Jefferson Davis and the Confederate Generals* by F. Gutekunst. Author's collection.

FIGURE 51. *Gen. Robert E. Lee at Fredericksburg, December 13, 1862* by Henry A. Ogden.
Author's collection.

FIGURE 52. *"I Will Be Moving Within the Hour"* by Mort Künstler. From the original painting by Mort Künstler, "I Will Be Moving Within the Hour," © 1993 Mort Künstler, Inc., www.mkunstler.com.

FIGURE 53. *Council of War—July 2, 1863* by Don Stivers, as shown in a promotional flyer. Author's collection.

FIGURE 54. *Pickett's Charge, Battle of Gettysburg* by Charles Prosper Sainton. Author's collection.

FIGURE 55. *Forward With The Colors* by Dale Gallon. Image courtesy of Gallon Historical Art, Gettysburg, Pa., www.gallon.com.

FIGURE 56. *The High Tide* by Mort Künstler. From the original painting by Mort Künstler, "The High Tide," © 1993 Mort Künstler, Inc., www.mkunstler.com.

FIGURE 57. *Starke's Brigade Fighting with Stones Near the "Deep Cut"* by Allen C. Redwood. From Robert Underwood Johnson and Clarence Clough Buel, eds., *Battles and Leaders of the Civil War*, 4 vols. (New York: Century, 1887–88), 2:534.

FIGURE 58. *The Diehards* by Don Troiani. Paintings by Don Troiani, www.historicalimagebank.com.

FIGURE 59. *"Until We Meet Again"* by Mort Künstler. From the original painting by Mort Künstler, "Until We Meet Again," © 1990 Mort Künstler, Inc., www.mkunstler.com.

FIGURE 60. *Thompson's Station, Tennessee, March 5, 1863* by John Paul Strain, as shown in a promotional flyer. Author's collection.

with the hat held aloft on Armistead's sword. Virtually all modern artists—including Troiani, Gallon, Künstler, and Rocco—have painted at least one version, and sometimes more, of the storied southern assault. Confederate battle flags fly prominently in most recent paintings, and descriptive texts touch on Lost Cause themes of tragedy, heroism, and a southern "high water mark."[42]

Two examples convey these qualities. In Dale Gallon's *Forward With The Colors* (1997; fig. 55), a piece ablaze with the vivid reds and blues of the St. Andrew's Cross flag, "Armistead leads the gallant remnants of Pickett's Division into the Union lines at the 'High Water Mark' at Gettysburg." Künstler's *The High Tide* (1993; fig. 56), with eight flags in evidence, shows Confederate attackers confronting "a solid line of blue infantrymen . . . who will not let Pickett's men go any farther." Selected for the dust jacket of *Gettysburg: The Paintings of Mort Künstler*, this painting portrays what Künstler describes, in good Lost Cause fashion, as the defining moment of the conflict: "This is the climax of the Battle of Gettysburg—the culmination of the Confederacy's hopes, and the victory so desperately needed to save the Union." The inclusion of multiple flags in recent artworks, it must be noted, accords with historical fact. Regimental standards bunched together as Confederate casualties mounted toward the end of the attack. The interesting point lies in the seemingly obligatory modern emphasis on flags that is often missing from artworks produced during the Lost Cause era.[43]

One other pair of images from an eastern battle underscores the ties between recent and Lost Cause era art. At Second Bull Run on August 30, 1862, some of Stonewall Jackson's Louisiana troops ran out of ammunition and hurled rocks at oncoming Federals. This incident became famous as a frequently embellished example of Rebels adopting extreme measures to fend off more numerous and better-supplied Federals. A veteran of Lee's army named Allen C. Redwood produced *Starke's Brigade Fighting with Stones Near the "Deep Cut"* (fig. 57) in the 1880s for Century's Battles and Leaders series. Two Rebel flags flutter amid the action, with defenders on the Confederate right silhouetted against black powder smoke. Don Troiani's *The Diehards* (1991; fig. 58) reverses the perspective, looking toward the Confederate left, but otherwise follows Redwood's lead very closely—down to the pair of flags and smoke at the far end of the southern line. Copy from a flyer describes Confederates fighting against intimidating odds: "In a scene recalling David and Goliath, the stones of the Southern stalwarts subdued the Northern giant. . . .

Here, with ammunition almost gone, the men of Louisiana still do not fail to do their duty."[44]

Original Lost Cause art interpreted African Americans as carrying out their quotidian labors without challenging the Confederacy's slave-based social structure. Black people in The Burial of Latané, arrayed in semishadow next to the casket, fit within that model—though the man who dug the grave seems disengaged from the proceedings. A few recent artworks mount a bold effort to take the "happy and loyal slave" cliché to a new level by claiming black men served in the Confederate army. Still in its infancy, this trend has yielded some disquieting items.

Press Forward, Men! by Bradley Schmehl depicts Stonewall Jackson and his Confederate infantry during the flank attack at Chancellorsville on May 2, 1863. A St. Andrew's Cross flag adds color to the center of the picture; more important, it frames a black soldier in line with white infantrymen. "In painting Stonewall Jackson at the apogee of his greatest military triumph at Chancellorsville," remarks the artist (whose advertisements sometimes show him in Confederate uniform), "I have frozen him in a moment of time, in an aggressive, urgent posture, that I think epitomizes the image and attitude of the General which endeared him to his men and to the patriotic hearts of Southerners, and which struck fear and awe into the hearts of his enemies." A possible spoof of the explanatory text comes readily to mind: "To General Jackson's right front, frozen in a moment of time, is a steadfast, loyal, black Confederate, framed against the banner of a nation that held so much promise for him and thousands of his black comrades." Released in 2003, both Press Forward, Men! and Ron Maxwell's Gods and Generals cast Jackson, without benefit of supporting historical documentation, as a man well out of step with most fellow Confederates in terms of his relationship with black people. Schmehl later painted The Grim Harvest of War—The Valley Campaign, in which a black man in partial military dress succors a fallen Confederate under Stonewall's approving eye.[45]

The "Forgotten in Gray" website specializes in artworks designed to recover the valor and service of "Confederates of Color and foreign origin." "After more than six years of searching and dozens of artists considered," the site's organizers found someone "both properly motivated and sufficiently talented to honor the Forgotten Confederates as a series of fine art prints." The first print, titled The Chandler Boys, shows an African American named Silas Chandler tending to Andrew Chandler, his former owner, after the battle of Chickamauga. According to a detailed description, Andrew suffered a serious wound at Chickamauga that threatened loss of a leg. As surgeons prepared to amputate, "Silas used a piece of gold given to him by Andrew's mother to buy whiskey to bribe the surgeons to release him." He then "carried Andrew on his back for several miles and loaded him onto a boxcar heading to Atlanta—once there Andrew was taken to a hospital, where Silas cared for him until the family could join them—his leg, and possibly his life, were saved by Silas' attention and efforts." The website promises other artworks and offers information calculated to prove the existence of numerous black Confederates. No "Forgotten in Gray" pieces have appeared in the advertising pages of popular Civil War magazines, which suggests that the market for this niche remains very small.[46]

Women occupy a somewhat more prominent place than African Americans in recent artworks dealing with Confederate subjects. Unlike so many of the Lost Cause era's prints on military topics, The Burial of Latané has inspired no modern counterparts. The home front comes into play mainly with wives or sweethearts saying good-bye to their uniformed menfolk or with town dwellers watching generals and soldiers march through their communities. Generals and their wives—especially General and Mrs. Stonewall Jackson— often stand in for all couples. Künstler's "Until We Meet Again" (1990; fig. 59), typical of many other pieces, portrays the Jacksons in Winchester during the winter of 1862. An advertisement for a limited reissue in 2006 pronounced the piece Künstler's "Most Popular Picture!"—"an unforgettable artwork depicting the tender farewell between General Stonewall Jackson and his wife, Mary Anna." In the late 1990s, Dale Gallon launched a Romance of the Civil War series that focused solely on the theme of farewells. "Let these works stand as a constant reminder," reads a text directing readers' attention to the home front, "that not all sacrifices are made on the battlefield." This treacly subgenre has grown rapidly since the mid-1990s but lacks a single piece that approaches the power of The Burial of Latané.[47]

Prints of Nathan Bedford Forrest stand in glaring contrast to those portraying tender farewells. The most painted Confederate general who did not fight with Lee, Forrest compiled a winning record as a cavalry commander in Tennessee, Georgia, Mississippi, and elsewhere. He had a hair-trigger temper and a ferocious approach to combat that placed him at risk on many battlefields. More than two dozen horses were shot out from under him, and he claimed to have killed at least thirty Federals with his own hand. His admirers, Shelby Foote among them, call attention to his lack of formal military training in pronouncing him a genius who used speed, deception, and aggressiveness to baffle opponents. Forrest distilled his understanding of warfare into seven words: "War means fightin', and fightin' means killin'." The many prints featuring Forrest play up his undeniable qualities as a leader. John Paul Strain's Thompson's Station, Tennessee, March 5, 1863 (1997; fig. 60) celebrates a typical Forrest moment: "The Northern cavalry charged Forrest—and Forrest then 'charged too.' Astride a favorite mount—'Roderick'—Forrest led the counterattack. When 'Roderick' was shot down and he was unhorsed, Forrest scrambled to his feet and led the charge on foot. Such a ferocity was too much for the enemy, who scattered or surrendered." Thompson's Station became "part of the Forrest legend . . . a display of the up-front leadership that enabled Nathan Bedford Forrest to rise from private to lieutenant general and made him famous as the 'Wizard of the Saddle.'"[48]

Forrest's appeal as a subject for prints likely operates on several levels. He is the untutored general who beats Yankee West Pointers at their own game and shows respect for Academy graduates in Confederate service only if they earn it on the battlefield (he famously threatened Braxton Bragg, his army commander, with physical harm after the battle of Chickamauga). A self-made son of the Tennessee frontier, he suits the needs of anyone who rails against class privilege. For those in search of inveterate Yankee haters, no Confederate surpasses Forrest and his ruthless war-making. Even the hard-bitten William Tecumseh Sherman paid him a grim, if typically hyperbolic, compliment, vowing to have subordinates "follow Forrest to the death if it costs 10,000 lives and breaks the Treasury." In fact, Forrest never performed on a stage large enough to affect the strategic sweep of the war in any decisive way—a point often lost amid effusive praise from the Forrest camp.[49]

There is a disturbing side to Forrest almost completely overlooked in artworks and advertisements—though probably not by a few of those who purchase prints. He prospered as a slave trader before the war, commanded the soldiers who executed black troops when they tried to surrender at Fort Pillow in April 1864, and probably served as the first Grand Wizard of the Ku Klux Klan. These unsavory elements of Forrest's life inspired Thomas Nast to include him in a cartoon titled "This Is a White Man's Government." Published during the 1868 presidential campaign, it depicts Forrest, a Wall Street financier, and a simian Irish thug as representative of the Democratic Party. Nast placed Forrest at the center of the cartoon with a dagger inscribed "The Lost Cause" held aloft, a slaver's whip protruding from his back pocket, and one foot on the back of a prostrate black man clutching a United States flag.

Many of Forrest's modern devotees explain away Fort Pillow; others openly champion his activities with the Klan. One of the latter, writing in the late 1980s and perhaps fresh from a viewing of *The Birth of a Nation*, called Forrest "the perfect choice to lead this daring band . . . [who,] by 1867, was named *Grand Wizard of the Imperial Empire*. Sweeping across the South, meting out punishment to the guilty, the Ku Klux Klan reclaimed the lost rights of southerners to such an extent that Forrest ordered it disbanded in 1869 and withdrew from it."[50]

My own experience has yielded many examples of the centrality of race for some who celebrate Forrest. One instance will suffice. As the guest on a nationally televised program in 2006, I took issue with Shelby Foote's placing Forrest alongside Lincoln as "one of the two authentic geniuses of the Civil War." My comment provoked angry calls during the live broadcast and a flurry of e-mails over the next several days. One listener compared U. S. Grant to "a pimple on the Wizard of the Saddle's ass" and went on to state: "If after the war the triumphant North had followed the great wisdom of repatriating the freed slaves back to Africa, we wouldn't be suffering from [the] presence of these hordes of intolerable, moronic black thugs and the deadly cancer their rapes, muggings & murders represent to our society. THAT is the tragic lesson of the war deliberately ignored by social Marxist historians like you." Many other listeners made similar points, and one closed with: "WHAT WOULD FORREST DO? KEEP UP THE SKEER!" This person referred to Forrest's belief that "having gotten the 'skeer'" (the general's pronunciation of "scare") into an enemy, "you had to keep it there." The "skeer" was also the weapon Forrest wielded to terrorize targets of the Klan during the postwar years. As I thought about angry listeners who had called or sent e-mails, I could not help imagining that prints of Forrest adorned walls in some of their homes.[51]

 ### Gettysburg, Joshua L. Chamberlain, and the Irish Brigade: The Northern War in Recent Art

Artists and printmakers paid ample attention to the North's Civil War in the decades following the conflict.[52] Unlike those working with Confederate themes, they often focused on subjects that occupy only secondary or marginal positions in recent prints and sculptures. Apart from Lincoln, their three leading figures were Ulysses S. Grant, William Tecumseh Sherman, and Philip H. Sheridan—the triumvirate whose victories secured the Union in 1864–65. Gettysburg and other battles in the Eastern Theater did not predominate as they did in Lost Cause art from the period. Indeed, western victories such as Shiloh, Vicksburg, Chattanooga, and Atlanta were well represented. A series of impressive chromolithographs published in the 1880s by Louis Prang of Boston, for example, included ten western battles among the total of eighteen (six of them naval engagements). Grant and Sheridan each graced two and Sherman one; nine of the eighteen depicted battles in which one of these three generals commanded United States forces. New York's Currier and Ives and Chicago's Kurz and Allison, firms that produced a number of garish battle prints, also paid considerable attention to the Western Theater. They commissioned artworks on Grant's victories at Fort Donelson, Shiloh, Vicksburg, and Chattanooga, as well as on less famous non-Eastern Theater engagements such as Corinth, Kennesaw Mountain, Pea Ridge, Wilson's Creek, and Olustee. In the 1880s, artists painted huge cycloramas of Shiloh, Lookout Mountain, and Atlanta as well as of Gettysburg and Second Bull Run.[53]

A number of Union generals attracted long-term attention in the print market, and Grant eventually surpassed Lincoln in popularity. "While the fashion endured for portrait prints of Civil War luminaries," note Mark E. Neely Jr. and Harold Holzer in their book that provides the most detailed examination of northern iconography, "Ulysses S. Grant reigned supreme." A major catalog in the 1890s offered a dozen portraits of Sherman and six of Sheridan—as well as eleven of George B. McClellan, six of Ambrose E. Burnside, and five of George G. Meade. McClellan and Burnside, who both relinquished command of the Army of the Potomac with their actions in question, might impress modern collectors as odd choices. Meade's victory at Gettysburg positions him more favorably, though his record during the twenty-two months between July 1863 and Appomattox leaves little doubt that he, unlike Grant, lacked the skills necessary to orchestrate final United States victory. H. A. Ogden painted eight generals—the six named above plus Joseph Hooker and George H. Thomas—on storied battlefields, a set that served as frontispieces for a series of books reproducing Mathew B. Brady photographs in 1912. Ogden's scenes, claims an introductory text, show "what a great man is in his greatest moment and measures him, sums him, comprehends him." Joining pieces on Grant at Shiloh and Sherman at Kennesaw Mountain is one devoted to Sheridan at Five Forks on April 1, 1865 (1897; fig. 61). Ogden's Sheridan exudes energy and success. Mounted on his celebrated horse, Rienzi, and holding a guidon aloft with his right hand, he leaps across a breastwork as Confederates cower or throw up their hands in surrender.[54]

No other Federal general provided more dramatic potential than Sheridan, whom artists often portrayed amid pulsing action. The two Prang chromolithographs, both by Swedish-born military artist Thure de Thulstrup, draw on Sheridan's 1864 Valley campaign. In *Sheridan's Final Charge at Winchester* (1886), the pugnacious general leads his cavalry in a sweeping assault against the exposed left flank of Jubal Early's Army of the Valley on September 19. In *Sheridan's Ride, October 19, 1864* (1886; fig. 62), "Little Phil" carries a guidon while galloping along the Union line at Cedar Creek following a twelve-mile ride from Winchester to the battlefield. "Sheridan's Ride" to Cedar Creek, made famous by Thomas Buchanan Read's wartime poem and early postwar painting (both titled *Sheridan's Ride*), remained a staple of northern iconography into the early twentieth century. As late as 1930, D. W. Griffith included an extended treatment of the incident in *Abraham Lincoln*. The exuberant narrative accompanying Prang's chromolithographs pulls out all the stops regarding Sheridan's Ride, asserting that it "lights up the sombre pages of the history of the Great Rebellion, even as the 'Charge of the Six Hundred' sparkles among the shadows of European warfare." Kurz and Allison's *Battle of Cedar Creek* (1890) positions Sheridan in the middle foreground, a fearless general brandishing his saber as Confederates raise the white flag.[55]

Although far less interesting to most white northerners than the exploits of Grant, Sherman, or Sheridan, African American military service nonetheless attracted attention from some publishers. Four Kurz and Allison prints feature black soldiers, most notably *Storming Fort Wagner* (1890; fig. 63), devoted to the 54th Massachusetts Infantry's assault led by Robert Gould Shaw in July 1863, and *The Fort Pillow Massacre* (1892), an unflinching portrayal of the cold-blooded execution of black soldiers on April 12, 1864, by Nathan Bedford Forrest's Confederates.[56] Currier and Ives also offered *Gallant Charge of the Fifty Fourth Massachusetts (Colored) Regiment* (1863); like all that company's battle prints, it combines bright colors, fanciful composition, and crude execution. A few other items from the decades following the war deal with other aspects of African American military service or the theme of emancipation.[57]

By far the most impressive acknowledgment of black soldiers came from the hands of a sculptor rather than a painter. Augustus Saint-Gaudens's monument to Colonel Shaw and the 54th Massachusetts (fig. 64), unveiled on Boston Common on May 31, 1897, belongs in the front rank of all artworks dealing with the Civil War. One eminent art historian remarked that it "may well be the greatest piece of public sculpture ever made in the United States, the one which embodies best our country's most enduring tragedy, its hope, and our common fate." Saint-Gaudens positioned Shaw in the middle of the sculpture, riding alongside his marching men (some critics have carped about Shaw's being on a horse and thus elevated above his African American troops—a complaint possible only from someone unaware of the fact that colonels usually rode horses and infantrymen, whatever their color, did not). The soldier's individual faces suggest purpose and strength, their powerful stride indicating an eagerness to get on with the task of ending slavery. Overall, the monument met the original intent of those who hoped it would "mark the public gratitude to the fallen hero [Shaw]" while also commemorating "that great event wherein he was a leader by which the title of colored men as citizen soldiers was fixed beyond recall."[58]

Neither the North's three leading military figures nor black soldiers have inspired much interest among modern artists. Grant receives far less attention than Lee and several second-echelon Confederate generals.[59] Sherman has been banished to the fringe of recent artworks, and Sheridan, so popular with the North's wartime generation, has fared no better. Battles in the Western Theater where Grant, Sherman, and Sheridan made their reputations trail far behind some less important eastern contests where Stonewall Jackson fought. And what about Grant and Sherman as the war's most important command team? Artists have manifested almost no interest in their collaborations at Shiloh, Vicksburg, or Chattanooga. In *How the West Was Won* John Ford imagined the two Union heroes' discussion at Shiloh on the night of April 6, 1862, but no artist has offered anything remotely comparable to Julio's *Last Meeting* or its many recent incarnations. Moreover, artists seldom treat any of the top Union leaders with the reverence generally accorded Lee and Jackson. To judge from recent artworks, not a single Union commander read to children from the Bible or attended church with young people.

Mort Künstler's "*On To Richmond*" (1991; fig. 65) typifies a modern sensibility regarding Grant. It shows the general on May 7, 1864, as the Army of the Potomac marches away from the Wilderness battlefield. Silhouetted against the orange-red flames of burning woods, Grant, staring straight ahead with a cigar clenched in his teeth, rides past cheering soldiers who have just realized their commander means to press the Rebels as strongly as possible. "This non-descriptive [sic] general on horseback was determined to finish what had been started so long ago," a restrained text informs potential purchasers, "and there would be no recrossing of the Rapidan. Truly, this moment amongst the thick woods of the Wilderness could be called the turning point in the east, and perhaps in the war." One of the few pieces relating to

Sheridan, Don Stivers's "*To Make Hell Tremble*" (1990; fig. 66), adopts a more subdued tone than the rousing Civil War era prints. Surrounded by subordinates near Five Forks on April 1, 1865, the general uses his sword to trace tactical movements in the dirt. As the accompanying text explains, "Sheridan conveying both the plan and spirit of the attack by drawing in the enemy's very soil his design for victory—literally carving his will with his saber into the enemy's territory—is the symbolic manifestation of a commander's role in any war." Planning an offensive surely represents one of a general's roles, but by taking Sheridan off his horse and out of the action Stivers forfeits the magnetic presence in combat prized by an earlier generation of artists.[60]

The shelf of books from leading artists in the Civil War field underscores how infrequently Grant, Sherman, and Sheridan turn up. In addition to "*On To Richmond*," Künstler's two major books offer Grant and Sherman twice each. Grant appears once in Don Troiani's *American Battles* and not at all in *Don Troiani's Civil War*, twice with Lee at Appomattox in Keith Rocco's *The Soldier's View*, and twice in John Paul Strain's *Witness to the Civil War* (in one of the two with Lee at Appomattox). Sherman does not grace the pages of Troiani's, Rocco's, or Strain's volumes. Just as tellingly, none of the artists includes a single episode in Philip Sheridan's Civil War career—though Künstler's *Sheridan's Men* (1982) shows a group of Union cavalry troopers during the 1864 Shenandoah Valley campaign. Lee and Jackson, by way of comparison, figure in more than 125 plates in the books. If either Jeb Stuart or Longstreet—roughly the equivalent of Sheridan in terms of their relationship to Lee—were added to the total, the Confederate margin would widen considerably.[61]

Recent art also relegates black soldiers to cameo appearances. Virtually absent from advertisements in the mainline Civil War magazines, they crop up occasionally in some of the artists' books. The men of the 54th Massachusetts, made famous in 1989 by *Glory*, garner more attention than any other black unit.[62] Don Troiani has moved beyond the 54th in paintings of the 29th United States Colored Troops at the battle of the Crater and a study of the 1st South Carolina Infantry. The South Carolinians, formed in late 1862 to fight for the Union and commanded by Harvard-educated Thomas Wentworth Higginson, preceded the 54th into service by many months and campaigned in the Deep South. Troiani's *1st South Carolina Volunteer Infantry* (1996; fig. 67) recognizes that the "Black soldier's place in the annals of the Civil War was hard fought and dearly won; calling for an extra measure of heroism to dispel the widespread opposition to their enlistment in the Union Army." The paucity of works devoted to United States Colored Troops suggests that in the arena of Civil War art, unlike in the public sphere and Hollywood, the Emancipation Cause remains elusive.[63]

Cinematic influences have certainly given a boost to two of the three northern subjects most often selected by recent artists. Gettysburg and Joshua Lawrence Chamberlain, inextricably linked for three days in July 1863, exemplify the northern war effort for many Americans who watched Burns's documentary and Maxwell's *Gettysburg*. Burns himself best describes how the battle and the soldier came to his attention. *The Killer Angels* "literally changed my life," he writes in an essay about his documentary. It "told the story of three of the most important days in American history; the high-water mark of the Confederacy, the mistake of all mistakes by Robert E. Lee . . . *Gettysburg*, the greatest battle ever fought in the Western hemisphere."

With the battle's preeminence established, Burns moves on to his hero: "But what was important to me about the book was that it introduced me, for the first time, to Joshua Lawrence Chamberlain. And for all intents and purposes, it was the life of Chamberlain which convinced me to embark on the most difficult and satisfying experience of my life." Burns sees Chamberlain as "the best kind of history, the best kind of American." A successful officer on many battlefields, the former college professor maneuvered his troops on Little Round Top in a manner "that saves the Union army and quite possibly the Union itself." Burns pronounces Appomattox to be Chamberlain's finest hour, in which he helped set the stage for successful reunion by honoring his Confederate opponents. Although Chamberlain's postwar writings had laid the groundwork for later admirers, Burns thought Maine's most famous Civil War soldier had been overlooked and through his documentary sought to remedy that situation. Together with Maxwell's film, his effort almost certainly succeeded to an extent greater than he could have imagined.[64]

If Burns could say that Chamberlain had been neglected, no one could say that Gettysburg had been underappreciated over the years. Artistic continuity with Civil War era precedents exists in the case of Gettysburg, which always has been a magnet for painters. Two massive works from the wartime generation marked the Union repulse of Pickett's Charge. Peter Rothermel's *The Battle of Gettysburg and Pickett's Charge* (1870), commissioned by the state of Pennsylvania, crowds an enormous number of figures into more than 535 square feet of action. General Meade hovers at one edge of the canvas, and soldiers from the Keystone State dominate the foreground. A smaller piece by Rothermel, titled *The Death of General Reynolds* (1870), shows the general's body being carried away from the battlefield on July 1. French artist Paul Phi-

FIGURE 61. *Sheridan at Five Forks* by Henry A. Ogden. Author's collection.

FIGURE 62. *Sheridan's Ride, October 19, 1864* by Thure de Thulstrup. Author's collection.

FIGURE 63. *Storming Fort Wagner* by Kurz and Allison. Author's collection.

FIGURE 64. Monument to Col. Robert Gould Shaw and the 54th Massachusetts Infantry by Augustus Saint-Gaudens. Photograph courtesy of Caroline E. Janney.

FIGURE 65. *"On To Richmond"* by Mort Künstler. From the original painting by Mort Künstler, "On To Richmond," © 1991 Mort Künstler, Inc., www.mkunstler.com.

FIGURE 66. *"To Make Hell Tremble"* by Don Stivers, as shown in a promotional flyer. Author's collection.

FIGURE 67. *1st South Carolina Volunteer Infantry* by Don Troiani. Paintings by Don Troiani, www.historicalimagebank.com.

FIGURE 68. *For God Sake Forward* by Don Troiani. Paintings by Don Troiani, www.historicalimagebank.com.

FIGURE 69. *Hancock's Ride* by Dale Gallon. Image courtesy of Gallon Historical Art, Gettysburg, Pa., www.gallon.com.

FIGURE 70. *Bayonet* by Don Troiani. Paintings by Don Troiani, www.historicalimagebank.com.

FIGURE 71. *Hold at All Costs* by Dale Gallon. Image courtesy of Gallon Historical Art, Gettysburg, Pa., www.gallon.com.

FIGURE 72. *Salute of Honor* by Mort Künstler. From the original painting by Mort Künstler, "Salute of Honor," © 2001 Mort Künstler, Inc., www.mkunstler.com.

FIGURE 73. *Honor Answering Honor* by Don Spaulding, as shown in a promotional flyer. Author's collection.

FIGURE 74. *The Proffered Wreath* by Don Stivers, as shown in a promotional flyer. Author's collection.

FIGURE 75. *"Clear the Way"* by Don Troiani. Paintings by Don Troiani,
www.historicalimagebank.com.

FIGURE 76. *Pride of Erin* by Dale Gallon. Image courtesy of Gallon Historical Art,
Gettysburg, Pa., www.gallon.com.

lippoteaux worked on a far larger scale in *Cyclorama of the Battle of Gettysburg* (1884), a 35 x 400-foot behemoth that affords a 360-degree view of the climax of Pickett's Charge. Generals Hancock and Armistead are among the identifiable figures in the cyclorama, described by one newspaper as "truly colossal . . . a marvel of artistic learning and sentiment."[65]

Over the past twenty years, northern characters and incidents prominent in Shaara's novel and Maxwell's film have become increasingly evident in artworks. Generals John Buford, John F. Reynolds, and Winfield Scott Hancock illustrate this trend. Mort Künstler's *There's the Devil to Pay* (1990) captures Buford and Reynolds on July 1 as Confederates approach the Union position on McPherson's Ridge. Buford gestures toward the Rebels; Reynolds surveys the field through his glasses; and artillerists work their guns at either margin of the print. Buford "forced the Confederates to accept battle on his terms," reads the flyer, "on terrain which would favor the Union forces. In the greater battle to follow, the strategic initiative of the Civil War would pass from the South to the North." In *For God Sake Forward* (1996; fig. 68) by Don Troiani, General Reynolds oversees deployment of the Iron Brigade just minutes after the moment Künstler painted in *There's the Devil to Pay*. The brigade hastens toward the developing action, and "Reynold's [sic] himself advanced to lead them on, calling 'Forward men, forward for God's Sake and drive those fellows out of those woods.' . . . The shaken Confederates began falling back, leaving hundreds behind to be taken prisoner." Dale Gallon's *Hancock's Ride* (1993; fig. 69) shifts to July 3 before Pickett's Charge. The general rides purposefully along his lines on Cemetery Ridge, past cheering members of the Irish Brigade, whose distinctive green flag adds interest to the scene. "Fifty years after that epic day," reads the flyer, "one veteran recalled how 'Hancock . . . by his magnificent presence, inspired his men with courage and determination.'"[66]

Nearly invisible in art before the 1980s, Joshua Chamberlain dominates all his comrades-in-arms—including Buford, Hancock, and Reynolds—as the hero of action on Little Round Top's smoke-filled slope. His trajectory most clearly reveals the enormous impact of Shaara's novel, Burns's documentary, and Maxwell's *Gettysburg*. Within the overall genre of artworks devoted to northern themes, Chamberlain boasts more than twice as many pieces as Grant and five times the number of Sherman, Sheridan, McClellan, and Meade combined. Of nearly 100 items listed with secondary-market values on a flyer from Dale Gallon in 2003, prints of Chamberlain occupied the first and third positions. Moreover, he is by far the most painted Union commander in the five major books by Troiani, Künstler, Strain, Rocco, and Gallon; his two dozen images exceed the combined total for Hancock, Grant, Buford, and Reynolds—the next four most-painted officers.[67]

Chamberlain on Little Round Top has come to symbolize the decisive moment of Gettysburg and possibly the war. The colonel brandishes his sword while sprinting downhill toward stunned Confederates in Don Troiani's *Bayonet* (1988; fig. 70). "On July 2, 1863, there occurred one of those moments where history was changed by a band of resolute men," affirms the text. Against an "overwhelming force of Confederates" (actually one regiment—the 15th Alabama), the 20th Maine seized the initiative: "The heroes in blue rushed into their attackers with new ferocity, driving the shocked foe back, . . . and saving the day—and perhaps the Battle of Gettysburg—for the Union." In Gallon's *Hold at All Costs* (1991; fig. 71), Chamberlain stands erect amid smoke from his regiment's musket fire, his left arm casually resting on his hip as he peers directly at the viewer. He personifies coolness under fire. "I have always been impressed with Joshua Chamberlain and his quality of leadership," writes Gallon. "His actions on 2 July 1863 at Gettysburg make him one of the great Civil War commanders."[68]

The fate of Chamberlain's counterpart at the opposite end of the Union line on July 2, 1863, provides a useful contrast. Colonel David Ireland and his 137th New York Infantry faced far greater odds on Culp's Hill than did the 20th Maine on Little Round Top. Chamberlain's men confronted one regiment of Alabamians who represented the far right flank of a single southern brigade; Ireland's regiment found itself opposite one big Confederate brigade supported closely by another. At one point, the 137th absorbed Confederate fire from three directions. Ireland saw his soldiers fall in exactly the same proportion as those in the 20th Maine. The 137th entered the fight with 423 men and lost 137 (32.4 percent); the 20th suffered 125 casualties of 386 engaged (32.4 percent). The New Yorkers lost a third more killed than their comrades from Maine. William F. Fox, a respected nineteenth-century chronicler of Union military units that suffered heavy casualties, praised the New Yorkers and Chamberlain's men equally. The 137th "won special honors at Gettysburg" for its defense "against a desperate attack of vastly superior force." The New Yorkers and the rest of George S. Greene's brigade defended Culp's Hill in "one of the most noteworthy incidents of the war." As for the 20th Maine, it "did much to save the day at Gettysburg" in "an episode which forms a conspicuous feature in the history of that battle." Yet Ireland's name and his unit's service on Culp's Hill remain almost completely unknown, and no artist has chosen them as a subject. Perhaps a novelist, screenwriter, or filmmaker will yet take up this cause.[69]

Artists have not neglected Chamberlain's role at Appomattox. One of the two most obvious expressions of the Reconciliation Cause in recent artworks (depictions of Grant and Lee at Appomattox would be the other), paintings of Chamberlain at the surrender ceremony on April 12, 1865, focus on his ordering Union soldiers to shoulder arms as Confederate infantry units approached to lay down their weapons. Maj. Gen. John B. Gordon, whose troops surrendered to Chamberlain's, wrote admiringly after the war about Chamberlain's behavior. Artworks such as Troiani's *The Last Salute* (1988), Künstler's *Salute of Honor* (2001; fig. 72), and Don Spaulding's *Honor Answering Honor* (1988; fig. 73) credit Chamberlain with setting an important conciliatory tone. All draw on Chamberlain's postwar account in *The Passing of the Armies* quoted in Chapter 1 above—a version of the surrender proceedings historian William Marvel has described as "Chamberlain's glorified version of events." Künstler observes that Chamberlain ordered a "soldier's salute, delivered in respect to the defeated Southerners. . . . Gordon immediately recognized this remarkable, generous gesture offered by fellow Americans—and responded with a like salute. A new day had begun—built on this salute of honor at Appomattox."[70]

Don Stivers's *The Proffered Wreath* (1989; fig. 74) takes Chamberlain beyond Appomattox to the Grand Review of United States forces in late May 1865. In *The Passing of the Armies*, Chamberlain adopts his usual flowery style to describe a key moment: "Now a girlish form, robed white as her spirit, presses close; modest, yet resolute, eyes fixed on her purpose. She reaches up towards me with a wreath of rare flowers, close-braided, fit for a viking's arming, or victor's crown." *The Proffered Wreath* depicts this scene. Turning to his left as Charlemagne, his battle-scarred horse, rears on cobblestoned Pennsylvania Avenue, Chamberlain looks down at the woman holding out a "victory wreath." The text explains why she would offer it to Chamberlain: "Of countless souls associated with the Army of the Potomac over its four years of life and death, none could come to symbolize its very essence more than Joshua L. Chamberlain." More than the Army of the Potomac seems to be in play, though the artist's text does not acknowledge it. With United States flags to his left and right and the new Capitol dome gleaming behind, Stivers's Chamberlain can be read as a symbol of the triumphant nation itself.[71]

The third popular northern subject taps into enthusiasms for both the Civil War and Irish American history. The Irish Brigade fought with the Army of the

Potomac, its members shedding blood profligately at Antietam and Fredericksburg and fighting hard in the Wheat Field at Gettysburg. Although not given to painting their faces blue before entering battle, the men otherwise fit the stereotype of wild Celtic warriors eager to launch headlong attacks (if Hollywood were to make a film about the brigade, Mel Gibson would seem to be the obvious choice for director). A leading scholar of the brigade accentuates its costly combat record: "During the war, two soldiers died of disease or accident for every one who died as a consequence of battle. For the Irish Brigade, however, this ratio was reversed: two died of battle wounds for every one who died of disease or accident." For William F. Fox, the "Irish Brigade was, probably, the best known of any brigade organization, it having made an unusual reputation for dash and gallantry."[72] Colorful leaders such as Brig. Gen. Thomas Francis Meagher, a native of Waterford, Ireland, and distinctive green banners adorned with gold shamrocks and harps enhance the brigade's value as a subject for artists. *Gettysburg* includes a scene depicting the Irish Brigade before going into battle, while *Gods and Generals* makes much of the brigade's doomed assault up Marye's Heights at Fredericksburg.[73]

Like Gettysburg, the Irish Brigade attracted artistic attention in the nineteenth century. Paul Wood's *Absolution Under Fire* (1891) offered a rare fusion of religion and patriotism in a northern subject. It paid tribute to Father William Corby, who climbed atop a large rock on Cemetery Ridge and gave a general absolution to the brigade's many Catholics before they entered combat on July 2. Because the soldiers were about to face death, Wood's painting exuded an urgency absent in the more relaxed religious atmosphere of Buttre's *Prayer in Stonewall Jackson's Camp*. This well-known episode with the Irish Brigade found its way into Maxwell's film and attracts attention from visitors to Gettysburg National Military Park, where a statue of Corby stands on the spot.[74]

Modern painters typically follow the brigade into one of its many ghastly actions. No other artist distills all the elements of the unit's attraction into one image more successfully than Don Troiani in *"Clear the Way"* (1987; fig. 75)—the most valuable of the artist's prints on northern subjects. Set at Fredericksburg, where the brigade lost roughly 550 of its 1,200 men attacking well-protected Confederates on Marye's Heights, it conveys a wild determination, Irish pride beneath a striking green banner (only the 28th Massachusetts, among the brigade's five regiments, carried a green flag at Fredericksburg), and certain loss on ground already thick with fallen comrades. "For the battle-hardened veterans of the dauntless Irish Brigade," reads a text much concerned with ethnicity and valor, "this unflinching assault . . . embodied the proud, resolute spirit contained in the Gaelic motto of one of its units: Faugh-a-Ballagh! Clear the way!" A quotation from the most dominant historical figure in recent Civil War art clinches the case for the brigade's valor: " 'Never were men so brave,' recalled Robert E. Lee after the war."[75]

Mort Künstler's *"Raise the Colors and Follow Me"* (1991) and Dale Gallon's *Pride of Erin* (1992; fig. 76) deal with Antietam and Gettysburg respectively. In the former, Brig. Gen. Meagher and the brigade's famous flag stand out among soldiers attacking Confederates in the infamous Sunken Road. Künstler's narrative stresses Celtic aggressiveness and willingness to absorb huge casualties. "In a word, Meagher's soldiers 'ached for a good fight.' . . . Again and again, Meagher led his men toward the blazing road. . . . The terrible testament to the valor of the Irish Brigade was written in blood on September 17th, 1862. Names of the dead on wooden boards which filled the green pastures of the Roulette Farm were the only monuments to their bravery at Antietam." Gallon's piece shows the brigade attacking through the Wheat Field on July 2, green flags dotting their line and casualties littering the ground behind them: "With men falling at every step and the source of the fire hidden by the smoke and shadows from the tree covered Stony Hill, the Irishmen, with their banners flying, had displayed the stoic courage of seasoned veterans. Now, face to face with their tormentors, it was payback time!"[76]

 Bringing What Past to Life?

A mailing from the Postal Commemorative Society in early 2007 graphically demonstrates which side has paid back the other in the world of Civil War art. Touting a "stamps collection" that "includes every U.S. Civil War stamp ever issued," it probably struck the unwary as an offering from the United States Postal Service. Images of seven stamps from the 1930s through the 1990s adorn the cover. "This exclusive Civil War collection," claims the brochure's colorful text, "brings the past to life as never before!" Purchasers can expect to derive insights into the historical watershed that, more than any other, "transformed our nation so dramatically." Stamps alone could not accomplish so much, but the ones in this collection are "enhanced by the art of renowned artist Mort Künstler in a stirring history of the War Between the States."[77]

The design of the brochure smacks of something suitable for publication by the Confederacy's Post Office Department—had it survived to target Civil War enthusiasts with a philatelic bent. A detail from Künstler's *The*

Last Rally (1991), which shows Lee holding a St. Andrew's Cross battle flag at Sayler's Creek, provides the front cover's background (fig. 77). Three of the seven stamps on the cover commemorate Lee, Jackson, and their victory at Chancellorsville. Pages 2–5 of the six-page brochure reproduce a half-dozen stamps: the United Confederate Veterans from the 1930s; the Lee, Jackson, Chancellorsville, and Gettysburg stamps from a set issued in 1995; and a stamp from the 1930s with portraits of Grant, Sherman, and Sheridan. Four of the six accompanying paintings by Künstler focus on the Army of Northern Virginia's high command; Lee, Jackson, and Stuart are each in three and Longstreet in one. The other two paintings show the climax of Pickett's Charge and—the one paired with the stamp featuring Grant, Sherman, and Sheridan—the battle of Chattanooga. The six paintings contain eleven Confederate and two United States flags. None includes an identifiable United States officer; indeed, the piece devoted to Chattanooga examines the battle from a Confederate perspective.[78]

An accompanying letter from the director of the Postal Commemorative Society refers to the stamp collection as a "great gift for any history lover" that will be "cherished for generations to come." Robert E. Lee also had future generations in mind when he wrote Jubal Early in late 1865 about hoping "to transmit, if possible, the truth to posterity, and do justice to our brave Soldiers."[79] Could he have envisioned a brochure more than 140 years hence that sold United States stamps while laying out a pro-Confederate artistic history celebrating "J. E. B. Stuart's dashing spirit, reflected in his long, flowing beard and plumed hat . . . Stonewall Jackson's unflinching courage at First Bull Run . . . and Lee's compelling ability to inspire his officers and troops"? Or a brochure that names him before Grant on a list of the war's leaders, refers to the conflict as the War between the States, and never mentions which side triumphed? The answer is almost certainly no.

The Lost Cause's Confederacy of gallant leaders and storied victories in defense of home ground retains enormous vitality in recent artworks. "Happy Birthday General Lee" proclaims an advertisement for three prints tied to the 200th anniversary of the general's birth.[80] Grant receives fewer such gestures, and his cause, which confirmed American nationalism and forced a redefinition of United States citizenship, has been reduced to little more than prints of a battle in Pennsylvania, a college professor who did well as a soldier, and a few thousand men who fought under green flags.[81]

FIGURE 77. Cover of a brochure for the Postal Commemorative Society's Civil War Stamps Collection. Author's collection.

Epilogue

uring the spring of 2003, the four Civil War interpretive traditions clashed over a piece of public art in Richmond, Virginia. Adherents of the Reconciliation and Emancipation Causes vanquished those of the Lost Cause, with the Union Cause typically relegated to a secondary position. Controversy centered on a statue depicting Lincoln and his son Tad during their visit to the Confederate capital on April 4–5, 1865. Commissioned by a nonprofit organization and donated to the Richmond National Battlefield Park, New York sculptor David Frech's life-size statue (fig. 78) was dedicated on the 138th anniversary of the event. The bronze piece rests on a hill overlooking the James River at historic Tredegar Iron Works, readily visible to tourists and others who enter the National Park Service visitor center for the Richmond battlefields. Lincoln's presence departs from a venerable Lost Cause tradition in Richmond. More than 18,000 Rebel dead lie in the city's Hollywood Cemetery, often termed the Confederacy's Arlington; impressive statues of Lee, Jefferson Davis, Jeb Stuart, and Stonewall Jackson erected between 1890 and 1919 greet motorists along Monument Avenue; and the White House of the Confederacy, now hemmed in by buildings of Virginia Commonwealth University's Health System, stands a few blocks from the state capitol, where the Confederate Congress met. No other city contains so much evidence of how white southerners remembered the Confederate war.[1]

Supporters of the Lincoln statue most often trumpeted it as an emblem of reconciliation. Historian Harold Holzer, a Lincoln scholar and co-chairman of the U.S. Lincoln Bicentennial Commission, called plans to erect the statue "an historic symbol of unity and reconciliation." Although Holzer's mention of unity addressed the overriding goal of those who saw the conflict as a struggle for Union, the thrust of his comments dealt with reconciliation. "In my Lincoln writings," he stated, "I have quoted a journalist who recalled Lincoln's visit to Richmond: 'He came not as a conqueror, not with bitterness in his heart, but with kindness. He came as a friend, to alleviate sorrow and suffering—to rebuild what has been destroyed.'" A fund-raising appeal for the statue took a similar tack. Inviting any "Fellow Admirer of Abraham Lincoln" to purchase a miniature of Frech's statue (the proceeds would help pay for the monument), the mailing asserted that "most Virginians and most Ameri-

FIGURE 78. Statue of Abraham Lincoln and his son Tad by David Frech.
Photograph © Chris Heisey, reproduced with his permission.

cans, of course, welcome—as long overdue—this symbol of reconciliation in Richmond." It also quoted James M. McPherson's observation that Lincoln's journey to Richmond represented "the most unforgettable scene of this unforgettable war." A month earlier, the mailing continued, "in his Second Inaugural Address Lincoln had passionately urged all Americans to strive, 'with malice toward none, with charity for all . . . to bind up the nation's wounds' in order to prepare the way for peace." At the statue's dedication, the nonprofit group's chairman predicted that Frech's bronze commemorating Lincoln's "visit of reconciliation" would bring Americans together in the future.[2]

The statue also carried an emancipationist message. Fund-raising literature included a memorandum from the Reverend Alice W. Harris pronouncing the Lincoln statue "of special interest" because her grandmother was a slave. "To me, and to many other people like me, this will be a truly great moment—almost a miraculous moment," Harris wrote. "To me, the statue will represent the freedom that I enjoy and the emancipation that President Lincoln issued for my ancestors and so many others." Other mailings emphasized Lincoln's warm reception by former slaves. One quoted a northern observer: "It was the great deliverer meeting the delivered. . . . Such wild indescribable joy I never witnessed. The majority of the thousands who crowded the streets and hindered our advance were slaves. Now they were free, beholding him who had given them their liberty." Former Virginia governor L. Douglas Wilder, the first African American to hold that office, described the statue as "fantastic" and termed Lincoln "a part of history that just cannot be ignored." The "vitriol and stridency" of those who opposed the statue amazed Wilder, but, as he said, "Time marches on. They will be left in their own time." Although perhaps taken aback by the depth of antipathy toward the statue, Wilder knew public monuments stirred fierce emotions. Less than a decade earlier, Richmond had debated whether to place a statue of Arthur Ashe, the city's most famous black athlete, on Monument Avenue. Challenged by Richmonders who insisted the avenue should remain a site of Confederate commemoration, the statue went up in 1996.[3]

The Sons of Confederate Veterans spearheaded opposition to Lincoln at Tredegar. The commander of the Virginia division of the scv attacked the statue as "a slap in the face of a lot of brave men and women who went through four years of unbelievable hell fighting an invasion of Virginia led by President Lincoln." Placed at Tredegar "ostensibly for reconciliation," asserted an scv press release two years later, the statue had been "promoted by career bureaucrats of the National Park Service"; the city's "business, political and educational establishment were sucked into believing that this statue would help business and improve Richmond's 'image.'" A few dozen protesters, some of whom had gathered earlier at Jefferson Davis's grave in Hollywood Cemetery, attended the dedication. One brandished a poster with Lincoln's face that read: "WANTED: For War Crimes." A small plane circled overhead pulling a banner emblazoned with *Sic Semper Tyrannis* (Thus Always to Tyrants), the Virginia state motto, which John Wilkes Booth shouted just after shooting Lincoln at Ford's Theater. Some of those most angry about the ceremony likened Lincoln to Hitler, Osama Bin Laden, and other war criminals of the twentieth and twenty-first centuries.[4]

Ironically, neo-Confederates mentioned Union about as often as did the statue's admirers. They did so within the context of anti-Lincoln writings by Thomas DiLorenzo and others, who, remarked an officer of the SCV, "have focused on Lincoln's ambition, motives, deceits, and illegalities." Reporters covering the dedication quoted DiLorenzo, who charged Lincoln with the behavior of "a military dictator and a tyrant" in perpetrating a number of horrors. "The Union of the founding fathers was a voluntary union," wrote DiLorenzo in stalwart Lost Cause fashion, but "he destroyed the voluntary union and created a coerced union."[5]

What would Lincoln have made of all this? On April 5, 1865, he wrote a brief statement about his conditions for peace. Appomattox lay just four days in the future, though he knew only that the killing would not continue much longer. "As to peace," he stated, "I have said before, and now repeat, that three things are indispensable. 1. The restoration of the national authority throughout all the States. 2. No receding by the Executive of the United States on the slavery question. . . . 3. No cessation of hostilities short of an end of the war, and the disbanding of all force hostile to the government." Union, emancipation, and peace based on unconditional Confederate military surrender—in that order—dominated the president's mind. He would address the nature of reconstruction a few days later but had told Grant in late March that, apart from the conditions listed above, he wanted to extend lenient terms to the Rebels. Attention to reconciliation and emancipation in the Tredegar affair would please him, as would the marginal status of neo-Confederate bitterenders. But what about his conception of Union as a democratic beacon and an expression of nationhood tested and strengthened by war? Its absence at Tredegar, which mirrors its fate in recent films and modern artworks, surely would leave him puzzled in contemplating the landscape of recent Civil War memory.[6]

Notes

INTRODUCTION

1. For observations by a number of leading scholars about Hollywood's handling of historical subjects, see Mark C. Carnes, "Hollywood History," *American Heritage* 46 (September 1995): 74–84.

2. This is not to say that the 1970s were bereft of good titles on the Civil War. For example, the final two volumes of Allan Nevins's magisterial *The War for the Union* appeared in 1971 and the third volume of Shelby Foote's *The Civil War: A Narrative* in 1974. Yet Michael Shaara had difficulty finding a publisher for his novel about Gettysburg titled *The Killer Angels*, finally placing it with New York publisher David McKay. The novel won the Pulitzer Prize for fiction in 1975 and went on to become a highly influential and best-selling title. On the Centennial, see Robert J. Cook, *Troubled Commemoration: The American Civil War Centennial, 1961–1965* (Baton Rouge: Louisiana State University Press, 2007). Bruce Catton, the most widely read Civil War historian of the era, reflected on the Centennial's meanings in "Lest We Forget," *American Heritage* 12 (August 1961): 26–27. For a clever spoof of Centennial excesses, see T. Lawrence Connelly, *Will Success Spoil Jeff Davis? The Last Book about the Civil War* (New York: McGraw-Hill, 1963).

3. Matthew Hodgson, "New Challenges, New Opportunities," in *Books from Chapel Hill, 1922–1997: A Complete Catalog of Publications from the University of North Carolina Press* (Chapel Hill: University of North Carolina Press, 1997), xxx. On Civil War publishing at the UNC Press, see Gary W. Gallagher, *The Civil War at Chapel Hill: The University of North Carolina Press and the Great American Conflict* (Wilmington, N.C.: Broadfoot, [1989]). Not all publishers shunned the Civil War in the 1970s and early 1980s — most notably Louisiana State University Press, which led the field in the number and quality of titles. Since 1985, the UNC Press has published, on average, more than four titles per year on the Civil War broadly defined; two series published by the press, Civil War America and Military Campaigns of the Civil War, both of which I edit, contain more than 70 titles between them.

4. For a thoughtful look at the ebb and flow of interest in the Civil War during the last forty years of the twentieth century, see Drew Gilpin Faust, "'We Should Grow Too Fond of It': Why We Love the Civil War," *Civil War History* 50 (December 2004): 368–83. Faust counted the number of Civil War books reviewed in the *Journal of Southern History* from the 1970s forward: "In 1976 the JSH reviewed 13 Civil War books. In 2002 it reviewed 66. That is a fivefold increase. How did we get from there to here?

From 1976 through 1987 the numbers average 13 a year, varying between a low of 7 in 1980 to a high of 21 in 1982. . . . Then in 1989 there is a dramatic rise—to 27 books. . . . For four years the number of books hovers at this level, and then we see a second significant increase, in 1993, to 45 books. Over the next decade the average number per year is 48, though the two most recent years, with totals of 64 and 66, may represent the beginning of a third, still higher, phase" (p. 374). See also Greg Brooking, "SCWH Meets in Birmingham," in Society of Civil War Historians Newsletter 20 (Winter 2007): [1, 3], for comparative data about publishing trends. The article gives the following totals for Civil War titles: 713 in 1960–64, 471 in 1980–84, and 1,455 in 2000–2004.

5. Jim Weeks, Gettysburg: Memory, Market, and an American Shrine (Princeton, N.J.: Princeton University Press, 2003), 171–72; Staff of Civil War Times Illustrated, "The Commemorative Years," Civil War Times Illustrated 27 (March 1988): 24–29.

6. On the fight over Manassas in 1988, see chapter 10 of Joan M. Zenzen, Battling for Manassas: The Fifty-Year Preservation Struggle at Manassas National Battlefield Park (University Park: Penn State University Press, 1998). Zenzen argued that the "Manassas mall controversy raised public awareness about historic preservation in ways no other previous issue had" (p. 133). In addition to a number of local preservation groups, two national nonprofit preservation organizations were founded in the late 1980s and early 1990s, the Association for the Preservation of Civil War Sites (1987) and the Civil War Trust (1991), which merged in 1999 to form the Civil War Preservation Trust (CWPT). By the end of 2006, the CWPT boasted a membership of more than 75,000 and land acquisitions of nearly 25,000 acres at ninety-five sites in eighteen states (Civil War Preservation Trust, Hallowed Ground 7 [Winter 2006]: 3).

7. John E. Stanchak, "Behind the Lines," Civil War Times Illustrated 27 (September 1988): 18; William C. Davis to Gary W. Gallagher, June 14, 2007 (e-mail).

8. Robert Brent Toplin, ed., Ken Burns's "The Civil War": Historians Respond (New York: Oxford University Press, 1996), xv–xvi; Geoffrey C. Ward, Ric Burns, and Ken Burns, The Civil War: An Illustrated History (New York: Knopf, 1990), dust jacket text; Robert C. Kenzer to Gary W. Gallagher, March 24, 2007 (e-mail). Toplin's volume contains nine essays that discuss how well Burns handled various themes relating to the war. Newsweek devoted its cover story on October 8, 1990, to Burns's series. The letters to Newsweek's editor printed on pp. 14–15 of the October 29 issue underscore the Civil War's ability to provoke passionate reactions. I am indebted to Professor Kenzer for figures regarding comparative airtime for Burns's talking heads. Foote's word count came to 7,677 (72.3 percent of the total), while that for the rest combined was 2,944.

9. Craig Haffner, "Foreword," in William C. Davis, Brian C. Pohanka, and Don Troiani, eds., *Civil War Journal: The Leaders* (Nashville, Tenn.: Rutledge Hill Press, 1997), vi–vii. The other two volumes, from the same editorial trio and press, are *Civil War Journal: The Battles* (1998) and *Civil War Journal: The Legacies* (1999).

10. A growing literature has explored debates over public displays of Lost Cause symbols. See, for example, John M. Coski, *The Confederate Battle Flag: America's Most Embattled Emblem* (Cambridge, Mass.: Harvard University Press, 2005), especially chapters 13–14; K. Michael Prince, *Rally 'Round the Flag, Boys! South Carolina and the Confederate Flag* (Columbia: University of South Carolina Press, 2004); and J. Michael Martinez, William D. Richardson, and Ron McNinch-Su, eds., *Confederate Symbols in the Contemporary South* (Gainesville: University Press of Florida, 2000), especially chapters 4–11.

11. *Wall Street Journal*, February 10, 1995, 1; *U.S. News & World Report*, March 10, 1997, 13; *Time*, March 10, 1997, 21. For representative examples of coverage regarding controversies over Lost Cause symbols, see *Washington Post*, December 16, 1999, A39 (South Carolina flag); *U.S. News & World Report*, December 6, 1999, 34 (South Carolina flag); *Washington Post*, January 31, 2001, A2 (Georgia flag); *U.S. News & World Report*, February 12, 2001, 28 (Mississippi flag); *Washington Post*, January 13, 2001, A21, April 22, 2001, B1, B4 (Mississippi flag); *Chronicle of Higher Education*, March 3, 2000, B13 (Confederate monuments on university campuses); *Daily Texan* [student newspaper at the University of Texas at Austin], September 23, 1999, 4 (Confederate monuments on university campuses); *Richmond Times-Dispatch*, June 4, 1999, A1, A14 (Lee's image on flood wall); [Hampton Roads] *Virginian-Pilot*, March 22, 2001, B10, March 25, 2001, J3 (Confederate History Month in Virginia); *Washington Post*, January 29, 2001, A19 (Lost Cause symbols as a whole). In the piece on February 12, 2001, *U.S. News* alluded to Georgia and South Carolina while examining an upcoming statewide vote in Mississippi regarding a proposed new state flag: "Last week, Georgia began flying a new state flag after the legislature there voted to dramatically shrink the size of the Confederate emblem gracing it. . . . [This] came in the wake of South Carolina's decision last year to stop waving a Confederate banner over its capitol." In light of such moves, wondered the magazine, "Is this the end of the Confederacy?"

12. Admirers of the Confederacy fought back, including a pair of groups made up of descendants of Confederate soldiers—the Sons of Confederate Veterans and the Military Order of the Stars and Bars. In the mid-1980s, the two groups resurrected *Confederate Veteran*, which from 1893 to 1931 had been "published monthly in the interest of Confederate associations and kindred topics." In 1996, the *Veteran* excori-

ated Hollywood, television, and major newspapers for linking the Confederate flag to racist hate groups. "The Sons of Confederate Veterans is engaged in a constant war on two fronts," it observed. "We admonish those groups which misappropriate our Confederate symbols for their own vile use. And then confront those groups which call for a complete ban on all things Confederate. The media continually seizes upon these abuses and false charges. The media portrays to the world that the Confederate Battle Flag stands for nothing but perverted honor" (*Confederate Veteran* 4 [1996]: 6–7). The contents page of the new *Confederate Veteran* carries this vintage Lost Cause sentiment: "Though men deserve, they may not win, success; the brave will honor the brave, vanquished none the less."

13. For information about the memorial, which stands at 10th Street and Vermont Avenue, see <http://www.afroamcivilwar.org/photogallery/four.html>. Cook, *Troubled Commemoration*, 272, observes that "few whites ever see" the memorial.

14. Among the twelve directors, Costner, Lee, Minghella, and Scorsese have won Oscars for best director. Zwick has twice been nominated in the best director category at the Golden Globes and won an Oscar as producer of *Shakespeare in Love*. Frankenheimer won a best director Emmy Award for *Andersonville*.

15. Jakes wrote a third Civil War era novel, titled *Heaven and Hell* (1987), which was turned into a miniseries in the early 1990s. Several other made-for-television programs are worth studying with an eye toward interpretive traditions (if not for the excellence of their acting and staging). These include a miniseries titled *The Blue and the Gray* (1982) and the films *Ironclads* (1991) and *The Hunley* (1999), which deal with, respectively, the clash between the *Monitor* and the *Virginia* and the Confederate submarine *Hunley*.

16. For an annotated list of Civil War films from the late nineteenth century through 1961, see Paul C. Spehr, comp., *The Civil War in Motion Pictures: A Bibliography of Films Produced in the United States since 1897* (Washington, D.C.: Library of Congress, 1961). The list includes theatrical as well as documentary films and comprises 868 entries, a large majority of them for productions of the silent era.

17. C. Peter Jorgensen, "The Making of 'Glory,'" *Civil War Times Illustrated* 28 (December 1989): 59. See also Brian C. Pohanka, "Working for Glory," *Civil War: The Magazine of the Civil War Society*, issue 23 (May–June 1990): 40–45. A historian who worked as an adviser on the film, Pohanka concluded that "Hollywood will probably always take liberties with history." He also described *Glory* as "the most authentic Civil War film to date" (p. 45).

18. For the thoughts of a leading Civil War historian on the impact of *Gone with the Wind*, see Albert Castel, "The Film that Made Me," *Civil War Times Illustrated* 28 (Summer 1989): 10, 66.

19. *Battle Cry of Freedom* (New York: Oxford University Press, 1988) has sold between 600,000 and 700,000 copies in all editions (James M. McPherson to Gary W. Gallagher, June 20, 2007 [e-mail]).

20. Robert Fowler in *Civil War Times Illustrated* 1 (April 1962): 2; David E. Roth and Robin P. Roth in *Blue & Gray Magazine* 1 (August-September 1983): 4; Keith Poulter in *North & South* 1 (November 1997): 5.

21. Chris Lewis to Gary W. Gallagher, June 15, 2007 (e-mail); Keith Poulter to Gary W. Gallagher, June 14, 2007 (e-mail); discussion with Chris Lewis, July 12, 2007. Lewis notes that numbers have declined over the past fifteen years. In the mid-1990s, *Civil War Times Illustrated* reached twice as many readers. Lewis adds: "There are many theories about what has happened: increased print competition, competition from the internet, general decline in the popularity of history magazines, and for that matter, magazines in general." At its peak, *Civil War Times Illustrated* had no significant competitors but now has three (the two used for this book plus *America's Civil War*, which is published by the same company that owns *Civil War Times Illustrated* and has a circulation of 40,000–45,000). The total number of readers interested enough to purchase a popular magazine devoted to the Civil War may have remained roughly the same, or even increased slightly, over the past thirty years. The demise in 2007 of *American Heritage*, which was the oldest and most prestigious popular magazine devoted to United States history, underscored Lewis's point about a general decline in the genre. (Lewis to Gallagher, June 18, 2007 [e-mail].)

22. For a libertarian view, see Jeffrey Rogers Hummel, *Emancipating Slaves, Enslaving Free Men: A History of the American Civil War* (Chicago: Open Court, 1996). Hummel concludes with this sentence about the effect of Union victory: "In contrast to the whittling away of government that had preceded Fort Sumter, the United States had commenced its halting but inexorable march toward the welfare/warfare State of today" (p. 359).

23. For a condemnation of Union commanders such as U. S. Grant, William Tecumseh Sherman, and Philip H. Sheridan as proponents of "total war" that engulfed Confederate civilians and, a few years later, Native Americans, see Harry S. Stout, *Upon the Altar of the Nation: A Moral History of the Civil War* (New York: Viking, 2006). Stout laments the rise of a nation state that embraced the example of Grant and his lieutenants—as well as what he sees as the tendency of Americans to view the conflict uncritically. At the end of his text, Stout specifically ties the Civil War to modern conflicts (with Iraq no doubt in mind): "Why is it important to finally write the moral history of the Civil War? It's important because we are its legates, and if we question nothing from that costly conflict, then we need question nothing in conflicts of the present and future. Issues of discrimination and proportionality re-

cur in every war. The Civil War does not provide an especially encouraging model in this regard, especially if the crimes go largely unnoticed beneath the natural urge to forget and move on. But as with the Holocaust, if we forget, we do so at great peril to our own humanity" (p. 461).

24. On nation and nationalism in the Civil War era, see Earl J. Hess, *Liberty, Virtue, and Progress: Northerners and Their War for the Union* (New York: New York University Press, 1988); Susan-Mary Grant, *North Over South: Northern Nationalism and American Identity in the Antebellum Era* (Lawrence: University Press of Kansas, 2000); Melinda Lawson, *Patriot Fires: Forging a New American Nationalism in the Civil War North* (Lawrence: University Press of Kansas, 2002); Nicholas Onuf and Peter Onuf, *Nations, Markets, and War: Modern History and the American Civil War* (Charlottesville: University of Virginia Press, 2006); John McCardell, *The Idea of a Southern Nation: Southern Nationalists and Southern Nationalism, 1830–1860* (New York: Norton, 1979); Emory M. Thomas, *The Confederate Nation: 1861–1865* (New York: Harper & Row, 1979); Drew Gilpin Faust, *The Creation of Confederate Nationalism: Ideology and Identity in the Civil War South* (Baton Rouge: Louisiana State University Press, 1988); Gary W. Gallagher, *The Confederate War* (Cambridge, Mass.: Harvard University Press, 1997); and Anne Sarah Rubin, *A Shattered Nation: The Rise and Fall of the Confederacy, 1861–1868* (Chapel Hill: University of North Carolina Press, 2005). For an argument that the Confederacy never developed a real sense of nationalism, see Richard E. Beringer, Herman Hattaway, Archer Jones, and William N. Still, Jr., *Why the South Lost the Civil War* (Athens: University of Georgia Press, 1986).

25. See Brian Steel Wills, *Gone with the Glory: The Civil War in Cinema* (Lanham, Md.: Rowman & Littlefield, 2006), xi, for further evidence of *Shenandoah*'s impact on young Civil War enthusiasts. Wills's book offers a useful overview of Hollywood's treatment of the war, with special attention to whether films have gotten historical details correct.

CHAPTER 1

1. For examples of the Confederate emphasis on numbers, see Walter H. Taylor, *Four Years with General Lee* (New York: D. Appleton, 1877), and Jubal A. Early, "The Campaigns of Gen. Robert E. Lee. An Address by Lieut. General Jubal A. Early, before Washington and Lee University, January 19th, 1872," in Gary W. Gallagher, ed., *Lee the Soldier* (Lincoln: University of Nebraska Press, 1996). For a Union response, see Adam Badeau, *A Military History of Ulysses S. Grant, from April, 1861, to April, 1865,* 3 vols. (New York: D. Appleton, 1885). For a specific exchange, see Jubal A. Early, *The Relative Strength of the Armies of Genl's Lee and Grant. Reply of Gen. Early to the Letter*

of Gen. Badeau to the London Standard (n.p.: n.p., [1870]). Taylor and Badeau served respectively on the wartime staffs of Lee and Grant. The ebb and flow of debates among officers on the same side can be traced in the pages of the *Southern Historical Society Papers* in the 1870s and 1880s, where the Gettysburg controversy played out in its most virulent form, and in the Century Company's Battles and Leaders of the Civil War series in the 1880s.

2. For early examples of studies that explored constitutional issues and the place of slavery in the history of secession and war, see Alfred T. Bledsoe, *Is Davis a Traitor; or, Was Secession a Constitutional Right Previous to the War in 1861?* (Baltimore: Innes and the author, 1866), and Henry Wilson, *History of the Rise and Fall of the Slave Power in America*, 3 vols. (Boston: J. R. Osgood, 1872–77).

3. The Lost Cause has received a good deal of scholarly attention. For some of the more important works, see Rollin G. Osterweis, *The Myth of the Lost Cause, 1865–1900* (Hamden, Conn.: Archon, 1973); Thomas L. Connelly, *The Marble Man: Robert E. Lee and His Image in American Society* (New York: Knopf, 1977); Charles Reagan Wilson, *Baptized in Blood: The Religion of the Lost Cause, 1865–1920* (Athens: University of Georgia Press, 1980); Gaines M. Foster, *Ghosts of the Confederacy: Defeat, the Lost Cause, and the Emergence of the New South, 1865–1913* (New York: Oxford University Press, 1987); Mark E. Neely Jr., Harold Holzer, and Gabor S. Boritt, *The Confederate Image: Prints of the Lost Cause* (Chapel Hill: University of North Carolina Press, 1987); Jim Cullen, *The Civil War in Popular Culture: A Reusable Past* (Washington, D.C.: Smithsonian Institution Press, 1995); Gary W. Gallagher and Alan T. Nolan, eds., *The Myth of the Lost Cause and Civil War History* (Bloomington: Indiana University Press, 2000); David Goldfield, *Still Fighting the Civil War: The American South and Southern History* (Baton Rouge: Louisiana State University Press, 2002); Karen L. Cox, *Dixie's Daughters: The United Daughters of the Confederacy and the Preservation of Confederate Culture* (Gainesville: University Press of Florida, 2003); Alice Fahs and Joan Waugh, eds., *The Memory of the Civil War in American Culture* (Chapel Hill: University of North Carolina Press, 2004); and Caroline E. Janney, *Burying the Dead but Not the Past: Ladies' Memorial Associations and the Lost Cause* (Chapel Hill: University of North Carolina Press, 2008). For photographs of, and summary facts about, more than 1,000 monuments in twenty-seven states and the District of Columbia, see Ralph W. Widener Jr., *Confederate Monuments: Enduring Symbols of the South and the War Between the States* (Washington, D.C.: Andromeda, 1982). For comparable information about Union monuments, see Mildred C. Baruch and Ellen J. Beckman, *Civil War Union Monuments* ([Washington, D.C.]: Daughters of Union Veterans of the Civil War, 1978). Thomas J. Brown's *The Public Art of Civil War Commemoration: A Brief History with Documents* (Boston and

New York: Bedford/St. Martin's, 2004) combines excellent analysis and useful primary evidence.

4. Robert E. Lee and Jubal A. Early, who had served under Lee as a division and corps commander in the Army of Northern Virginia, exchanged correspondence in the early postwar years that addressed the question of establishing a published record supporting the Confederate point of view. Lee planned to write a history of his army's operations, he explained to Early in November 1865, "to transmit, if possible, the truth to posterity, and do justice to our brave Soldiers." Early touched on the same point in a letter to Lee three years later: "The most that is left to us is the history of our struggle, and I think that ought to be accurately written." (Lee to Early, November 22, 1865, George H. and Katherine Davis Collection, Howard-Tilton Memorial Library, Tulane University, New Orleans; Early to Lee, November 20, 1868, box 25, folder titled "Introductory Chapter [Notes & Pages of a Rough Draft] I," John Warwick Daniel Papers, Alderman Library, University of Virginia, Charlottesville.)

5. For the process by which Lee became a national hero, see Connelly, *The Marble Man*. Readers should be aware that Connelly's book combines insights and distortions in roughly equal measure. Connelly is especially misleading in insisting that Lee was not the primary Confederate military idol from early 1863 through the end of the war. See also chapter 10 of Gary W. Gallagher, *Lee and His Generals in War and Memory* (Baton Rouge: Louisiana State University Press, 1998), and Ella Lonn, "Reconciliation between the North and the South," *Journal of Southern History* 13 (February 1947): 25–26. Lonn's presidential address to the Southern Historical Association emphasizes the importance of Lincoln and Lee as the leading popular figures of the conflict. Diverse evidence illustrates how Lee's popularity surpassed that of Grant for much of the twentieth century. For example, the United States Navy launched the ballistic missile submarine USS *Robert E. Lee* (SSBN 601) on December 18, 1959; the USS *Ulysses S. Grant* (SSBN 631), a vessel in the same class, followed on November 2, 1963. (Robert Hallmark kindly pointed out this interesting example of Lee's precedence in a note to the author dated September 20, 2006.) The past several years have seen Grant's reputation swing upward. On this phenomenon, see Janny Scott, "A Bull Market for Grant, A Bear Market for Lee: History's Judgment of the 2 Civil War Generals Is Changing," *New York Times*, September 30, 2000, B9–B11.

6. *Southern Historical Society Papers*, ed. J. William Jones and others, 52 vols. (1876–1959; reprint with 3-vol. index, Wilmington, N.C.: Broadfoot, 1990–92), 2:6–7; Early, "Campaigns of Gen. Robert E. Lee," 65.

7. See B. A. C. Emerson, *Historic Southern Monuments: Representative Memorials of the Heroic*

Dead of the Southern Confederacy (New York and Washington, D.C.: Neale, 1911) for information about more than 150 Confederate monuments, including inscriptions they bear. (Neither the Austin nor the Charlottesville monument is included in Emerson's book.)

8. Jon L. Wakelyn, ed., *Southern Pamphlets on Secession, November 1860–April 1861* (Chapel Hill: University of North Carolina Press, 1996), 405–6; Jefferson Davis's message to the Confederate Congress, April 29, 1861, in *Jefferson Davis Constitutionalist: His Letters, Papers and Speeches*, ed. Dunbar Rowland, 10 vols. (Jackson: Mississippi Department of Archives and History, 1923), 5:72. The secession convention in Davis's home state of Mississippi put the matter equally bluntly: "Our position is thoroughly identified with the institutions of slavery—the greatest material interest of the world. . . . A blow at slavery is a blow at commerce and civilization. That blow has been long aimed at the institution, and was at the point of reaching its consummation. There was no choice left us but submission to the mandates of abolition, or a dissolution of the Union, whose principles had been subverted to work out our ruin" (Mississippi Secession Convention, *Journal of the State Convention and Ordinances and Resolutions Adopted in January, 1861, with an Appendix* [Jackson: E. Barksdale, 1861]).

9. Alexander H. Stephens, *A Constitutional View of the Late War between the States; Its Causes, Character, Conduct, and Results*, 2 vols. (Philadelphia: National Publishing Company, 1868, 1870), 1:10; Jefferson Davis, *The Rise and Fall of the Confederate Government*, 2 vols. (1881; reprint, New York: DaCapo, 1990), 1:67. The Lost Cause argument about slavery's tertiary importance has reappeared in various forms ever since Stephens and Davis wrote. Two recent examples are Thomas J. DiLorenzo, *The Real Lincoln: A New Look at Abraham Lincoln, His Agenda, and an Unnecessary War* (Roseville, Calif.: Forum, 2002), and Charles Adams, *When in the Course of Human Events: Arguing the Case for Southern Secession* (Lanham, Md.: Rowman & Littlefield, 2000). Both books display what can only be termed a casual approach to the use of evidence.

10. "Honor for the Old-Time Negro," *Confederate Veteran* 20 (September 1912): 410; Jubal A. Early, *The Heritage of the South* (Lynchburg, Va.: Brown-Morison, 1915), 114–16. For another article about loyal slaves during the war, see "Intended Honor to a Confederate Negro," *Confederate Veteran* 13 (November 1905): 499. For a modern example of the same type of argument, see Daniel W. Barefoot, *Let Us Die Like Brave Men: Behind the Dying Words of Confederate Warriors* (Winston-Salem, N.C.: Blair, 2005), 135–38.

11. *Southern Historical Society Papers*, 6:144. See Early, "Campaigns of Gen. Robert E. Lee," 70–73, for an excellent example of how Lost Cause writers handled Lee, Jackson, and Grant. On the comparisons of Washington and Lee, see Richard B. McCaslin,

Lee in the Shadow of Washington (Baton Rouge: Louisiana State University Press, 2001).

12. John B. Gordon, *Reminiscences of the Civil War* (1903; reprint, Dayton, Ohio: Morningside, 1993), 158. On Pickett's Charge in the American imagination, see Carol Reardon, *Pickett's Charge in History and Memory* (Chapel Hill: University of North Carolina Press, 1997). Douglas Southall Freeman's *R. E. Lee: A Biography* (4 vols., New York: Scribner's, 1934–35), by far the most influential of all biographies of Lee, concluded that Gettysburg marked "the turning-point in the history of the Army of Northern Virginia." Freeman attributed the outcome at Gettysburg to the absence of Stonewall Jackson and the reorganization of the army that followed the death of Lee's most famous lieutenant (3:153).

13. Shelby Foote, a proud Mississippian whose work otherwise fit quite comfortably within a Lost Cause interpretive framework, criticized the literature's imbalance between Lee's theater and the rest of the strategic landscape: "In all too many of these works, long and short, foreign and domestic, the notion prevailed that the War was fought in Virginia, while elsewhere—in an admittedly large but also rather empty region known vaguely as 'the West'—a sort of running skirmish wobbled back and forth, presumably as a way for its participants, faceless men with unfamiliar names, to pass the time while waiting for the issue to be settled in the East" (Foote, *The Civil War: A Narrative*, 3 vols. [New York: Random House, 1958–74], 3:1064–65).

14. Margaret Ann Vogtsberger, *The Dulanys of Welbourne: A Family in Mosby's Confederacy* (Berryville, Va.: Rockbridge, 1995), 188–89; Jubal A. Early, *A Memoir of the Last Year of the War for Independence in the Confederate States* (1867; reprint, Harrisburg, Pa.: Archive Society, 1996), 73; Cornelia Phillips Spencer, *The Last Ninety Days of the War in North Carolina* (1866; reprint, Wilmington, N.C.: Broadfoot, 1993), 95.

15. George Cary Eggleston, *A Rebel's Recollections* (1875; reprint, Baton Rouge: Louisiana State University Press, 1996), 83; Matthew Page Andrews, comp., *Women of the South in War Times* (Baltimore: Norman Remington, 1927), 3. The pages of *Confederate Veteran* abound with tributes to Confederate women. For examples, see 8 (October 1900): 454; 9 (May 1901): 230; 14 (January 1906): 33.

16. John R. Neff uses the term "the Cause Victorious" to describe an overall "Northern mythology" that sought "to explain what . . . victory ultimately meant for the nation, and in some way demonstrate the truth of that national victory" (Neff, *Honoring the Civil War Dead: Commemoration and the Problem of Reconciliation* [Lawrence: University Press of Kansas, 2005], 8–10).

17. Daniel Webster, *The Papers of Daniel Webster*, Series 4, *Speeches and Formal Writings, 1800–1852*, ed. Charles M. Wiltse, 2 vols. (Hanover, N.H.: University Press of New

England, 1986–88), 2:550–51; Susan-Mary Grant, *North Over South: Northern Nationalism and American Identity in the Antebellum Era* (Lawrence: University Press of Kansas, 2000), 61; Sean Wilentz, *The Rise of American Democracy: Jefferson to Lincoln* (New York: Norton, 2005), 321.

18. William E. Gienapp, ed., *This Fiery Trial: The Speeches and Writings of Abraham Lincoln* (New York: Oxford University Press, 2002), 97, 99–100, 184. On opposition to emancipation in the North, see chapters 2–4 of Forrest G. Wood, *Black Scare: The Racist Response to Emancipation and Reconstruction* (Berkeley: University of California Press, 1968), and chapters 2–5 of Joel H. Silbey, *A Respectable Minority: The Democratic Party in the Civil War Era, 1860–1868* (New York: Norton, 1977).

19. James M. McPherson, *What They Fought For, 1861–1865* (Baton Rouge: Louisiana State University Press, 1994), 29, 33; Wilbur Fisk, *Hard Marching Every Day: The Civil War Letters of Private Wilbur Fisk, 1861–1865*, ed. Emil and Ruth Rosenblatt (Lawrence: University Press of Kansas, 1992), 5, 326–27.

20. William Tecumseh Sherman, *Memoirs of W. T. Sherman* (1875; reprint, New York: Library of America, 1990), 171; Frederic Denison, *Sabres and Spurs: The First Rhode Island Cavalry in the Civil War, 1861–1865* (1876; reprint, Baltimore: Butternut and Blue, 1994), 25.

21. David Power Conyngham, *The Irish Brigade and Its Campaigns* (1867; reprint, New York: Fordham University Press, 1994), 5–6; William McCarter, *My Life in the Irish Brigade: The Civil War Memoirs of Private William McCarter, 116th Pennsylvania Infantry*, ed. Kevin E. O'Brien (Campbell, Calif.: Savas, 1996), 221.

22. The outpouring of national grief at Grant's death in 1885 attested to his stature. On this point, see Joan Waugh, "'Pageantry of Woe': The Funeral of Ulysses S. Grant," in Edward J. Blum and W. Scott Poole, eds., *Vale of Tears: New Essays on Religion and Reconstruction* (Macon, Ga.: Mercer University Press, 2005), 212–18.

23. Hennig Cohen, ed., *The Battle-Pieces of Herman Melville* (New York: Yoseloff, 1963), [31]; Maria Lydig Daly, *Diary of a Union Lady, 1861–1865*, ed. Harold Earl Hammond (1962; reprint, Lincoln: University of Nebraska Press, 2000), 352; J. A. Mowris, *A History of the One-Hundred and Seventeenth Regiment, N.Y. Volunteers, (Fourth Oneida,) from the Date of Its Organization, August, 1862, Till that of Its Muster Out, June, 1865* (1866; reprint, Hamilton, N.Y.: Edmonston, 1996), 223–25. Melville first published *Battle-Pieces* in 1866.

24. William Swinton, *Campaigns of the Army of the Potomac: A Critical History of Operations in Virginia, Maryland, and Pennsylvania from the Commencement to the Close of the War, 1861–5* (1866; reprint, Secaucus, N.J.: Blue & Grey Press, 1988), 622.

25. Baruch and Beckman, *Civil War Union Monuments*, 105, 63, 55, 40. Some northern

monuments honor both the Union and Emancipation Causes. The text on one in Antrim, New Hampshire, praises men who "Fought For Liberty, Union, And Equal Rights For All Mankind" (ibid., 111).

26. For a modern incarnation of the argument that emancipation gave true meaning to Union victory, see Ira Berlin, Barbara J. Fields, Steven F. Miller, Joseph P. Reidy, and Leslie S. Rowland, *Slaves No More: Three Essays on Emancipation and the Civil War* (New York: Cambridge University Press, 1992). These essays and the massive Freedmen and Southern Society Project out of which they originated emphasize the role of African Americans in "the drama of emancipation" (p. xv).

27. Gienapp, ed., *This Fiery Trial*, 184, 220–21.

28. David W. Blight, *Frederick Douglass' Civil War: Keeping Faith with Jubilee* (Baton Rouge: Louisiana State University Press, 1989), 229; Frederick Douglass, *Autobiographies* (1845, 1855, 1893; reprint, New York: Library of America, 1994), 851.

29. J. William Jones, *Life and Letters of Robert Edward Lee: Soldier and Man* (1906; reprint, Harrisonburg, Va.: Sprinkle, 1986), 482–83; James M. McPherson, ed., *The Most Fearful Ordeal: Original Coverage of the Civil War by Writers and Reporters of the New York Times* (New York: St. Martin's, 2004), 399; Blight, *Frederick Douglass' Civil War*, 229.

30. Thomas J. Pressly, *Americans Interpret Their Civil War* (Princeton, N.J.: Princeton University Press, 1954), 39–40. Just as Lost Cause arguments have their modern counterparts, so do Emancipation Cause interpretations. Henry Wilson and Frederick Douglass would have been cheered by Leonard L. Richards's *The Slave Power: The Free North and Southern Domination, 1780–1860* (Baton Rouge: Louisiana State University Press, 2000) and Charles B. Dew's *Apostles of Disunion: Southern Secession Commissioners and the Causes of the Civil War* (Charlottesville: University Press of Virginia, 2001), which attest to the power of antebellum slaveholding interests and to the absolute centrality of slavery in the process of secession. See also James L. Huston, *Calculating the Value of the Union: Slavery, Property Rights, and the Economic Origins of the Civil War* (Chapel Hill: University of North Carolina Press, 2003), which underscores the enormous wealth invested in slaves and places debates over property rights at the heart of the secession crisis.

31. W. R. Kiefer, *History of the One Hundred and Fifty-Third Regiment, Pennsylvania Volunteers Infantry, Which Was Recruited in Northampton County, Pa., 1862–1863* (1909; reprint, Baltimore: Butternut and Blue, 1996), 1–2.

32. Kathleen Ann Clark, *Defining Moments: African American Commemoration and Political Culture in the South, 1863–1913* (Chapel Hill: University of North Carolina Press, 2005), 15, 24–25. See also William Blair, *Cities of the Dead: Contesting the Memory of the Civil War in the South, 1865–1914* (Chapel Hill: University of North Carolina Press, 2004).

33. Joseph T. Wilson, *The Black Phalanx: African American Soldiers in the War of Independence,*

the War of 1812, and the Civil War (1887; reprint, New York: DaCapo, 1994), 460 (more than 80 per cent of Wilson's book deals with the Civil War); Luis F. Emilio, *History of the Fifty-Fourth Regiment of Massachusetts Volunteer Infantry, 1863–1865* (1894; reprint, New York: Arno, 1969), 319–20.

34. David W. Blight's *Race and Reunion: The Civil War in American Memory* (Cambridge, Mass.: Harvard University Press, 2001) argues that reconciliationists succeeded in virtually erasing emancipation and black participation from the nation's Civil War narrative. Although more recent works have somewhat softened this picture (especially regarding the degree to which white Union veterans turned their backs on black comrades), Blight's book has been extremely influential. On the North and reunion, see Nina Silber, *The Romance of Reunion: Northerners and the South, 1865–1900* (Chapel Hill: University of North Carolina Press, 1993). For an argument that "black and white Union veterans formulated a joint vision of the war at odds with the more reconciliationist, segregationist, and racist trends found in postwar society as a whole," see Andre Fleche, "'Shoulder to Shoulder as Comrades Tried': Black and White Union Veterans and Civil War Memory," *Civil War History* 51 (June 2005): 175–201 (quotation, p. 201).

35. Clement A. Evans's introduction to Myrta Lockett Avary, *Dixie After the War: An Exposition of Social Conditions Existing in the South, During the Twelve Years Succeeding the Fall of Richmond* (New York: Doubleday, Page, 1906), [v].

36. *The Grand Army Record* 10 (November 1895): 84; Mary R. Dearing, *Veterans in Politics: The Story of the G.A.R.* (Baton Rouge: Louisiana State University Press, 1952), 410.

37. Ulysses S. Grant, *Ulysses S. Grant: Memoirs and Selected Letters* (New York: Library of America, 1990), 146–47, 735, 779–80. On Grant's death as a spur to reconciliation, see Waugh, "'Pageantry of Woe,'" 223–34.

38. Gordon, *Reminiscences*, 19.

39. Ibid., 463–65; Southern Lyceum Bureau, *General Gordon's Great Lecture on "The Last Days of the Confederacy"* (n.p.: n.p., [ca. 1900]), [2]. McKinley's quotation is one of many testimonials printed in the bureau's unpaginated pamphlet; the others are from northern and southern newspapers. Most of the quotations praise Gordon's reconciliationist rhetoric.

40. Joshua Lawrence Chamberlain, *"Bayonet! Forward": My Civil War Reminiscences,* comp. Stan Clark Jr. (Gettysburg, Pa.: Stan Clark Military Books, 1994), 193, 195, 198. This book gathers a number of Chamberlain's reports, speeches, letters, and other writings.

41. Joshua Lawrence Chamberlain, *The Passing of the Armies: An Account of the Final Campaign of the Army of the Potomac, Based upon Personal Reminiscences of the Fifth Army Corps* (1915; reprint, Lincoln: University of Nebraska Press, 1998), 260, 382. On the ways

in which Appomattox has been used and misused as a symbol of reconciliation, see Gary W. Gallagher, "'There is Rancor in Our Hearts . . . Which You Little Dream Of,'" *Civil War Times Illustrated* 39 (May 2000): 52–55, and David W. Blight, "Legacies and Memory," in National Park Service Division of Publications, *Appomattox Court House* (Washington, D.C.: Government Printing Office, 2003), 82–102.

42. Theodore Roosevelt's speech, titled "Lincoln and the Race Problem," is at <http://www.theodore-roosevelt.com/trlatrp.html>.

43. Avary, *Dixie After the War*, 419.

44. Woodrow Wilson, *Robert E. Lee: An Interpretation* (Chapel Hill: University of North Carolina Press, 1924), 11–12, 21–22; "An Address at the Gettysburg Battlefield," July 4, 1913, in Woodrow Wilson, *The Papers of Woodrow Wilson*, ed. Arthur S. Link, 69 vols. (Princeton, N.J.: Princeton University Press, 1966–94), 28:23.

45. "Address at the Dedication of the Memorial on the Gettysburg Battlefield, Gettysburg, Pennsylvania," July 3, 1938, in Franklin D. Roosevelt, *The Public Papers and Addresses of Franklin D. Roosevelt*, comp. Samuel I. Rosenman, 13 vols. (New York: various publishers, 1938–50), 6:420; Jack McLaughlin, *Gettysburg: The Long Encampment* (New York: Appleton-Century, 1963), 225–30.

CHAPTER 2

1. Bruce Chadwick, *The Reel Civil War: Mythmaking in American Film* (New York: Knopf, 2001), 132, 187.

2. No prints of Ince's film survive. See Frank Thompson, "A Moving Picture," *Civil War Times Illustrated* 35 (April 1996): 56–61. According to one account, the packed house at *The Battle of Gettysburg*'s initial screening "actually went wild as the stirring scenes and exciting incidents of the memorable battle were once more enacted before their very eyes." D. W. Griffith himself had produced a number of short Civil War films before 1915, including *In the Border States* (1910; 16 minutes), *The House with Closed Shutters* (1910; 17 minutes), *The Fugitive* (1910; 17 minutes), *His Trust* (1910; 14 minutes), *His Trust Fulfilled* (1910; 11 minutes), *Swords and Hearts* (1911; 16 minutes), and *The Battle* (1911; 17 minutes). For a discussion of pre-1915 films, see Chadwick, *Reel Civil War*, chapters 1–2. For titles and plot synopses, see Paul C. Spehr, comp., *The Civil War in Motion Pictures: A Bibliography of Films Produced in the United States since 1897* (Washington, D.C.: Library of Congress, 1961).

3. North Carolinian Thomas F. Dixon (1864–1946) wrote three novels on Reconstruction: *The Leopard's Spots: A Romance of the White Man's Burden* (1902), *The Clansman: An Historical Romance of the Ku Klux Klan* (1905), and *The Traitor: A Story of the Rise and Fall of the Invisible Empire* (1907). Acquainted with Woodrow Wilson when the future president was a graduate student at The Johns Hopkins University, Dixon helped

Griffith set up a screening of *The Birth of a Nation* at the White House. Dixon later claimed that Wilson responded to the film by stating, "It is like writing history with lightning. And my only regret is that it is all so terribly true." On Dixon, Griffith, and Wilson, see John Hope Franklin, "Silent Cinema as Historical Mythmaker," in Steven Mintz and Randy Roberts, eds., *Hollywood's America: United States History Through Its Films* (St. James, N.Y.: Brandywine, 1993), 42–47; Robert Brent Toplin, *Reel History: In Defense of Hollywood* (Lawrence: University Press of Kansas, 2002), 186–87; and Chadwick, *Reel Civil War*, 121–24.

4. Joan L. Silverman, "Birth of a Nation," in Charles Reagan Wilson and William Ferris, eds., *Encyclopedia of Southern Culture* (Chapel Hill: University of North Carolina Press, 1989), 947; Francis Hackett, "Brotherly Love," *The New Republic* 1 (March 20, 1915), 185; Chadwick, *Reel Civil War*, 131–32; Franklin, "Silent Cinema," 48. Franklin's essay offers a good overview of the negative reaction to the film.

5. Bob Thomas, *The Story of Gone With the Wind* (New York: National Publishers, 1967), [3, 29].

6. Ibid., [31]; Roy Kinnard, *The Blue and Gray on the Silver Screen: More than 80 Years of Civil War Movies* (Secaucus, N.J.: Carol Publishing, 1996), 60. After its premiere in 1939, *Gone with the Wind* was re-released in the United States in 1941, 1942, 1947, 1954, 1961 (tied to the Civil War Centennial celebration), 1967 (with the original 35mm negative converted to 70mm), 1989, and 1998. In 1986, historian Jack Temple Kirby predicted that the publication of Alex Haley's *Roots: The Saga of An American Family* and its subsequent production as a hugely successful television miniseries would mark the end of *Gone with the Wind* as a cultural force: "This venerable relic of racism and romance had been turned inside out, and probably vanquished at last in both Margaret Mitchell's printed medium and on television" (Kirby, *Media-Made Dixie: The South in the American Imagination*, rev. ed. [Athens: University of Georgia Press, 1986], 165). Although there are no available comparative figures, *Gone with the Wind* probably has been more widely seen than *Roots* over the past twenty-five years.

7. Selznick originally had planned for 2,500 extras as wounded soldiers in the scene at the railroad station, changing to 1,600 humans and 1,200 dummies because of budgetary constraints. The Screen Extras Guild insisted that all the "wounded" be real bodies. Selznick agreed, but the Guild could supply no more than 1,500 people. (Thomas, *Story of Gone With the Wind*, [23].)

8. "Bummer" was a term applied to soldiers who ventured out as foragers from Sherman's main columns—with or without permission from officers. For a good brief discussion of the term, see Joseph T. Glatthaar, *The March to the Sea and Beyond: Sherman's Troops in the Savannah and Carolinas Campaigns* (New York: New York University Press, 1985), 122–23. The crowd at the premiere in Atlanta erupted in sustained

applause when Scarlett, with Melanie nearby holding the sword, shot the Union soldier in the head. (Thomas, *Story of Gone With the Wind*, [29].)

9. Claude G. Bowers, *The Tragic Era: The Revolution After Lincoln* (1929; reprint, Boston: Houghton Mifflin, 1962), 307–8.

10. For an interesting discussion of Selznick's decisions relating to African American characters and race in *Gone with the Wind*, see Leonard J. Leff, "*Gone With the Wind* and Hollywood's Racial Politics," *Atlantic Monthly* 284 (December 1999): 106–14.

11. This scene must be problematical for those who, in a quixotic effort to get the Confederacy right on the issue of slavery, pretend there were tens of thousands of African Americans who "served" in southern armies. The scene correctly indicates that the slaves did not volunteer to dig trenches; rather, they were deployed in that capacity according to an arrangement between a Confederate government that needed their labor and the O'Hara family, which allowed them to go to Atlanta (most slaveholders would have taken Gerald O'Hara's rather than his wife's position on this issue). For an example of neo-Confederate speculation about black Confederate "soldiers," see Charles Kelly Barrow, J. H. Segars, and R. B. Rosenburg, eds., *Forgotten Confederates: An Anthology about Black Southerners* ([Murfreesboro, Tenn.]: Southern Heritage Press, 1995), 3. For other books of this type, see J. H. Segars and Charles Kelly Barrow, comps., *Black Southerners in Confederate Armies: A Collection of Historical Accounts* (Atlanta: Southern Lion Books, 2001); Richard Rollins, ed., *Black Southerners in Gray: Essays on Afro-Americans in Confederate Armies* (Murfreesboro, Tenn.: Southern Heritage Press, 1994).

12. Thomas, *Story of Gone With the Wind*, [31].

13. John Lee Mahin and Martin Rackin wrote the screenplay, based on the 1956 novel of the same title by Harold Sinclair.

14. William Blair, *Virginia's Private War: Feeding Body and Soul in the Confederacy, 1861–1865* (New York: Oxford University Press, 1998), 125.

15. Other films of this type include *Major Dundee*, directed by Sam Peckinpah and starring Charlton Heston and Richard Harris (1965); *A Time for Killing*, starring Glenn Ford and George Hamilton (1967); and *The Last Rebel*, a showcase for football player Joe Namath's limited acting skills (1971). By the 1960s, Hollywood had a long tradition of including Civil War themes in westerns, a topic examined in chapter 12 of Chadwick, *Reel Civil War* and, without scholarly trappings, in chapter 8 of John M. Cassidy, *Civil War Cinema: A Pictorial History of Hollywood and the War between the States* (Missoula, Mont.: Pictorial Histories Publishing Company, 1986).

16. The main characters in *Gettysburg* are Robert E. Lee (Martin Sheen), James Longstreet (Tom Berenger), George E. Pickett (Stephen Lang), Lewis A. Armistead (Richard Jordan), A. J. L. Fremantle (James Lancaster), James L. Kemper (Royce D.

Applegate), Joshua L. Chamberlain (Jeff Daniels), Buster Kilrain (Kevin Conway), and Tom Chamberlain (C. Thomas Howell). For a discussion of the historical accuracy of Shaara's novel, see D. Scott Hartwig, *A Killer Angels Companion* (Gettysburg, Pa.: Thomas, 1996). For a thoughtful essay on the film, see William Blair, "The Brothers' War: *Gettysburg* the Movie and American Memory," in William Blair and William Pencak, eds., *Making and Remaking Pennsylvania's Civil War* (University Park: Penn State University Press, 2001), 245–60.

17. On Gettysburg as an overblown turning point, see Gary W. Gallagher, "Gettysburg: A 2003 Perspective," in *Gettysburg Commemorative Issue*, a joint special issue from the editors of *Civil War Times Illustrated, Civil War Times*, and *Military History* (Summer 2003): 80–90.

18. The reenactors playing Confederate soldiers broke into unscripted applause and shouting when Martin Sheen, as Lee, rode by during shooting. Ron Maxwell decided to keep the scene in the film. For a historical example of this phenomenon, see Edward Porter Alexander, *Fighting for the Confederacy: The Personal Recollections of General Edward Porter Alexander*, ed. Gary W. Gallagher (Chapel Hill: University of North Carolina Press, 1989), 345–46. Lee's best artillerist, Alexander likened the outpouring of emotion to "a military sacrament."

19. James Longstreet's reputation underwent a remarkable transformation in the late 1980s and 1990s, due in large measure to the flattering portrayals in Shaara's *The Killer Angels* and Maxwell's *Gettysburg*. In July 1998, admirers unveiled a statue of "Old Pete" on the battlefield at Gettysburg. For more on this monument, see below, pp. 140–41.

20. *The Killer Angels* does not include a scene with Tom Chamberlain interrogating captured Confederates. The younger Chamberlain merely recounts the conversation, and the allusion to "rats," to his brother Joshua.

21. Longstreet's *From Manassas to Appomattox: Memoirs of the Civil War in America* (Philadelphia: Lippincott, 1896) makes no mention of freeing slaves. Longstreet's most recent biographer notes that when Lee asked his lieutenant's opinion about enrolling slaves as soldiers in the last winter of the war, Longstreet "opposed the idea because it would mean the 'necessity' of abolishing slavery in the future without 'materially aiding us in the present'" (Jeffry D. Wert, *General James Longstreet: The Confederacy's Most Controversial Soldier, A Biography* [New York: Simon and Schuster, 1993], 397).

22. Kent Masterson Brown, *Retreat from Gettysburg: Lee, Logistics, and the Pennsylvania Campaign* (Chapel Hill: University of North Carolina Press, 2005), 49–50, estimates that "there must have been anywhere from 6,000 to 10,000 slaves laboring for Lee's troops." Other scholars place the likely number at about half of Brown's estimate. A. J. L. Fremantle, a British soldier who accompanied Lee's army during the cam-

paign, wrote on June 25, 1863, that in the "rear of each regiment were from twenty to thirty negro slaves." Lee's army comprised 169 infantry regiments during the campaign, which by Fremantle's reckoning would have contained between 3,380 and 5,070 slaves. Slaves accompanying the thirty cavalry regiments and sixty-eight artillery batteries would have added to the number. (Fremantle, *Three Months in the Southern States: April–June, 1863* [1864; reprint, Lincoln: University of Nebraska Press, 1991], 234.)

23. Mort Künstler (art) and James M. McPherson (text), *Gettysburg: The Paintings of Mort Künstler* (Atlanta: Turner Publishing, 1993), 7. On Lee as a nationalist, see Gary W. Gallagher, *Lee and His Army in Confederate History* (Chapel Hill: University of North Carolina Press, 2001), 162–75.

24. The main characters in *Sommersby* are John "Jack" Sommersby (Richard Gere), Laurel Sommersby (Jodie Foster), Judge Barry Conrad Isaacs (James Earl Jones), Joseph (Frankie Faison), and Orin Meecham (Bill Pullman).

25. Journalist John T. Trowbridge's travels through Tennessee immediately after the war revealed considerable white antipathy toward freed slaves. From near Memphis, he described the reaction among "Southern ladies and gentlemen" on a train who looked out of their car to see homeless black people camped near the tracks. "That's freedom!" they said scornfully. "That's what the Yankees have done for 'em!" "They'll all be dead before spring. Niggers can't take care of themselves. How much better off they were when they were slaves!" (Trowbridge, *The Desolate South, 1865–1866*, ed. Gordon Carroll [New York: Duell, Sloan and Pierce, 1956], 176.) It is worth mentioning that the Ku Klux Klan was organized by Confederate veterans in Pulaski, Tennessee, in the early summer of 1866, suggesting the degree to which Sommersby's ideas about race would have stood out among the views of his white peers.

26. The main characters in *Pharaoh's Army* are John Hull Abston (Chris Cooper), Sarah Anders (Patricia Clarkson), Boy (Will Lucas), Chicago (Robert Joy), Newt (Huckleberry Fox), Rodie (Richard Tyson), Neely (Frank Clem), and Preacher (Kris Kristofferson).

27. Kentucky sent 51,743 white and 23,703 black men into United States military service and approximately 35,000 into the Confederate army. A number of generals on both sides claimed Kentucky as their home state.

28. The main characters in *Andersonville* are Henry Wirz (Jan Triska), Colonel Chandler (William H. Macy), Sergeant McSpadden (Frederic Forrest), Martin Blackburn (Ted Marcoux), Tyce (Justin Henry), and Billy (Jayce Bartok).

29. [J. William Jones], "The Treatment of Prisoners during the War between the States," in *Southern Historical Society Papers*, ed. J. William Jones and others, 52 vols. (1876–

1959; reprint with 3-vol. index, Wilmington, N.C.: Broadfoot, 1990–92), 1:115. A recent encyclopedia of the Civil War notes that "Andersonville's reputation for its exceptionally brutal conditions has made it the best known of all Civil War prisons" (David S. Heidler and Jeanne T. Heidler, eds., *Encyclopedia of the American Civil War: A Political, Social, and Military History*, 5 vols. [Santa Barbara, Calif.: ABC-CLIO, 2000], 1:48).

30. Kantor's novel created quite a stir. On October 30, 1955, in a front-page review, the *New York Times Book Review* observed: "Onto the warp of history Mr. Kantor has woven with the stuff of imagination an immense and terrible pattern, a pattern which finally emerges as a gigantic panorama of the war itself, and of the nation that tore itself to pieces in war. Out of fragmentary and incoherent records, Mr. Kantor has wrought the greatest of our Civil War novels." On modern neo-Confederates who deplore the novel as a "Northern-biased account" of Andersonville, see Tony Horwitz, *Confederates in the Attic: Dispatches from the Unfinished Civil War* (New York: Pantheon, 1998), 328–30.

31. William Marvel, "Andersonville: The Myth Endures," *Civil War Times Illustrated* 35 (April 1996): 10.

32. The best study of Andersonville is William Marvel, *Andersonville: The Last Depot* (Chapel Hill: University of North Carolina Press, 1994). On conditions in Union and Confederate prisons generally, see Charles W. Sanders Jr., *While in the Hands of the Enemy: Military Prisons of the Civil War* (Baton Rouge: Louisiana State University Press, 2005).

33. The main characters in *Ride with the Devil* are Jacob "Jake" Roedel (Tobey Maguire), Jack Bull Chiles (Skeet Ulrich), George Clyde (Simon Baker), Daniel Holt (Jeffrey Wright), Sue Lee Shelley (Jewel Kilcher), and Pitt Mackeson (Jonathan Rhys Meyers).

34. *Ride with the Devil* does not exaggerate the brutality of Missouri's war. See Michael Fellman, *Inside War: The Guerrilla Conflict in Missouri during the Civil War* (New York: Oxford University Press, 1989), and Albert Castel and Thomas Goodrich, *Bloody Bill Anderson: The Short, Savage Life of a Civil War Guerrilla* (Mechanicsburg, Pa.: Stackpole, 1998).

35. The main characters in *Gods and Generals* are Robert E. Lee (Robert Duvall), Thomas J. "Stonewall" Jackson (Stephen Lang), Joshua Lawrence Chamberlain (Jeff Daniels), Buster Kilrain (Kevin Conway), Thomas Chamberlain (C. Thomas Howell), Jim Lewis (Frankie Faison), Anna Morrison Jackson (Kali Rocha), Jane Beale (Mia Dillon), Martha Beale (Donzaleigh Abernathy), and Fanny Chamberlain (Mira Sorvino).

36. *New York Times*, March 9, 2003, The Word, 14; *Washington Post*, February 21, 2003, C1,

C4; *Journal of American History* 90 (December 2003): 1123 [review by Steven E. Wood-worth].

37. John E. Stanchak, "Gods and Generals," *Civil War Times* 41 (December 2002): 37; Dennis E. Frye, "The Making of 'Gods and Generals,'" *North & South* 5 (October 2002): 24; Bill Kauffman, "The Civil War Returns," *American Enterprise* 14 (March 2003): 25. See also Kathryn Jorgensen, "'Gods & Generals' Opens Nationally; Movie Critics Boo," *Civil War News* 28 (April 2003): 1, 30.

38. In Shaara's book, Union officers Winfield Scott Hancock and Joshua Lawrence Chamberlain have much larger parts and Jackson a much smaller one. In terms of northern civilians, Francis Preston Blair Sr., long a figure on the Washington political scene, appears early in the film to offer Lee command of United States forces mustering outside Washington.

39. Jane Howison Beale's journal has been published as *The Journal of Jane Howison Beale of Fredericksburg, Virginia, 1850–1862* ([Fredericksburg, Va.]: Historic Fredericksburg Foundation, 1979). In it, Beale expresses considerable concern about slaves who have run away to Union forces. Her entries concerning the battle of Fredericksburg mention Martha just once—on December 11, 1862: "We were aroused before day by Gen. Lee's 'Signal guns,' but not knowing their special significance, we did not hurry ourselves, until 'Martha' our chamber maid came in and said in a rather mournful tone, 'Miss Jane the Yankees are coming, they have got two pontoons nearly across the river'" (p. 69).

40. In March 1868, Lee remarked to a former Confederate staff officer that he told Jefferson Davis "often and early in the war that the slaves should be emancipated, that it was the only way to remove a weakness at home and to get sympathy abroad, and to divide our enemies, but Davis would not hear of it." No wartime documents corroborate this statement. (William Allan, "Memoranda of Conversations with General Robert E. Lee," in Gary W. Gallagher, ed., *Lee the Soldier* [Lincoln: University of Nebraska Press, 1996], 12.) Very late in the war, Lee did support placing slaves in the Confederate army and granting freedom to those who served honorably. There is no evidence that he advanced such an idea during the period covered in *Gods and Generals*.

41. Stanchak, "Gods and Generals," 37. A recent book that seems to take the film's handling of Jackson and Jim Lewis as a point of departure is Richard G. Williams Jr., *Stonewall Jackson: The Black Man's Friend* (Nashville, Tenn.: Cumberland House, 2006), for which James I. Robertson Jr. wrote an appreciative introduction that describes Jackson as "a spiritual teacher for scores of slaves and freedmen as well as the best friend many of them ever had" (p. 12). Robertson's *Stonewall Jackson: The Man, The Soldier, The Legend* (New York: Macmillan, 1997), 191–92, summarizes the general's

views about slavery in less enthusiastic terms. The historical record offers little to support Williams's flattering portrait.

42. Mort Künstler (art) and James I. Robertson Jr. (text), *Gods and Generals: The Paintings of Mort Künstler* (Shelton, Conn.: The Greenwich Workshop Press, 2002), 13. A consultant for the film, Robertson defended Maxwell's interpretive stance.

43. The main characters in *Cold Mountain* are Inman (Jude Law), Ada Monroe (Nicole Kidman), Ruby Thewes (Renée Zellweger), Teague (Ray Winstone), Reverend Monroe (Donald Sutherland), Reverend Vessey (Philip Seymour Hoffman), Sally Swanger (Kathy Baker), and Sara (Natalie Portman).

44. *USA Today*, December 24, 2003, 1D; *Washington Post*, December 25, 2003, C1; *Journal of American History* 91 (December 2004): 1128–29 [review by John C. Inscoe]; *New York Times*, December 21, 2003, section 2, p. 28. For a discussion of the film by historians Edward L. Ayers, Stephen Cushman, and Gary W. Gallagher, see Bob Thompson, "Civil War, Take 2," in *Washington Post*, December 24, 2003, C1, C8. For a discussion of the historical accuracy of Frazier's novel, see Paul Ashdown, *A Cold Mountain Companion* (Gettysburg, Pa.: Thomas, 2004).

45. *Los Angeles Times*, December 28, 2003, E39. For an assessment of the film aimed at Civil War enthusiasts, see John E. Stanchak, "Cold Mountain," *Civil War Times Illustrated* 42 (February 2004): 32–39.

46. For a study of elite Confederate women as increasingly skeptical about the war, see Drew Gilpin Faust, *Mothers of Invention: Women of the Slaveholding South in the American Civil War* (Chapel Hill: University of North Carolina Press, 1996). In "Altars of Sacrifice: Confederate Women and the Narratives of War," *Journal of American History* 76 (March 1990): 1228, Faust made the case more directly: "Historians have wondered in recent years why the Confederacy did not endure longer," she wrote. "In considerable measure, . . . it was because so many women did not want it to. . . . It may well have been because of its women that the South lost the Civil War." See also George C. Rable, *Civil Wars: Women and the Crisis of Southern Nationalism* (Urbana: University of Illinois Press, 1989), and LeeAnn Whites, *The Civil War as a Crisis in Gender: Augusta, Georgia, 1860–1890* (Athens: University of Georgia Press, 1995).

47. David Williams, *A People's History of the Civil War: Struggles for the Meaning of Freedom* (New York: The New Press, 2005), builds on earlier scholarship highlighting disaffection in the Confederacy to craft a picture similar to that presented in *Cold Mountain*. A much different interpretation emerges in a number of recent studies that describe considerable tenacity and sense of purpose on the Confederate home front. For examples, see Blair, *Virginia's Private War*; Gary W. Gallagher, *The Confederate War* (Cambridge, Mass.: Harvard University Press, 1997); Anne Sarah Rubin, *A Shattered Nation: The Rise and Fall of the Confederacy, 1861–1868* (Chapel Hill: University of North

Carolina Press, 2005); Mark V. Wetherington, *Plain Folk's Fight: The Civil War and Reconstruction in Piney Woods Georgia* (Chapel Hill: University of North Carolina Press, 2005).

48. Several hundred North Carolina Cherokees fought for the Confederacy. For a good overview of their service and overall Native American participation in the war, see Laurence M. Hauptman, *Between Two Fires: American Indians in the Civil War* (New York: The Free Press, 1995). The DVD version of *Cold Mountain* includes a deleted scene in which a Confederate soldier shoots a wounded USCT private.

49. For a forceful argument against the idea that southern white women harbored serious doubts about slavery, see Elizabeth Fox-Genovese, *To Be Worthy of God's Favor: Southern Women's Defense and Critique of Slavery*, 32nd Annual Robert Fortenbaugh Memorial Lecture (Gettysburg, Pa.: Gettysburg College, 1993).

50. Martin Crawford, *Ashe County's Civil War: Community and Society in the Appalachian South* (Charlottesville: University Press of Virginia, 2001), presents a complicated picture of loyalty and disaffection in one North Carolina county. For firsthand testimony from across the state, see W. Buck Yearns and John G. Barrett, eds., *North Carolina Civil War Documentary* (Chapel Hill: University of North Carolina Press, 1980). Phillip Shaw Paludan, *Victims: A True Story of the Civil War* (Knoxville: University of Tennessee Press, 1981), explores the murder of thirteen Unionist prisoners in western North Carolina.

51. The film is denoted a "Spike Lee Presentation," though Willmott wrote and directed it and Lee receives no producing credit.

52. Willmott's film represents a satirical addition to a body of work that imagines the history of the United States following a Confederate victory in the war. See for example, MacKinlay Kantor, *If the South Had Won the Civil War* (New York: Bantam, 1961); Mark Nesbitt, *If the South Won Gettysburg* (Gettysburg, Pa.: Reliance, 1980); Harry Turtledove, *How Few Remain* (New York: Ballantine, 1997); and, with a title exactly like Willmott's save for an article, Howard Means, *C.S.A.: Confederate States of America* (New York: Morrow, 1998).

53. "Lincoln's 2nd Arrival Divides Richmond," *Washington Post*, April 6, 2003, C6.

CHAPTER 3

1. On the phenomenon of placing emancipation alongside preservation of the Union, see Barry Schwartz and Howard Schuman, "History, Commemoration, and Belief: Abraham Lincoln in American Memory, 1946–2001," *American Sociological Review* 79 (April 2005), especially pp. 194–96. For specific examples, see Michael Fellman, Lesley J. Gordon, and Daniel E. Sutherland, *This Terrible War: The Civil War and Its*

Aftermath (New York: Longman, 2003), 147–49, and Brooks D. Simpson, *America's Civil War* (Wheeling, Ill.: Harlan Davidson, 1996), 127–28.

2. Barbara J. Fields, "Who Freed the Slaves?," in Geoffrey C. Ward, Ric Burns, and Ken Burns, *The Civil War: An Illustrated History* (New York: Knopf, 1990), 178–81. Lincoln's government, observed Fields, "discovered that it could not accomplish its narrow goal—union—without adopting the slaves' nobler one—universal emancipation" (181).

3. *Band of Angels* features the theme of miscegenation, with which Hollywood has shown a tenacious fascination. In this instance, Clark Gable's southern planter falls in love with one of his slaves, played by Yvonne De Carlo, who turns out to be half white. Poitier's character recoils from De Carlo's behavior and runs off to enlist in the Union army.

4. Metro-Goldwyn-Mayer hoped *Raintree County* would duplicate the success of *Gone with the Wind*. Despite a multimillion dollar budget and front-rank stars Elizabeth Taylor and Montgomery Clift, the film fell far short of that lofty goal. The *New York Times* dismissively noted that MGM had failed to extract a good screenplay from Ross Lockridge Jr.'s "great flowing, formless amoeba of a novel" (Roy Kinnard, *The Blue and Gray on the Silver Screen: More than 80 Years of Civil War Movies* [Secaucus, N.J.: Carol Publishing, 1996], 166–67, quoting from the *Times*.)

5. The main characters in *Glory* are Col. Robert Gould Shaw (Matthew Broderick), Private Trip (Denzel Washington), John Rawlins (Morgan Freeman), Jupiter Sharts (Jihmi Kennedy), Thomas Searles (Andre Braugher), Col. James Montgomery (Cliff De Young), Cabot Forbes (Cary Elwes), and Sergeant Major Mulcahy (John Finn). The screenplay drew on Richard Benson and Lincoln Kirstein, *Lay This Laurel: An Album of the Saint-Gaudens Memorial on Boston Common Honoring Black and White Men Together Who Served the Union Cause with Robert Gould Shaw and Died with Him on July 18, 1863* (New York: Eakins, 1973); Peter Burchard, *One Gallant Rush: Robert Gould Shaw and His Brave Black Regiment* (New York: St. Martin's, 1965); and Shaw's letters in the collections of Harvard University. For the letters, unpublished when the film was made, see Russell Duncan, ed., *Blue-Eyed Child of Fortune: The Civil War Letters of Colonel Robert Gould Shaw* (Athens: University of Georgia Press, 1992).

6. Lynne M. Bonenberger, "Bound for Glory," *Ohio State* (December 1989): 7–8; "For Washington, 'Glory' was a lesson," undated clipping [ca. December 1989] from the *West Chester Daily Local News* supplied to the author by John Haas. The statement about audience reaction is based on discussions with many people who saw *Glory* in theaters, as well as on my own experience at a showing in New York City shortly after the film debuted. I stood in the foyer of the theater after the show ended to

listen to comments. By far the most common observation from both black and white members of the audience was, "I didn't know there were black soldiers in the Civil War." The January 8 and 15, 1990, issue of the *New Republic* devoted its cover, an essay by historian James M. McPherson, and a favorable review by film critic Stanley Kauffmann to *Glory*. Kauffmann applauded the film's success in "making credible" to a modern audience "the black men's eagerness to fight"—its "depiction of oppressed men with the means at hand to end the oppression" (pp. 29–30).

7. For the importance of emancipation to men of the 54th, see Virginia M. Adams, ed., *On the Altar of Freedom: A Black Soldier's Civil War Letters from the Front, Corporal James Henry Gooding* (Amherst: University of Massachusetts Press, 1991). On motivation among African American soldiers more generally, see Edwin S. Redkey, ed., *A Grand Army of Black Men: Letters from African-American Soldiers in the Union Army, 1861–1865* (New York: Cambridge University Press, 1992).

8. Adams, ed., *On the Altar of Freedom*, 26–27.

9. On the importance of flags and color-bearers, see James M. McPherson, *For Cause and Comrades: Why Men Fought in the Civil War* (New York: Oxford University Press, 1997), 84–85; Bell I. Wiley, *The Life of Billy Yank: The Common Soldier of the Union* (Indianapolis: Bobbs-Merrill, 1952), 93–94. For the 54th's flag during the assault on Fort Wagner, see Adams, ed., *On the Altar of Freedom*, 38–39.

10. Historians cannot precisely say how many Union soldiers considered emancipation a vital goal for the United States, but James M. McPherson offers a thoughtful discussion in *For Cause and Comrades*, 117–18. He estimates that fewer than one in ten had a strong interest in emancipation as a goal worthy in itself. But if defined to mean "a perception that the abolition of slavery was inseparably linked to the goal of preserving the Union, then three in ten Union soldiers whose letters and diaries form the basis of this book took that position during the first eighteen months of the war, and many more were eventually converted to it. While restoration of the Union was the main goal for which they fought, they became convinced that this goal was unattainable without striking against slavery." Chandra Manning's *What This Cruel War Was Over: Soldiers, Slavery, and the Civil War* (New York: Knopf, 2007) argues that significant numbers of Union soldiers embraced emancipation in late 1861 and early 1862. Her findings, though comforting to twenty-first-century sensibilities, are at odds with most other scholarship on the topic.

11. The film gets Chamberlain's views correct. On April 12, 1866, he wrote about the meaning of the war: "We fought for that 'more perfect Union,' which the Constitution announced as its object: we fought for the completion of those great ideas which inspired the souls of our fathers; for the extirpation of that fatal Calhoun heresy which would destroy the very existence of our nationality, and in defence of

a united and indivisible country. We fought for liberty, in its widest and best sense" (Jeremiah E. Goulka, ed., *The Grand Old Man of Maine: Selected Letters of Joshua Lawrence Chamberlain, 1865–1914* [Chapel Hill: University of North Carolina Press, 2004], 16).

12. The main characters in *Little Women* are Jo March (Winona Ryder), "Marmee" March (Susan Sarandon), young Amy March (Kirsten Dunst), Beth March (Claire Danes), Meg March (Trini Alvarado), Laurie (Christian Bale), John Brooke (Eric Stoltz), Friedrich Bhaer (Gabriel Byrne), and Mr. March (Matthew Walker). Earlier cinematic adaptations of Louisa May Alcott's novel, all of which fall far short of the 1994 version, include George Cukor's in 1933 (starring Katharine Hepburn) and Mervyn LeRoy's in 1949 (starring Elizabeth Taylor).

13. In contrast to the film's implication, Harvard men served the Union cause in large numbers. More than half of Harvard's class of 1860 and two-thirds of the class of 1861 donned blue uniforms, and the war claimed the lives of more than a third of all Harvard-connected Union soldiers. For one regiment in which many Harvard graduates served as officers, see Richard F. Miller, *Harvard's Civil War Regiment: A History of the Twentieth Massachusetts Volunteer Infantry* (Lebanon, N.H.: University Press of New England, 2005).

14. Louisa May Alcott, *Hospital Sketches* (1863; reprint, Bedford, Mass.: Applewood Books, 1993), 32, 50–51, 77, 95–96.

15. C.S.A.'s treatment of Lincoln reflects two strands of the historical literature that paint the sixteenth president as a hypocritical racist: (1) neo-Confederate books such as Thomas J. DiLorenzo, *The Real Lincoln: A New Look at Abraham Lincoln, His Agenda, and an Unnecessary War* (Roseville, Calif.: Forum, 2002), and (2) works such as Lerone Bennett Jr.'s *Forced Into Glory: Abraham Lincoln's White Dream* (Chicago: Johnson, 2000) that deplore Lincoln's receiving credit for work carried out by black and white abolitionists. Other than their zeal to undo the heroic image of Lincoln, these two strands share little interpretively. The mass of scholarship on Lincoln leaves no doubt about his personal hatred of slavery.

16. Tony Horwitz, *Confederates in the Attic: Dispatches from the Unfinished Civil War* (New York: Pantheon, 1998), 136–37. On the debate about interpretation at National Park Service sites, see the September 30, 2002, issue of *U.S. News & World Report*. Under the headline "Who Won the Civil War? A New Fight to Reshape the Nation's History," the magazine states that the Park Service's interpretation at Gettysburg, documentaries, Hollywood movies, and works of fiction all have portrayed the war as "America's epic, a heroic conflict both sides fought for freedom. The same tale is told at battlefields across the country. And it's wrong." In trying to honor soldiers from both sides, the article notes, battlefields as sites of reconciliation have avoided

discussing what the war was about, thereby conveying a subtly pro-Confederate message (pp. 56–68, quotation, p. 58). See also chapter 13 of Gary W. Gallagher, *Lee and His Generals in War and Memory* (Baton Rouge: Louisiana State University Press, 1998). Superintendent John Latschar of Gettysburg National Military Park has done an excellent job of broadening interpretation at the most-visited of all National Park Service Civil War battlefields. According to Latschar, texts on more than 1,300 monuments at Gettysburg include a great deal of praise for soldiers' valor, some mention of Union, and virtually no recognition of emancipation (notes from a conversation with Latschar on November 10, 2004, in Seattle, Washington). A detailed examination of the monuments would shed a good deal of light on the interpretive conventions of the period 1880–1920.

17. U.S. Postal Service, *Civil War: June 29, 1995, Gettysburg, Pennsylvania* (n.p.: U.S. Postal Service, 1995), [6].

18. On fraternization, see Wiley, *Life of Billy Yank,* 351–55; James I. Robertson Jr., *Soldiers Blue and Gray* (Columbia: University of South Carolina Press, 1988), 139–44. On Crane's character Henry Fleming, see Perry Lentz, *Private Henry Fleming at Chancellorsville: "The Red Badge of Courage," and the Civil War* (Columbia: University of Missouri Press, 2006).

19. Stephen Crane, *Prose and Poetry* (New York: Library of America, 1984), 87, 207–8.

20. The leave-taking Armistead recalls occurred on June 15, 1861, in Los Angeles. Almira Hancock's *Reminiscences of Winfield Scott Hancock* (New York: Charles L. Webster, 1887), 69–70, describes the evening. "The most crushed of the party," she recalls, "was Major Armistead, who, with tears, which were contagious," told his friend Hancock, "Good-by; you can never know what this has cost me." In a biographical sketch of Armistead, Robert K. Krick notes that it was Col. Albert Sidney Johnston's wife rather than Almira Hancock who "sang some romantic songs with a deep emotion that moved the whole group" (Robert K. Krick, "Armistead and Garnett: The Parallel Lives of Two Virginia Soldiers," in Gary W. Gallagher, ed., *The Third Day at Gettysburg and Beyond* [Chapel Hill: University of North Carolina Press, 1994], 111–12).

21. For Fremantle on Gettysburg, see his *Three Months in the Southern States: April–June, 1863* (1864; reprint, Lincoln: University of Nebraska Press, 1991), 251–72. Fremantle's engaging diary includes classic vignettes of Longstreet at Gettysburg but alludes to no discussion during the battle about the Revolution or the War of 1812.

22. W. A. Smith, *The Anson Guards: Company C, Fourteenth Regiment North Carolina Volunteers, 1861–1865* (1914; Wendell, N.C.: Broadfoot, 1978), 170. George C. Rable's *Fredericksburg! Fredericksburg!* (Chapel Hill: University of North Carolina Press, 2002), 146–47, discusses the phenomenon of fraternization at Fredericksburg. Rable suggests

that most of the contact between pickets "centered on what was commonly called 'blackguarding.'" A dispassionate Pennsylvanian stated that men from both sides used "insulting slang and profanity." Reconciliationists typically echoed W. A. Smith in casting fraternization at Fredericksburg in far more uplifting terms.

23. William E. Gienapp, ed., *This Fiery Trial: The Speeches and Writings of Abraham Lincoln* (New York: Oxford University Press, 2002), 105.

24. See also Lincoln's message to Congress of December 3, 1861, which reaffirmed his desire to "keep the integrity of the Union prominent as the primary object of the contest on our part." (Gienapp, ed., *This Fiery Trial*, 112.)

25. Peter Clayton Luebke, "To Transmit and Perpetuate the Fruits of This Victory: Union Regimental Histories, 1865–1866, and the Meaning of the Great Rebellion" (M.A. thesis, University of Virginia, 2007), 27, 30–31. Luebke's study rests on evidence from fifty-one regimental histories published in the first nineteen months after the war.

26. Wilson believed the white South had suffered at the hands of what he considered manipulating northern opportunists who exploited black southerners. In *A History of the American People*, vol. 5 (New York: Harper & Brothers, 1902), 98–99, he wrote that Radical Republican policies caused "the temporary disintegration of southern society," forcing white men "to rid themselves, by fair means or foul, of the intolerable burden of governments sustained by the votes of ignorant negroes and conducted in the interest of adventurers." Wilson introduced the Ku Klux Klan by observing that white men "took the law into their own hands, and began to attempt by intimidation what they were not allowed to attempt by the ballot or by any ordered course of public action." For similar language, see Wilson's *Division and Reunion, 1829–1889* (New York: Longmans Green, 1898), 268–69.

27. William Archibald Dunning, *Reconstruction Political and Economic, 1865–1877* (New York: Harper, 1907), 122; Wilson, *History of the American People*, 98–99.

28. Walter Huston plays Lincoln in the film, crafting a performance that rises above Griffith's glacial direction to achieve some very impressive moments.

29. George F. Root, a prolific northern composer, wrote the words and music for "Battle Cry of Freedom" in 1862. He composed two sets of lyrics—one to rally civilians and one a battle song. The song was so sprightly and engaging that H. L. Schreiner and W. H. Barnes created a Confederate version. Schreiner adapted Root's tune, and Barnes came up with pro-southern lyrics. See Paul Glass and Louis C. Singer, *Singing Soldiers: A History of the Civil War in Song* (1964; reprint, New York: DaCapo, 1993), 36–39, for both the northern and southern incarnations of the composition.

30. Louisa May Alcott, *Little Women, Little Men, Jo's Boys* (New York: Library of America, 2005), 51–52.

31. Federal prisoners who joined the Confederate army were called "galvanized Yankees" (a term later applied to Confederates who joined the United States Army). Nearly 200 Union soldiers left the stockade at Andersonville to don Confederate uniforms during a three-day period in January 1865. On galvanized Yankees at Andersonville, see William Marvel, *Andersonville: The Last Depot* (Chapel Hill: University of North Carolina Press, 1994), 223–24, 231, 234, 300 n. 27.

32. David Power Conyngham, *The Irish Brigade and Its Campaigns* (1867; reprint, New York: Fordham University Press, 1994), ix–x. Lawrence Frederick Kohl's introduction to Conyngham's book discusses "the surprisingly strong Union sentiment among the Irish" in 1861–62. By the time of the riots, he notes, Lincoln's stance on emancipation and other factors soured most Irish Americans on the war. The draft riots "brought to a boil the simmering Irish resentment at sacrificing their lives for the advancement of their hated black adversaries. Many Irish-Americans continued to enlist and to fight in the Union army, but neither their numbers nor their spirit matched the early days of the war" (pp. xiv–xvi). For a summary of the Irish Brigade's service and casualties, see William F. Fox, *Regimental Losses in the American Civil War, 1861–1865* (1898; reprint, Dayton, Ohio: Morningside, 1974), 118. Iver Bernstein, *The New York City Draft Riots: Their Significance for American Society and Politics in the Age of the Civil War* (New York: Oxford University Press, 1990), 113, observes: "Being Irish or Irish Catholic did not necessarily predispose one against the war or the wartime government—to the contrary. Though the Irish were known for their commitment to the Democratic Party and enmity toward blacks, they were frequently deeply loyal to the Union." Bernstein notes that the 69th New York Infantry was among the units sent from the Army of the Potomac to battle the rioters, duty the regiment's men carried out with "sangfroid."

33. The most detailed recent study of New York City during the war gives full attention to class tensions and political conflict but concludes that "the city dwellers, in the main, gave their support to the Union, and they gain our admiration, but it was not an easy decision for them. Even after minds were made up, many remained disturbed and disconsolate" (Ernest A. McKay, *The Civil War and New York City* [Syracuse, N.Y.: Syracuse University Press, 1990], xii). A later, shorter treatment chronicles the city's contributions in volunteers and conscripts, supply, and benevolent activities. Did "the metropolis contribute its full share of manpower to the Union cause? Using the state census of 1865, I conclude that it did not" (Edward K. Spann, *Gotham at War: New York City, 1860–1865* [Wilmington, Del.: Scholarly Resources, 2002], xiv).

34. On the relative absence of Union brutality, see Mark Grimsley, *The Hard Hand of War: Union Military Policy toward Southern Civilians, 1861–1866* (New York: Cambridge University Press, 1995). On the vicious war along the margins, see Michael Fell-

man, *Inside War: The Guerrilla Conflict in Missouri during the Civil War* (New York: Oxford University Press, 1989), and Robert R. Mackey, *The Uncivil War: Irregular Warfare in the Upper South, 1861–1865* (Norman: University of Oklahoma Press, 2004).

35. For an engaging discussion of World War II in film, see Bernard F. Dick, *The Star-Spangled Screen: The American World War II Film* (Lexington: University Press of Kentucky, 1985). On Clint Eastwood's reshaping of the genre in *Flags of Our Fathers* and *Letters From Iwo Jima*, see David J. Morris, "The Image as History: Clint Eastwood's Unmaking of an American Myth," *Virginia Quarterly Review* 83 (Spring 2007): 95–107. For two sets of essays on various aspects of Hollywood's handling of Vietnam, see Michael A. Anderegg, ed., *Inventing Vietnam: The War in Film and Television* (Philadelphia: Temple University Press, 1991), and Linda Dittmar and Gene Michaud, eds., *From Hanoi to Hollywood: The Vietnam War in American Film* (New Brunswick, N.J.: Rutgers University Press, 1990).

36. Federals at the battle of New Market admired the conduct of the cadets from VMI but showed them no special consideration. The chief Union signal officer recalled the cadets' charge against northern artillery: "They came on steadily up the slope, swept as it was by the fire of these guns. . . . As they advanced, our guns played with utmost vigor upon their line; at first with shrapnel, then, as they came nearer, with canister, and finally, with double loads of canister." More than 20 percent of the cadets, whose average age was under eighteen years, were killed or wounded in the fighting (Jennings C. Wise, *The Military History of the Virginia Military Institute from 1839 to 1865* [Lynchburg, Va.: J. P. Bell, 1915], 326–27).

37. On the burning of Darien, see Spencer B. King Jr., *Darien: The Death and Rebirth of a Southern Town* (Macon, Ga.: Mercer University Press, 1981).

38. Corporal Gooding wrote on July 20, 1863, that the 54th marched toward the beach to form for the assault "amid the cheers of the officers and soldiers" (Adams, ed., *On the Altar of Freedom*, 38). The redemptive power of the white cheers for the 54th undoubtedly struck a chord with viewers. On March 11, 1990, *The Lancaster* [Pa.] *Sunday News* used "Give 'em Hell, 54th!" as the lead sentence in a front-page story on the film, suggesting camaraderie between white and black Civil War soldiers the movie does not depict. A color illustration of nine white reenactors purchasing tickets for the film accompanied the article.

39. Adrian Cook's *The Armies of the Streets: The New York City Draft Riots of 1863* (Lexington: University Press of Kentucky, 1974) includes four useful appendixes: "The Dead," "The Wounded," "The Arrested," and "The Rioters." See also the chapter titled "Riot" in McKay, *The Civil War and New York City*.

40. Stephen Hunter, "Dances With Swords," *Washington Post*, December 5, 2003, C1, C4.

41. The main characters in *Seraphim Falls* are Col. Morsman Carver (Liam Neeson), Captain Gideon (Pierce Brosnan), Parsons (Ed Lauter), Rose Carver (Angie Harmon), and Madame Louise Fair (Angelica Huston).

42. Richard M. Weaver, *The Southern Tradition at Bay: A History of Postbellum Thought* (Washington, D.C.: Regnery, 1968), 53, front and back dust jacket flaps; Walter Brian Cisco, *War Crimes Against Southern Civilians* (Gretna, La.: Pelican, 2007), 17, front dust jacket flap. The blurb for Cisco's book, provided by David Aiken, offers numbers for lost property and civilian deaths far beyond those generally accepted by historians. In *Battle Cry of Freedom: The Civil War Era* (New York: Oxford University Press, 1988), 619 n. 53, James M. McPherson estimates that as many as 50,000 civilians may have died. For a clue about the trustworthiness of Cisco's scholarship, see p. 17 of his book, where he rewrites Weaver's sentence that I have quoted in the text in this fashion: "It scarcely needs pointing out that from the military policies of [William T.] Sherman and Sheridan there lies but an easy step to the total war of the Nazis, the greatest affront to Western civilization since its founding." Perhaps Cisco thought Weaver merely overlooked the opportunity to compare Sherman and Sheridan to Nazis and sought to rectify the failing. For a more measured assessment of Sherman in a popular forum, see Jay Tolson, "The Man Who Would Shape the Future of War," *U.S. News & World Report* 143 (July 2–7, 2007): 38–39.

CHAPTER 4

1. Chris W. Lewis (editor of *Civil War Times Illustrated*) to Gary W. Gallagher, October 10, 2006 (e-mail); Jason L. Roth (general manager of *Blue & Gray Magazine*) to Gallagher, November 6, 2006 (e-mail); Keith Poulter (publisher of *North & South*) to Gallagher, October 4, 2006 (e-mail); conversation between Gallagher and Poulter, September 9, 2003. According to Poulter, the breakdown by region for *North & South* changed little between 2000 and 2006. The top five states in number of subscribers to *Civil War Times Illustrated* are, in order, Pennsylvania, Ohio, New York, California, and Virginia.

2. See Tony Horwitz, *Confederates in the Attic: Dispatches from the Unfinished Civil War* (New York: Pantheon, 1998), on how modern Confederates easily outnumber their Federal opponents at reenactments.

3. *Confederate Veteran* 37 (March–April 1988): 2–3, 47. The Sons of Confederate Veterans maintains a Heritage Committee that urges members to counter what it considers slanders against the Confederacy and its symbols—asserting that the flag represents southern heritage rather than white supremacy. Preprinted cards bound into issues of *Confederate Veteran* allow subscribers to register unhappiness with individuals or groups who criticize the Confederacy. One such card from 1996, addressed to the

editors of the *Atlanta Journal/Constitution*, read in part: "Accept this correspondence as demonstrating my vehement objection to the attacks on Confederate heritage by staff cartoonist Mike Luckovich. Mr. Luckovich libels my Confederate ancestors by portraying in a false light the real heritage of the Confederate Battle Flag."

4. Artist Don Troiani attributes much of Cleburne's popularity to his Irish background, which appeals to the sector of the market with interests in both the Civil War and Irish history or heritage (Don Troiani to Gary W. Gallagher, October 1, 2006 [e-mail]). Older Confederate art also seems to attract far more interest. The University of North Carolina Press has published two books on prints published during the war and the decades following Appomattox: Mark E. Neely Jr., Harold Holzer, and Gabor S. Boritt, *The Confederate Image: Prints of the Lost Cause* (1987), and Mark E. Neely Jr. and Harold Holzer, *The Union Image: Popular Prints of the Civil War North* (2000). The Confederate volume has enjoyed much higher annual sales. (David Perry, editor-in-chief of the UNC Press, to Gary W. Gallagher, June 19, 2007 [e-mail].)

5. The comparative popularity of Grant and Lee in some collecting circles stands out in *The Franklin Mint: 2003 Holiday Preview* (Franklin Center, Pa.: The Franklin Mint, 2003), 24–31. The pages of this catalog offer the following devoted to Lee: a Robert E. Lee collector's knife; a bronze statue of Lee on "Traveller"; a revolver "inspired by the one carried by Lee"; a Robert E. Lee walking stick; an "Official Robert E. Lee Confederate Ring"; a Robert E. Lee pocket watch; a sculpture of Lee, Jackson, and Longstreet on horseback; a Robert E. Lee tankard; and a bronze statue of Lee and Jackson's last meeting at Chancellorsville. For General Grant, there are just two items: a Civil War chess set featuring Grant as the Union king—who gazes across the board at Lee, the Confederate king—and a U. S. Grant bowie knife offered as part of a pair that includes a Lee bowie knife. The Franklin Mint, no doubt responding to some kind of survey regarding potential buyers, apparently could not imagine selling any Grant item unless it was linked to Lee.

6. Notably absent from the most-painted list is Lee's victory at the Seven Days in June–July 1862, an odd omission considering the campaign's scale of carnage and wide-ranging impact. Three factors likely account for this: (1) Stonewall Jackson performed poorly and thus presents no obvious heroic moments to paint; (2) the campaign figures in no major films; and (3) the fighting consisted of a number of individual battles spread over several days rather than one huge clash. On Union battle art of the late nineteenth century, see Neely and Holzer, *Union Image*, especially chapter 7.

7. On Burns's coverage of Eastern and Western Theater battles, see Gary W. Gallagher, "How Familiarity Bred Success: Military Campaigns and Leaders in Ken Burns's *The*

Civil War," in Robert Brent Toplin, ed., *Ken Burns's "The Civil War": Historians Respond* (New York: Oxford University Press, 1996), 46–50.

8. Flyer titled *It's About Time: Lt. General James Longstreet Memorial Fund* (quotation); Gary Casteel, *It's About Time: The Sculpting of the General James Longstreet Memorial* (Gettysburg, Pa.: Four Winds Studio, 1998), 16–17. The fund sold thirteen small reproductions of the equestrian statue for $5,000–$7,500. Casteel also produced a small standing figure of Longstreet, copies of which the fund sold to raise money for the project. (Flyers titled *Gary Casteel and the Longstreet Memorial Fund Present Longstreet at Gettysburg* and *Gary Casteel and the Longstreet Memorial Fund Presents Longstreet of the First Corps, ANV.* [(Sanford, N.C.): Longstreet Memorial Fund, n.d.].)

9. The bulk of this paragraph and the next paragraph rests on a series of e-mail communications from Don Troiani to Gary W. Gallagher, October 1, 2006, and June 11 and 17, 2007; an interview Gary W. Gallagher conducted with Gallon on June 7, 2007; and a telephone conversation Gallagher had with Mort Künstler on August 30, 2007. According to Troiani, a serious collector of military arms and accoutrements, the value of items associated with black soldiers increased significantly in the wake of *Glory*. Along with historians William C. Davis and Brian C. Pohanka, Troiani served as a principal consultant for *Civil War Journal*.

10. My own experience confirms Troiani's impressions about Chamberlain and Little Round Top. When I first visited Gettysburg in the summer of 1965 and climbed up Little Round Top as part of a frenetic day's touring, Brig. Gen. Gouverneur K. Warren rather than Chamberlain dominated interpretation of that phase of the battle. The regimental marker for Chamberlain's 20th Maine lacked even a formal path connecting it to the crest of the hill. Since Burns and Maxwell emphasized Chamberlain's role, the National Park Service has installed markers, a wide path, and other interpretive devices that call attention to the 20th Maine.

11. Don Troiani (art) and Brian C. Pohanka (text), *Don Troiani's Civil War* (Mechanicsburg, Pa.: Stackpole, 1995), xv; Keith Rocco (art) and Robert I. Girardi (text), *The Soldier's View: The Civil War Art of Keith Rocco* (Berkeley, Calif.: Military History Press, 2004), 4–5. For a larger selection of Troiani's military art that focuses heavily on the Civil War, see Don Troiani and others, *Don Troiani's American Battles: The Art of a Nation at War, 1754–1865* (Mechanicsburg, Pa.: Stackpole, 2006). For an interview in which Troiani discusses his pursuit of accuracy, see William J. Miller, "The Way It Looked: A Conversation with Don Troiani," *Civil War: The Magazine of the Civil War Society*, issue 58 (August 1996): 28–33.

12. Gallon Historical Art, *Dale Gallon Historical Art: Collectors Edition* (Gettysburg, Pa.: Dale Gallon Historical Art, 2007), 1, 3; Dale Gallon (art) and Wayne Motts (text), *The Civil War Art of Dale Gallon* (Gettysburg, Pa.: Dale Gallon Historical Art, 1996), [5]; flyer

titled *No Artist Closer to His Work* (Gettysburg, Pa.: Dale Gallon Historical Art, n.d.). In a 2007 interview, Gallon said, "People ask for Grant all the time" and expressed surprise that artists paint him so seldom. Gallon has painted Grant just twice because, he explained, "there is always something else in the way." Graduating classes at the U.S. Army War College often commission works of art to be distributed as prints to their members, and Gallon more than once has proposed ideas featuring Grant—including Grant and Sherman at Shiloh. To date, none of the classes has asked for a Grant piece. (Gallagher interview with Gallon, June 7, 2007.)

13. Gallagher telephone conversation with Künstler, August 30, 2007; Mort Künstler, *The Civil War Art of Mort Künstler* (Seymour, Conn.: Greenwich Workshop Press, 2004), 212–19; Mort Künstler (art) and James I. Robertson Jr. (text), *Jackson and Lee: Legends in Gray* (Nashville, Tenn.: Routledge Hill, 1995), 11. The photograph of Künstler in front of the Confederate flag also graces the back dust jacket flap of an earlier book, with text by James M. McPherson, titled *Images of the Civil War: The Paintings of Mort Künstler* (New York: Gramercy, 1992), as well as of some of the artist's flyers.

14. Mort Künstler (art) and James M. McPherson (text), *Gettysburg: The Paintings of Mort Künstler* (Atlanta: Turner Publishing, 1993), 7. For paintings with figures that resemble actors in the film, see *The Return of Stuart* (Lee), *Forming the Line* (Alexander, Longstreet), *Longstreet at Gettysburg* (Longstreet, Goree), and *Lee's Old War Horse* (Lee, Longstreet) in Künstler, *Künstler*, 150–53. See also Künstler and McPherson, *Gettysburg*, frontispiece, 58–59, 68–69, 70 (Pickett), 74–75 (Pickett); Künstler and Robertson, *Jackson and Lee*, 126–27, 128–29. Interestingly, none of the depictions of Lee in Mort Künstler (art) and James I. Robertson Jr. (text), *Gods and Generals: The Paintings of Mort Künstler* (Shelton, Conn.: Greenwich Workshop Press, 2002), a companion to Ron Maxwell's second Civil War film, looks like Martin Sheen. The one on pp. 62–63 summons thoughts of Robert Duvall, who played Lee in the film.

15. John Paul Strain [with Paul E. Fowler], *Witness to the Civil War: The Art of John Paul Strain* (Philadelphia: Courage Books, 2002), back dust jacket flap, [5], 6, 70, 26. The front flap of the jacket for Strain's book displays a color photograph of the artist "on his dapple-gray horse battling Federals at Wilson's Creek." A flyer for his painting titled *Morning of the Third Day*, a study of Lee and Longstreet at Gettysburg, includes a large color picture of a mounted Strain in full Confederate uniform.

16. Dr. Roy W. Heidicker (Classic Aviation and War Art) to Gary W. Gallagher, March 17, 2004; conversations with salespeople at Gettysburg Historical Print Shop and Gettysburg Frame Shop, July 28, 2004; Joe Fulginiti (Valor Art and Frame, LTD) to Gary W. Gallagher, October 1, 2006 (e-mail); Jerry Netherland (Civil War Enthusiasts) to Gary W. Gallagher, February 26, 2006.

17. *Don Troiani Limited Edition Prints Status Report* (Southbury, Conn.: Historical Art Prints,

Winter 1997); Dale Gallon, *Report from Gettysburg—2003* (Gettysburg, Pa.: Gallon Historical Art, 2003); Dale Gallon, *Report from Gettysburg* (Gettysburg, Pa.: Gallon Historical Art, [2007]). I also consulted similar lists issued by Troiani from 1988, 1989, 1991, 1992, and 1998. The lists do not offer prints for sale but do include information about dealers who handled "sold out" examples of Troiani's work.

18. Don Troiani to Gary W. Gallagher, June 17, 2007 (e-mail); Gallagher interview with Gallon, June 7, 2007; Heidicker to Gallagher, March 17, 2004; "Thomas Kinkade: A Success," article on the CBS News *60 Minutes* website, July 4, 2004, <http://www.cbsnews.com/stories/2001/11/21/60minutes/main318790.shtml>. "He produces paintings by the container load," observes the article about Kinkade: "He is to art what Henry Ford was to automobiles." For examples of the Buffalo Soldier genre, see Gallon Historical Art, *Dale Gallon Historical Art: Collectors Edition*, 24–37.

19. Gallagher telephone conversation with Künstler, August 30, 2007; Gallagher interview with Gallon, June 7, 2007; Troiani to Gallagher, October 1, 2006, June 11, 2007 (e-mails); Fulginiti to Gallagher, October 1, 2006 (e-mail). The books devoted to Künstler's and Strain's art contain numerous snow scenes; those of Troiani, Rocco, and Gallon do not. One flyer offers Künstler's *The Bravest of the Brave*, a study of the Confederate Black Horse Cavalry at Warrenton, Virginia, as the "Official 1999 Snow Print" (Gettysburg, Pa.: American Print Gallery, [1999]).

20. Gallagher telephone conversation with Künstler, August 30, 2007; Gallagher interview with Gallon, June 7, 2007; Troiani to Gallagher, June 11, 2007 (e-mail). Troiani described the process: "The ad copy for magazines is usually based on the certificates written by you historians. . . . Basically it needs to tell the public what's going on briefly. I have always left it up to the historians what to write for the certificates that accompany our prints, basically just checking them for typos etc." Many prominent historians have worked on texts for advertisements and books of paintings by Civil War artists, including Dale Gallon (Samuel W. Floca Jr. and Wayne E. Motts), Mort Künstler (Rod Gragg, James M. McPherson, and James I. Robertson Jr.), Keith Rocco (Peter Cozzens, D. Scott Hartwig, and Brian C. Pohanka); Don Troiani (William C. Davis, Robert K. Krick, Brian C. Pohanka, and many others). Only John Paul Strain appears not to have sought such help, though his book does credit Paul E. Fowler's "exhaustive knowledge of the Civil War" as being of "indispensable aid" (Strain [with Fowler], *Witness to the Civil War*, [2]). A number of years ago, I wrote the descriptive prose for Don Troiani's *Bonnie Blue Flag*, which depicted Stephen Dodson Ramseur's brigade at the battle of Spotsylvania on May 12, 1864. I assume Troiani selected me because I had written a biography of Ramseur. That proved to be my only experience working with artists.

21. For an excellent discussion of Lost Cause iconography, see Neely, Holzer, and Boritt, *Confederate Image*.

22. On Julio and his painting, see Harold Holzer and Mark E. Neely Jr., *Mine Eyes Have Seen the Glory: The Civil War in Art* (New York: Orion, 1993), 146–47, 150–53; Estill Curtis Pennington, *The Last Meeting's Lost Cause* (Spartanburg, S.C.: Robert M. Hicklin, Jr., Inc., 1988), 13–36; Neely, Holzer, and Boritt, *Confederate Image*, [xxv] plate 11, 133. The painting went unsold during the artist's lifetime. In 1909, an article in *Confederate Veteran* informed readers that Mrs. J. B. Richardson, who owned the painting, was "very desirous of disposing of the picture, which I believe should be in an art gallery, where it could be appreciated by the lovers of high and noble art" (*Confederate Veteran* 17 [March 1909]: 140). *The Last Meeting*, which measures approximately 13 feet by 9½ feet, is now in the collections of the Museum of the Confederacy in Richmond, Virginia.

23. The last meeting, which took place on the morning of May 2, is often confused with an earlier discussion between Lee and Jackson on the night of May 1 (see, for example, Neely, Holzer, and Boritt, *Confederate Image*, 133). The generals planned the flank attack during the evening conference and met for the last time the next morning as Jackson led his soldiers toward the point of attack.

24. Christiana Bond, *Memories of General Robert E. Lee* (Baltimore: Norman, Remington, 1926), 19–20; introduction by Viscount Garnet Wolseley in G. F. R. Henderson, *Stonewall Jackson and the American Civil War*, 2 vols. (London: Longmans, Green, 1909), 1:vii, ix. On the various engravings, see Pennington, *The Last Meeting's Lost Cause*, [xii] (a reversed version of an 1872 engraving), 12; Neely, Holzer, and Boritt, *Confederate Image*, [xxv] plate 11. For an advertisement that ran in 1985 and 1986, see *Civil War Times Illustrated* 24 (April 1985): 8; for two from 2004–5, see *Civil War Standard* (Holiday 2004): 11, (Summer 2005): 9.

25. Neely, Holzer, and Boritt, *Confederate Image*, ix–xiv, [xvii] plate 1; Drew Gilpin Faust, *The Creation of Confederate Nationalism: Ideology and Identity in the Civil War South* (Baton Rouge: Louisiana State University Press, 1988), 69–71. See also Faust's *Southern Stories: Slaveholders in Peace and War* (Columbia: University of Missouri Press, 1992), for an essay on *The Burial of Latané*.

26. *Confederate Veteran* 37 (May 1929), cover and article on p. 165; *Southern Historical Society Papers*, ed. J. William Jones and others, 52 vols. (1876–1959; reprint with 3-vol. index, Wilmington, N.C.: Broadfoot, 1990–92), 39:89–90. Neely, Holzer, and Boritt, *Confederate Image*, xiii, states: "*The Burial of Latane* became one of the most famous icons of the Lost Cause, a tribute to the vision of its artist, the skill of its engraver, and the marketing ingenuity of its publisher and promoters."

27. *Confederate Veteran* 16 (April 1908): xxxi, (May 1908): 196.

28. For details about publication, see Neely, Holzer, and Boritt, *Confederate Image*, 166. For recent reprints, see *The Civil War Standard* (Holiday 2003): 34, (Spring 2004): 29, (Summer 2005): 26.

29. Jubal A. Early, "The Campaigns of Gen. Robert E. Lee. An Address by Lieut. General Jubal A. Early, before Washington and Lee University, January 19th, 1872," in Gary W. Gallagher, ed., *Lee the Soldier* (Lincoln: University of Nebraska Press, 1996), 70–73.

30. Gallagher interview with Gallon, June 7, 2007; Troiani and others, *Don Troiani's American Battles*, 117.

31. A Confederate congressman saw Bruce's painting on January 31, 1865. "I have just been to the hall of the House of Delegates of Va. to see a life-size portrait of Gen Lee," wrote Warren Aiken of Georgia. "The picture does not come up to my expectation, but it is a good picture" (Warren Aiken, *Letters of Warren Aiken, Confederate Congressman*, ed. Bell Irvin Wiley [Athens: University of Georgia Press, 1959], 106–7). The original of Bruce's portrait has been lost. Peale's portrait of Washington is reproduced as the frontispiece of volume 4 of Douglas Southall Freeman, *George Washington: A Biography*, 7 vols. (New York: Scribner's, 1948–57). On the 1907 etching of Lee, see Neely, Holzer, and Boritt, *Confederate Image*, 165.

32. Advertisement, *For the Cause* in *Virginia Country's Civil War* 5 (1986): back cover; flyer titled *Bringing History to Life . . . Robert E. Lee by Michael Gnatek* (n.p.: Hamilton Mint, 1994). A native of Hadley, Massachusetts, Gnatek studied at Yale University's School of Design.

33. Waud's sketch is in John Esten Cooke, *A Life of Gen. Robert E. Lee* (1871; reprint, Harrisburg, Pa.: Archive Society, 1995), opposite p. 398; advertisements for Troiani and Abbett prints in *Virginia Country's Civil War* 2 (1984): inside back cover (Troiani), back cover (Abbett); Tunison sculpture in flyer from the American Print Gallery (Gettysburg, Pa., [n.d.]). On Waud, see Frederic E. Ray, *Alfred R. Waud: Civil War Artist* (New York: Viking, 1974).

34. Robert Underwood Johnson and Clarence Clough Buel, eds., *Battles and Leaders of the Civil War*, 4 vols. (New York: Century, 1887–88), 3:204; flyer for Künstler, *The Last Council* (Gettysburg, Pa.: American Print Gallery, [1990]). On William Ludwell Sheppard, see chapter 6 of Lauralee Trent Stevenson, *Confederate Soldier Artists: Painting the South's War* (Shippensburg, Pa.: White Mane, 1998).

35. Holzer and Neely, *Mine Eyes Have Seen the Glory*, 148, 151; flyer for Künstler, *General Thomas J. 'Stonewall' Jackson, Winchester, Virginia, May 25, 1862* (Gettysburg, Pa.: American Print Gallery, [1988]); advertisement for Künstler's print in *Blue & Gray Magazine* 6 (April 1989): back cover. Künstler also packaged the Winchester print as one of

twelve images in a set of postcards titled Legends in Gray: The Paintings of Mort Künstler.

36. Flyer for Maughan, *The Prayer Warrior* (Canton, Ga.: The Marks Collection, 1991); flyer for Gallon, *The General and His Chaplain* (Gettysburg, Pa.: Dale Gallon Historical Art, 1994); Gallagher interview with Gallon, June 7, 2007. A graduate of the Art Center College of Design in Los Angeles, Maughan has lived and worked on both the East and West Coasts. For another painting of a pious Jackson, see Künstler's *Divine Guidance* (2003) in Künstler and Robertson, *Gods and Generals: The Paintings of Mort Künstler*, 112–13. Gallon's *The General and His Chaplain* is reproduced in Gallon Historical Art, *Dale Gallon Historical Art: Collectors Edition*, 176–77.

37. Flyer for Maughan, *The Christian General* (Canton, Ga.: The Marks Collection, 1989); advertisement for *The Prayer* placed by Four Winds Studio & Gallery, Gettysburg, Pa. (undated clipping from *Civil War News*); flyer for collector's plate of *The Generals Were Brought To Tears* (Norwalk, Conn.: The Danbury Mint, n.d.). A color reproduction of Künstler's painting is in Künstler, *Civil War Art of Mort Künstler*, 111. John Paul Strain's *Battlefield Prayer* depicts Jeb Stuart, another devout Confederate, alongside Lee and Jackson on the day before the battle of Fredericksburg. (Advertisement for *Battlefield Prayer* in *North & South* 9 [May 2006]: inside front cover.)

38. Flyer for *Christian Patriots, C.S.A.* (Canton, Ga.: The Marks Collection, n.d.); Neely, Holzer, and Boritt, *Confederate Image*, 182–83; Early, "Campaigns of Gen. Robert E. Lee," 70.

39. Dixon Wecter, *The Hero in America: A Chronicle of Hero-Worship* (New York: Scribner's, 1972), 306. Originally published in 1941, Wecter's book devoted an admiring chapter to Lee and a very negative one to U. S. Grant. For a book-length treatment of Lee as a Christian published shortly before Roosevelt gave his speech, see William J. Johnstone, *Robert E. Lee the Christian* (New York: Abingdon, 1933). For the statue in Dallas, which depicts Lee with a mounted courier at his side, see Roy Meredith, *The Face of Robert E. Lee in Life and Legend* (New York: Scribner's, 1947), 141.

40. Cooke, *Life of Gen. Robert E. Lee*, 184. Ogden also painted other Confederate generals in famous campaigns, including Jeb Stuart (first "Ride Around McClellan"), James Longstreet and George E. Pickett (Gettysburg on July 3, 1863), and Stonewall Jackson (First Bull Run).

41. Flyer for Künstler, "*I Will Be Moving Within The Hour*" (Gettysburg, Pa.: American Print Gallery, n.d.); flyer for Stivers, *Council of War—July 2, 1863* (Gettysburg, Pa.: American Print Gallery, 1985). Künstler's image was the first of six in a Legends in Gray series devoted to Lee and Jackson together. A native of Wisconsin, Stivers received part of his training at the California College of Arts and Crafts in Oakland. His work focuses on military topics from different eras of United States history. (Bio-

graphical information on reverse of flyer for *Wilson's Charge* [Wilton, Conn.: Stivers Publishing, n.d.].)

42. For examples of paintings devoted to Pickett's Charge, see Troiani and Pohanka, *Don Troiani's Civil War*, 128–32; Rocco and Girardi, *The Soldier's View*, 120–23; Künstler, *Civil War Art of Mort Künstler*, 154–65. For a sculpture, see flyer for Ron Tunison's *Gen. Lewis Armistead* (Cairo, N.Y.: Historical Sculptures, 1994). The flyer states that the piece, which shows Armistead just before he received a mortal wound, "captures completely the fortitude and courage of the general at this powerful moment in history." A diligent search did not turn up a date for Sainton's *Pickett's Charge*. Harold Holzer, a leading expert on Civil War art, has never been able to date the piece, deeming it "something of a mystery" that "every copy I have seen has been undated" (Harold Holzer to Gary W. Gallagher, July 9, 2007 [e-mail]).

43. Dale Gallon, *Gallon: The Complete Print Collection*, 1; flyer for *The High Tide* ([Gettysburg, Pa.]: American Print Gallery, 1993).

44. Johnson and Buel, *Battles and Leaders*, 2:534; flyer for Troiani, *The Diehards* (Southbury, Conn.: Historical Art Prints, 1991). On Allen C. Redwood, see Stevenson, *Confederate Soldier Artists*, 111–15.

45. Advertisement for *Press Forward, Men!* in *Civil War Times Illustrated* 42 (June 2003): 55; descriptive text for the print at <http://www.somersethouse.com/product_detail .asp?Reference_ID=4376>; *Grim Harvest of War* on Schmehl's website at <http:// www.bradleyschmehl.biz/>. A native of Pennsylvania, Schmehl graduated from the Pennsylvania School of Art and design in Lancaster. According to his website, he "has been focusing almost exclusively on Civil War subjects since 1995, although some recent projects have him branching out into the Revolutionary War period as well as the contemporary 'Christian Cowboy' market."

46. The "Forgotten in Gray" website is at <http://www.37thtexas.org/html/FIG .html>.

47. Advertisement for *Until We Meet Again* in *Civil War Times Illustrated* 45 (October 2006): back cover; Gallon, *Gallon: The Complete Print Collection*, 16. For other farewell pieces, see John Paul Strain's *The Parting* (A. P. Hill and his wife) in flyer, *The Paintings of John Paul Strain, 1997–1998* (Gettysburg, Pa.: Gettysburg Military Publishing, 1998); Künstler, *Civil War Art of Mort Künstler*, 36–37, 48, 79, 102–03; and Gallon Historical Art, *Dale Gallon Historical Art: Collectors Edition*, 42–53. For one of the few home-front pieces that fall outside the farewell genre, see Keith Rocco's *The Patriots of '61* (1995), a study of three Confederate women sewing military flags. (Rocco and Girardi, *The Soldier's View*, 20–21.)

48. Flyer for Strain, *Thompson's Station, Tennessee, March 5, 1863* (n.p.: John Paul Strain Gettysburg Military Publishing, n.d.). For other prints of Forrest, see Troiani and

others, *Don Troiani's American Battles*, 214–15, 220–21; Gallon Historical Art, *Dale Gallon Historical Art: Collectors Edition*, 174–75; Strain [with Fowler], *Witness to the Civil War*, 52–59, 62–65.

49. Paul Ashdown and Edward Caudill, *The Myth of Nathan Bedford Forrest* (Lanham, Md.: Rowman & Littlefield, 2005), 42, 194; Brian Steel Wills, *A Battle from the Start: The Life of Nathan Bedford Forrest* (New York: HarperCollins, 1992), 29–34, 217, 336–37.

50. Michael Andrew Grissom, *Southern by the Grace of God*, rev. ed. (Gretna, La.: Pelican, 1989), 350–51. Nast's cartoon is reproduced in both Ashdown and Caudill's *Myth of Nathan Bedford Forrest* and Wills's *Battle from the Start*. The Democrats vowed in 1868 to restore white rule throughout the former Confederacy.

51. E-mail (name withheld) to Gary W. Gallagher, August 12, 2006; John M. Coski to Gary W. Gallagher, August 8, 2006 (e-mail), forwarding a number of postings to a southern heritage mail list. Dr. Coski, I hasten to emphasize, does not share the sentiments of the postings but thought I should be aware of them. The program was C-SPAN II's *In Depth*, which aired on August 6, 2006. On Forrest and "the skeer," see Wills, *Battle from the Start*, 213. On Forrest at Fort Pillow, see John Cimprich, *Fort Pillow, a Civil War Massacre, and Public Memory* (Baton Rouge: Louisiana State University Press, 2005), and Andrew Ward, *River Run Red: The Fort Pillow Massacre in the American Civil War* (New York: Viking, 2005). For an editorial that addressed Forrest's troubling dimensions as well as his military skills, see "Forrest Fires" in *Wall Street Journal*, March 2, 2001, W15; the author of the editorial opposed placing a bronze bust of Forrest on city property in Selma, Alabama.

52. For an argument that nineteenth-century painters failed to produce any great works relating to the Civil War, see Steven Conn, "Narrative Trauma and Civil War History Painting, or Why Are These Pictures So Terrible?," *History and Theory: Studies in the Philosophy of History* 41 (December 2002): 17–42. "In a war whose scope was unprecedented, whose destruction was quite literally unimaginable, and whose ultimate purpose and meaning was confused," wrote Conn, "old narrative conventions once used to make sense of very different kinds of historical events and placed in a very different context of historical understanding failed and needed to be replaced by new ones" (p. 42).

53. Neely and Holzer, *Union Image*, chapters 6–7; Harold Holzer, *Prang's Civil War Pictures: The Complete Battle Chromos of Louis Prang* (New York: Fordham, 2001), 146–79; Harold Holzer, "Saving the 'IMAX of Its Day,'" *American Heritage* 56 (August/September 2005): 38–45; Robert Wernick, "History From a Grandstand Seat," *Smithsonian* 16 (August 1985): 68–83. Prang's subjects are Sheridan at Third Winchester, laying pontoons at Fredericksburg, Sheridan's ride to Cedar Creek, the repulse of Pickett's Charge at Gettysburg, Antietam, the Bloody Angle at Spotsylvania, Chattanooga,

Kennesaw Mountain, Allatoona Pass, Atlanta, Vicksburg, Shiloh, the capture of New Orleans, the *Monitor* versus the *Merrimac*, Mobile Bay, the *Kearsarge* versus the *Alabama*, Port Hudson, and the capture of Fort Fisher. For excellent color reproductions of nineteen Kurz and Allison and fifteen Currier and Ives prints, see Margaret E. Wagner, *The American Civil War: 365 Days* (New York: Abrams and the Library of Congress, 2006). Two of the Civil War cycloramas have been restored: *The Battle of Gettysburg*, at Gettysburg National Military Park's visitor center, and *The Battle of Atlanta*, at the Atlanta Cyclorama and Civil War Museum in the city's Grant Park.

54. Neely and Holzer, *Union Image*, 179, 196–97; Benson J. Lossing, *Mathew Brady's Illustrated History of the Civil War, 1861–65* (1912; reprint, New York: Fairfax, n.d.), 2. For Ogden's eight color prints, see the unnumbered leaves between pp. 256 and 257 of the reprint of Lossing's book. Lossing's work first appeared in sixteen separately issued parts, each of which had a color frontispiece. In addition to Ogden's eight, the publishers selected eight of Prang's chromolithographs for frontispieces.

55. Holzer, *Prang's Civil War Pictures*, 31–32, 61.

56. Neely and Holzer, *Union Image*, 218, plates 14 and 21 between pp. 118 and 119. The other two Kurz and Allison prints with black soldiers are *Battle of Nashville* (1891) and *Battle of Olustee, Fla.* (1894), both of which show regiments of United States Colored Troops on the attack.

57. On African Americans in Civil War art, see chapter 7 of Holzer and Neely, *Mine Eyes Have Seen the Glory*, and the epilogue in Neely and Holzer, *Union Image*. The Prang series ignored black military service.

58. Eastern National, *The Shaw Memorial: A Celebration of an American Masterpiece* (Cornish, N.H.: Eastern National, 2002), vi–vii [quotation from art historian Vincent Scully's foreword], 19. For an excellent analysis of the Shaw memorial and its meanings, see Martin H. Blatt, Thomas J. Brown, and Donald Yacovone, eds., *Hope and Glory: Essays on the Legacy of the 54th Massachusetts Regiment* (Amherst: University of Massachusetts Press, 2001). For an article critical of Saint-Gaudens's placement of the black soldiers, see Gary Scharnhorst, "From Soldier to Saint: Robert Gould Shaw and the Rhetoric of Racial Justice," *Civil War History* 34 (December 1988): 308–22. According to Scharnhorst's perverse reading of the sculpture, "St. Gaudens depicted the colonel larger than life, figuratively if not literally. . . . The black rank and file depicted in the monument were, in turn, second-class soldiers almost incidental to its design" (pp. 317–18).

59. At the risk of echoing a point made in n. 5 of this chapter, see *Civil War Times Illustrated* 43 (April 2004). Grant graces the cover, which features the famous photograph from 1864 of a resolute general-in-chief in the field looking right at the photographer. Most of the issue relates to Grant. What about the advertisements for art

in this "Grant" issue? Lee is featured on the front and back covers, appears in three full-page ads, and shares a full-page ad with Grant, Jackson, and Sherman; Grant shares the full-page ad with Lee, Jackson, and Sherman and has one smaller ad of his own.

60. Flyer for Künstler, "On To Richmond" (Gettysburg, Pa.: American Print Gallery, n.d.); flyer for Stivers, "To Make Hell Tremble" (Wilton, Conn.: Stivers Publishing, n.d.).

61. For images of Grant and Sherman, see Künstler, Civil War Art of Mort Künstler, 170–71, 186, 193; Künstler and McPherson, Images of the Civil War, 90–91, 98–99, 138, 140–41, 156–57; Troiani and others, Don Troiani's American Battles, 194; Rocco and Girardi, The Soldier's View, 184–87; Strain [with Fowler], Witness to the Civil War, 78–81. As he does with Grant in "On To Richmond," Künstler associates Sherman with fire and destruction in "War Is Hell" (2001), wherein Sherman and his officers begin their March to the Sea against the backdrop of Atlanta in flames. (Künstler, Civil War Art of Mort Künstler, 193.) Although it includes no prints of Sheridan, The Civil War Standard's Holiday 2003 catalog, 36, offers a 10-inch, "hand-painted resin figure" of the general (part of a set of ten such figures).

62. Don Troiani notes that the "54th Mass. and black regiments were pretty popular for a few years after 'Glory' came out but that has faded as time went by" (Troiani to Gallagher, October 1, 2006 [e-mail].) For treatments of the 54th, see Colonel Robert Gould Shaw and the 54th Massachusetts (1991) in Künstler, Civil War Art of Mort Künstler, 120; Fort Wagner (2003) in Rocco and Girardi, The Soldier's View, 128–29. Unlike many artworks dealing with Fort Wagner, Rocco's piece does not include Shaw. Künstler's Images of the Civil War also includes Her Name Was Sojourner Truth (1977), a highly romanticized treatment (p. 16), and The Thirteenth Amendment is Passed (1982), a study of a black couple and their son (p. 133).

63. Troiani and others, Don Troiani's American Battles, 195, 226–278; Troiani and Pohanka, Don Troiani's Civil War, 69; flyer for 1st South Carolina Volunteer Infantry (Southbury, Conn.: Historical Art Prints, 1997). Troiani's piece on the 29th USCT is titled Mahone's Counterattack (2003). On the 1st South Carolina, see Thomas Wentworth Higginson's Army Life in a Black Regiment (Boston: Fields, Osgood, 1870). Although seldom advertised in the popular Civil War magazines, art devoted to African Americans during the conflict can be found and purchased on the Internet. See, for example, Black Camisards: African-American Civil War Art & Collectibles, which is described as the "Home of the United States Colored Troops," at <http://www.blackcamisards.com/>.

64. Ken Burns, "Four O'Clock in the Morning Courage," in Toplin, ed., Ken Burns's "The Civil War," 157–59.

65. Holzer and Neely, Mine Eyes Have Seen the Glory, 170–73, 198–201. On Rothermel's The

Battle of Gettysburg and Pickett's Charge and other paintings of the battle he executed, see Mark Thistlethwaite, "'Magnificent and Terrible Truthfulness': Peter F. Rothermel's *The Battle of Gettysburg*," in William Blair and William Pencak, eds., *Making and Remaking Pennsylvania's Civil War* (University Park: Penn State University Press, 2001), 211–43. For a series of twelve paintings of the battle by F. D. Briscoe that show Hancock and Reynolds, among others, see Frederick Tilberg, *Gettysburg National Military Park, Pennsylvania* (Washington, D.C.: Government Printing Office, 1962 [National Park Service Historical Handbook Series No. 9]), [51–63]. Philippoteaux painted four versions of his Gettysburg cyclorama, two of which survive.

66. Flyer for Troiani, *For God Sake Forward* (Southbury, Conn.: Historical Art Prints, 1996); flyer for Gallon, *Hancock's Ride* ([Gettysburg, Pa.]: Lower Marsh Creek Press, [1992]). Troiani's piece is part of his Epic of Gettysburg series. For another study of Buford on July 1, see flyer for Don Stivers's *Fighting for Time* (n.p.: Stivers Publishing, [1991]). Regarding Buford's work on McPherson's Ridge on July 1, Stivers's text states: "Buying time until the army came up saved the high ground for the infantry, and perhaps saved Gettysburg for the Union." See also Gallon, *Gallon: The Complete Print Collection*, [i] (print of Buford), 1 (Reynolds), 11 (Buford, Reynolds), 13 (Hancock), 14 (Hancock).

67. Gallon, *Report from Gettysburg — 2003*. See Troiani and Pohanka, *Don Troiani's Civil War*; Künstler, *Civil War Art of Mort Künstler*; Strain [with Fowler], *Witness to the Civil War*; Rocco and Girardi, *The Soldier's View*; Gallon and Motts, *Civil War Art of Dale Gallon*. The best biography of Chamberlain is Alice Rains Trulock, *In the Hands of Providence: Joshua L. Chamberlain and the American Civil War* (Chapel Hill: University of North Carolina Press, 1992). For a selection of Chamberlain's extensive writings about the war, see Joshua Lawrence Chamberlain, *"Bayonet! Forward": My Civil War Reminiscences*, comp. Stan Clark Jr. (Gettysburg, Pa.: Stan Clark Military Books, 1994).

68. Flyer for Troiani, *Bayonet* (Southbury, Conn.: Historical Art Prints, 1988); flyer for Gallon, *Hold At All Costs* (Fredericksburg, Va.: Fredericksburg Historical Prints, n.d.). In addition to the art books listed in n. 66 above, see also Mort Künstler's books to accompany the films *Gettysburg* and *Gods and Generals* for a number of paintings of Chamberlain.

69. John W. Busey and David G. Martin, *Regimental Strengths and Losses at Gettysburg*, 4th ed. (Hightstown, N.J.: Longstreet House, 2005), 134, 143; William F. Fox, *Regimental Losses in the American Civil War, 1861–1865* (1898; reprint, Dayton, Ohio: Morningside, 1974), 233, 135. For a brief discussion of Ireland's part in the battle on July 2, see Harry W. Pfanz, *Gettysburg: Cemetery Hill and Culp's Hill* (Chapel Hill: University of North Carolina Press, 1993), 220–21, 300, 302.

70. Troiani and Pohanka, *Don Troiani's Civil War*, 187–89; Künstler, *Civil War Art of Mort*

Künstler, 208–9; flyer with image of Spaulding's piece (Gettysburg, Pa.: American Print Gallery, n.d.); advertisement for Spaulding's *Honor Answering Honor* in large flyer (Gettysburg, Pa.: American Print Gallery, n.d.); William Marvel, *Lee's Last Retreat: The Flight to Appomattox* (Chapel Hill: University of North Carolina Press, 2002), 193–95, 278–79 n. 2. The Shipyard Brewing Company paid its own form of tribute to Gordon and Chamberlain in 2007 by including them among twelve generals on boxes of its "Battleground Ale." In addition to a dozen bottles of the ale, purchasers could savor a "special distinct commemorative boxed collection of exquisite portraits" designed by artist Ken Hendrickson. See <www.battlegroundale.com>.

71. Flyer for Stivers, *The Proffered Wreath* (Wilton, Conn.: Stivers Publishing, [1989]); Joshua Lawrence Chamberlain, *The Passing of the Armies: An Account of the Final Campaign of the Army of the Potomac, Based upon Personal Reminiscences of the Fifth Army Corps* (1915; reprint, Lincoln: University of Nebraska Press, 1998), 339–40. The reprint's publisher chose Stivers's painting for the cover. For a print showing Chamberlain in action at Petersburg on June 18, 1864, see flyer for Joe Umble's *Soul of the Lion* (Fredericksburg, Va.: Fredericksburg Historical Prints, [1992]): "Although diagnosed with a mortal wound" in the fighting, "Chamberlain will be miraculously restored to health. He will stand at Appomattox Courthouse 10 months later to salute his former enemies."

72. Lawrence Frederick Kohl, introduction, in David Power Conyngham, *The Irish Brigade and Its Campaigns* (1867; reprint, New York: Fordham University Press, 1994), x; Fox, *Regimental Losses*, 118. Fox notes that the brigade lost more than 4,000 soldiers killed and wounded—a higher number than ever served in its ranks at one time. By the time of Gettysburg, it had been reduced to 532 men, 198 of whom (37.2 percent) fell in the battle. At one time or another, the following infantry regiments served in the brigade: the 63rd, 69th, and 88th New York, 28th Massachusetts, and 116th Pennsylvania.

73. *Gods and Generals* plays up the Irish angle, imagining a touching confrontation between the attacking Irish Brigade and some Irish soldiers in Confederate units on Marye's Heights. For a refutation of this myth, see chapter 3 of Kelly J. O'Grady, *Clear the Confederate Way! The Irish in the Army of Northern Virginia* (Mason City, Iowa: Savas, 2000).

74. Holzer and Neely, *Mine Eyes Have Seen the Glory*, 298–300. In their research, Holzer and Neely turned up just two "Civil War paintings of any fame" and four "popular prints" that "embrace religious scenes."

75. Flyer for Troiani, *"Clear the Way"* ([Southbury, Conn.]: Historical Art Prints, 1987). Troiani also painted the brigade at Antietam and Gettysburg. See flyers for *Sons of Erin* (1996) in the Antietam Series and *Rock of Erin* (1997) in the Epic of Gettysburg

Series (Southbury, Conn.: Historical Art Prints, 1996, 1997). On values, see Troiani's *Limited Edition Prints Status Report* for Summer 1998 (Southbury Conn.: Historical Art Prints, 1998); *"Clear the Way"* ranks first with an estimated value of $2,850. For the brigade's attack at Fredericksburg from a Confederate perspective, see flyer for Joe Umble's *Never Were Men So Brave!* (Fredericksburg, Va.: Fredericksburg Historical Prints, [1993]). The flyer's text posits a confrontation between Irishmen in blue and gray: "Umble expertly brings to life the moment when [Brig. Gen. Thomas R. R.] Cobb's 24th Georgia, while cheering the valor of their fellow Irishmen, help tear Meagher's hapless command to pieces." For information about the green flags at Fredericksburg, see historian Lawrence F. Kohl's discussion in Troiani and others, *Don Troiani's American Battles*, 110.

76. Flyer for Künstler, *"Raise the Colors and Follow Me"* ([Gettysburg, Pa.]: American Print Gallery, [1991]); flyer for Gallon, *Pride of Erin* (Gettysburg, Pa.: Dale Gallon Historical Art, [1992]). For Irish Brigade pieces by painter Rick Reeves, see *69th New York Infantry* and *Remember Ireland and Fontenoy* on his website at <http://www.old gloryprints.com/reeves.htm>. On October 25, 1997, admirers of the Irish Brigade dedicated a monument to the unit at Antietam National Battlefield. Placed at one end of the Bloody Lane, it features a bas-relief of men advancing with the unit's distinctive flag.

77. Postal Commemorative Society, *The Civil War Stamp Collection* (Norwalk, Conn.: Postal Commemorative Society, 2007). A two-page letter signed in facsimile by Michael R. Wilbur, director of the society, accompanies the brochure.

78. For images of the six paintings, see Künstler, *Civil War Art of Mort Künstler*, 28, 58–59, 61, 118, 161, 175.

79. Robert E. Lee to Jubal A. Early, November 22, 1865, George H. and Katherine Davis Collection, Howard-Tilton Memorial Library, Tulane University, New Orleans.

80. The advertisement for three Künstler pieces is on the inside back cover of *Civil War Times Illustrated* 46 (February 2007). A Virginia license plate honoring Lee's bicentennial also featured a portrait by Künstler, and sculptor Gary Casteel created a bronze tablet of the general for a new Lee County courthouse in Sanford, North Carolina. (*Civil War News*, September 20007, 19, 45.)

81. Beyond his relative neglect in Civil War art, Grant remains mired near the bottom of presidential ratings. He ranked seventh in an article titled "The 10 Worst Presidents," *U.S. News & World Report* 142 (February 26, 2007): 40–53. The article does predict that his reputation, which has been lower in the past, "may continue to rise as a result of sympathetic studies — and because of renewed appreciation of his own memoir, considered to be the best ever produced by a former president" (p. 49).

EPILOGUE

1. On Monument Avenue, see Sarah Shields Driggs, Richard Guy Wilson, and Robert P. Winthrop, *Richmond's Monument Avenue* (Chapel Hill: University of North Carolina Press, 2001). A fifth Confederate statue, honoring oceanographer Mathew Fontaine Maury, went up in 1929.

2. "Lincoln is Returning to Richmond," *Civil War News*, February/March, 2003, 8; form letter from Martin J. Moran (president of the United States Historical Society) to "My Fellow Admirer of Abraham Lincoln," n.d.; "Lincoln's 2nd Arrival Divides Richmond," *Washington Post*, April 6, 2005, C1. On the history of the monument and the controversy that surrounded its placement, see Adam Dean, "Lincoln in Richmond: A Tale of the First Lincoln Statue in the South" (honor's thesis, Department of History, University of California, Los Angeles, 2005).

3. "A memo from . . . The Reverend Alice W. Harris," n.d. [part of mailing from the United States Historical Society]; Harold Holzer, "When Lincoln and Son Came to Richmond" ([Richmond, Va.: The U.S. Historical Society, n.d.]), [3]; "Lincoln's 2nd Arrival," C6; Driggs, Wilson, and Winthrop, *Richmond's Monument Avenue*, 88–96.

4. "Lincoln is Returning to Richmond," 8; Sons of Confederate Veterans, press release titled "The Lincoln Prize at Tredegar," April 19, 2005; "Lincoln's 2nd Arrival," C6; *Richmond Times-Dispatch*, April 6, 2003. The National Park Service estimated that approximately 850 supporters of the statue attended the dedication.

5. "The Lincoln Prize at Tredegar"; "Lincoln's 2nd Arrival," C6; Moran to "My Fellow Admirer of Abraham Lincoln." The SCV opposed Tredegar's hosting the Lincoln Prize dinner in April 2005, in part because books by DiLorenzo and other authors who share his views have never contended for the award. The Lincoln Prize, grouse members of the SCV, has gone to writers in the "mainstream historical community" who overlook DiLorenzo's evidence and repeat "time honored myths" regarding the sixteenth president. Lewis Lehrman, one of the donors who fund the Lincoln Prize, responded with a staunchly reconciliationist message. (*Richmond Times-Dispatch*, April 17, 2005, E1.) For other recent anti-Lincoln sentiment, see reports in Little Rock's *Arkansas Democrat-Gazette*, January 12, 2004 (a conference titled "Homage to John Wilkes Booth"); Charlottesville, Virginia's *The Daily Progress*, March 28, 2005 (a mock tribunal held at Liberty University that found Lincoln guilty of war crimes).

6. Lincoln to John A. Campbell, [April 5, 1865], in Abraham Lincoln, *The Collected Works of Abraham Lincoln*, ed. Roy P. Basler, 9 vols. (New Brunswick, N.J.: Rutgers University Press, 1953–55), 8:386–87; Moran to "My Fellow Admirer of Abraham Lincoln"; Edward L. Ayers, Gary W. Gallagher, and David W. Blight, *Appomattox Court House* (Washington, D.C.: Department of the Interior, 2003), 38.

Acknowledgments

The origins of this book lay in an invitation to deliver the Steven and Janice Brose Lectures in the Civil War Era at Penn State University. As one who spent the first dozen years of his academic life in the Department of History at Penn State, I eagerly accepted the invitation and thoroughly enjoyed my stay in State College to give the three lectures in April 2004. Susan Welch, Bill Blair, and Nan Elizabeth Woodruff provided gracious introductions for the talks, and I found time to see many other friends and former colleagues. The visit added to a store of fond memories of my time at Penn State.

Before I gave the Brose Lectures, I had participated in a conference at the Huntington Library in October 2003 titled "Crossing Boundaries: New Perspectives on Civil War Military and Cultural History." I used that opportunity to prepare an early version of my chapter on the Civil War in recent art. As always at the Huntington, Robert C. Ritchie provided a delightful forum for Civil War specialists to exchange ideas. Among the participants, David Blight, Joe Glatthaar, Alice Fahs, and Jim Marten offered a number of useful suggestions about my paper.

Many other friends generously took time to read and critique all or part of the manuscript. Ed Ayers, Bill Bergen, Steve Cushman, Ted Lendon, and Peter Onuf—all colleagues at the University of Virginia—raised excellent questions, caught many errors, and pushed me in directions that greatly improved the manuscript. Beyond Virginia, George Rable gave the manuscript a close and very helpful reading, as did an anonymous reader for the University of North Carolina Press. Harold Holzer, Robert Kenzer, and Lawrence F. Kohl responded cheerfully to queries about, respectively, nineteenth-century Civil War art, Shelby Foote as a talking head in Ken Burns's documentary, and the Irish Brigade. Chris Heisey allowed me to use two of his beautiful photographs. T. Michael Parrish shared many fascinating pieces of evidence relating to both films and art, one of which I have used as an illustration. Robert Hallmark pointed me toward an interesting example of Lee's and Grant's comparative popularity in the Centennial era, and John Haas provided a useful clipping regarding *Glory*. Chris W. Lewis of *Civil War Times Illustrated*, Keith Poulter of *North & South*, and Jason L. Roth of *Blue & Gray Magazine* answered a number of questions about circulations, regional distribution, and other aspects of their magazines. Steve Bailey, Paul Baker, Ken Hack, Dr. Roy W. Heidicker, Jerry Netherland, and Kendall R. Warren helped me understand the market for Civil War art.

Dale Gallon, Mort Künstler, and Don Troiani stand out among those who helped me.

As three of the artists whose work I discuss, they reasonably could have been wary of saying too much. Yet each took the time to respond to questions in ways that saved me from embarrassing errors and allowed me to make connections I otherwise would have missed (Dale over lunch at Avenue Restaurant in Gettysburg, Mort in a long telephone conversation, and Don in a series of e-mails over a period of eight months). All provided examples of their art to be used as illustrations without demanding or even requesting anything beyond copies of the book when it appears. With his understated sense of humor, Don closed one of his notes with this: "We'll see how happy I am after the book comes out." I hope they will be generally pleased, or at least not regretful that they talked so openly with an academic interloper in their world of paintings and markets.

Caroline E. Janney, Katherine A. Pierce, and Matthew A. Speiser, while doctoral candidates at Virginia, examined thousands of magazine pages in search of advertisements for artworks. Carrie tabulated those from 1982–2003, and Matt did the same for those after 2003. Their hard work was indispensable in creating the database on which I relied for my statistical comparisons. After she joined the Department of History at Purdue University, Carrie read my manuscript and offered a number of excellent suggestions, as well as giving permission to reproduce a photograph she took of the 54th Massachusetts Infantry monument in Boston.

I have worked with the unequaled staff at the University of North Carolina Press on twelve books. Editor-in-chief David Perry and I discussed this project more than any of the earlier ones, and always to good effect. Managing editor Ron Maner took over once the final manuscript arrived in Chapel Hill—as he has done many times in the past. I thank them both. As editor of The Steven and Janice Brose Lectures in the Civil War Era, Bill Blair exhibited the professionalism that marks all of his endeavors. I am very pleased to have a title in his series.

The dedication indicates that this book is for Joan Waugh. Whether walking up Tigertail Road in Brentwood or Canyon Road in Santa Fe, or making our way to the Lincoln Diner in Gettysburg or to Wild Greens in Charlottesville, we often discussed the war in art and films. Her thorough grounding in the field of Civil War memory helped me sharpen my arguments, and her steadfast encouragement helped me overcome several periods of doubt. Thanks to her, I have learned the true meaning of collaboration.

Index

and the Lost Cause, 56–57; and the Reconciliation Cause, 108, 110, 112; in recent art, 138, 140, 141, 142, 143, 144, 146, 159, 188, 206; in early Lost Cause art, 159

Lookout Mountain, battle of, 185

Lost Cause, 7, 11, 17, 132, 209, 212, 221 (n. 9); as an interpretative theme in films, 2, 17, 42, 51, 56–58, 67; central themes of, 18, 42–43, 66; diminished presence of in films, 52–55, 62, 65–66, 81–86; resurgence of in later films, 74, 76, 89; opposition to in films, 86–89; as an interpretive theme in art, 136–37, 143–46, 154–84 passim, 206; origin of in art, 148–54. See also Confederate flags

Louisiana State University Press, 214 (n. 3)

Love and War, 8

Loyal Leagues, 33

Lukey (character in The Horse Soldiers), 51

Mackeson, Pitt (character in Ride with the Devil), 70

Maguire, Tobey, 71

Maine units

—20th Infantry Regiment, 36, 100, 202; regimental marker at Gettysburg, 244 (n. 10). See also Chamberlain, Joshua Lawrence; Gettysburg; Gods and Generals

Mammy (Character in Gone with the Wind), 50, 76

Manassas National Battlefield Park, 5

March, Amy (character in Little Women), 120

March, Beth (character in Little Women), 120

March, Jo (character in Little Women), 101, 120

March, "Marmee" (character in Little Women), 117, 119, 120

March, Meg (character in Little Women), 117, 119, 120

Marcoux, Ted, 68

Marlowe, John (character in The Horse Soldiers), 51, 124

Martha (character in Gods and Generals), 76–77, 78

Marye's Heights, 204. See also Fredericksburg, battle of

Massachusetts units

—54th Infantry Regiment, 32–33, 55, 95–99, 125; in early postwar art, 186–87, 188; monument to, 186–87, 192, 252 (n. 58). See also Glory

Massey, Raymond, 51, 93

Matthews, G. B., 152, 153–54, 155

Mauldin, Bill, 126

Maughan, William L., 157, 169, 171

Maxwell, Ron, 1, 14, 58, 73, 136, 138, 139, 140, 142, 144, 148, 181, 189, 201, 204, 225 (n. 18)

McClellan, George B., 130; in recent art, 139, 201; in early postwar art, 185

McGuire, Dorothy, 93

McIntire, Tim, 53

McKinley, William, 36

McMullen, James, 53

McPherson, James M., 5, 10, 211, 236 (n. 10)

McPherson's Ridge, 201

Meade, Dr. (character in Gone with the Wind), 46

Meade, George G.: in recent art, 139, 148, 201; in early postwar art, 185, 189

Meagher, Thomas Francis, 204, 205

Meyers, Jonathan Rhys, 70

Military Order of the Stars and Bars, 215 (n. 12)

Minghella, Anthony, 81

Mississippi Secession Convention, 221 (n. 8)

Mitchell, Margaret, 42, 45

Monroe, Ada (character in *Cold Mountain*), 82–84, 86

Montgomery, James, 125

Monument Avenue (Richmond, Va.), 209, 211

Morgan, Harry, 118

Morgan, John Hunt, 93; in recent art, 144, 146

Morning Orders, 156

Murphy, Audie, 126

Nast, Thomas, 183

Nationalism

—Confederate, 12, 14, 24, 74, 80; diminished presence of in films, 58, 61, 70, 72, 110, 123; in Lost Cause art, 153, 154. *See also* Lost Cause

—United States, 25, 203, 206. *See also* Union Cause

National Park Service, 107, 209, 211, 237–38 (n. 16)

Native Americans, 121, 125, 127, 129, 133

Nazi Germany, 87, 89

Neeson, Liam, 132

Neo-Confederates, 89, 133, 212

New Market, battle of, 124, 241 (n. 36)

Newton, Wayne, 8

New York City Draft Riots, 128, 240 (n. 32)

New York units: 69th Infantry Regiment, 121, 123, 240 (n. 32); 137th Infantry Regiment, 202

North and South (novel), 8

North & South (periodical), 10–11, 136–37

North and South (television miniseries), 8

Ogden, Harry A., 159, 173, 185, 190

O'Hara, Gerald (character in *Gone with the Wind*), 50

O'Hara, Scarlett (character in *Gone with the Wind*), 46, 50, 59, 84, 104, 128

Olustee, battle of, 185

"On to Richmond," 187–88, 193

The Outlaw Josie Wales, 55

Overland campaign, 22, 146

The Passing of the Armies, 36, 203

Patton, Waller Tazewell, 1

Pea Ridge, battle of, 185

Peale, Charles Willson, 155

Pennsylvania units: 116th Infantry Regiment, 27; 153rd Infantry Regiment, 31

Peppard, George, 111

Perkins, Anthony, 94

Petersburg: siege of, 23; battles near, 58, 84; in recent art, 139

Pharaoh's Army, 8, 55, 62, 69; and the Reconciliation Cause, 64; and the Lost Cause, 65–66; and the Emancipation Cause, 103; and the Union Cause, 117, 119; image of Union soldiers in, 127, 128

Philippoteaux, Paul, 189, 201

Pickett, George E., 1, 56; in recent art, 138–39, 140, 144; in early Lost Cause art, 159

Pickett-Pettigrew assault, 23, 56, 58. *See also* Pickett's Charge

Pickett's Charge, 1, 113, 140; in recent art, 142, 143, 159, 180, 201, 206; in early postwar art, 189, 201

Pickett's Charge, Battle of Gettysburg, 159, 175

Poitier, Sidney, 93

Pork (character in *Gone with the Wind*), 50

Postal Commemorative Society, 205–6, 207

Prang, Louis, 185, 186

Prayer in Stonewall Jackson's Camp, 157, 168, 204

The Prayer Warrior, 157

Press Forward, Men!, 181

Pride of Erin, 200, 204

Prisoners from the Front, 57

Miami Dade College
Kendall Campus Library
11011 Southwest 104th Street
Miami, FL 33